From Patron
to Partner

From Patron to Partner

The Development of U.S.-Korean
Business and Trade Relations

Edited by
Karl Moskowitz
Harvard University

LexingtonBooks
D.C. Heath and Company
Lexington, Massachusetts
Toronto

Library of Congress Cataloging in Publication Data
Main entry under title:

From patron to partner.
 Includes bibliographical references and index.
 1. United States—Foreign economic relations—Korea
(South)—Addresses, essays, lectures. 2. Korea (South)—
Foreign economic relations—United States—Addresses,
essays, lectures. 3. United States—Commerce—Korea
(South)—Addresses, essays, lectures. 4. Korea (South)—
Commerce—United States—Addresses, essays, lectures.
I. Moskowitz, Karl, 1948–
HF1456.5.K6F76 1984   337.519′5′073   83–48028
ISBN 0–669–06837–3 (alk. paper)

Copyright © 1984 by D.C. Heath and Company

Published simultaneously in Canada

Printed in the United States of America on acid-free paper

International Standard Book Number: 0–669–06837–3

Library of Congress Catalog Card Number: 83–48028

Contents

Figures and Tables

Acknowledgments

Many people contributed to this book, and the success of the research efforts on which it is based. We owe our greatest appreciation to the Henry Luce Foundation, whose generous support carried the project from its conception to its conclusion. We were undertaking new research, and Martha Wallace and Robert Armstrong of the Henry Luce Foundation were most supportive as we moved from the idea stage to the practical logistics of coordinating two research groups based at Harvard University and Yonsei University in Seoul working according to different academic calendars.

At Harvard the Korea Institute of the Fairbank Center for East Asian Research served as the base from which the research was organized and coordinated. We owe thanks to Edward W. Wagner, Director of the Institute, and Philip A. Kuhn, Director of the Center, for their interest in the project. Special gratitude is due Song Cha, Dean of the School of Business and Economics of Yonsei University, for lending his personal support. Dean Song and Professors Kim Chong-bin and Pak Chin-gŭn, Director of the Industrial Management Research Center, kindly arranged a visiting faculty research fellow appointment and provided office space and research assistance during the editor's year of residence at Yonsei. Professor Hak Chong Lee of Yonsei, the senior Korean scholar contributing to the project, was particularly helpful to the progress of the research in Korea. A Fulbright Faculty Research Abroad Fellowship enabled the editor to spend a fruitful year of research in Korea. Harvard University provided research assistance and supplementary research funds. A grant from the Asan Welfare Foundation supported the translation and dissemination of the research results in Korean and provided supplementary research funds to the Korean scholars.

On August 15-16 of 1983, we gathered at Harvard with our colleagues to consider the research results. Discussion was intense and focused, and everyone benefited, particularly the contributing authors. We owe special thanks to C. William Emory, Lawrence G. Franco, Richard Moxon, James M. Utterback, David B. Yoffie, Kent E. Calder, Ki-bok Lee, and Kyung-il Ghymn, for it was their critical remarks as paper discussants that set the high tone of the debates and helped clarify issues and indicate directions for future research. Hakchung Choo, Teruo Komaki, Stephan Haggard, Bertrand Renaud, David Steinberg, Vincent Brandt, Carl Hammer, John Bennett, and many others contributed to the vigorous discussions.

Not least, the success of the Harvard meeting was due to the careful preparations by Sherrill Davis, who as the chief research assistant to the editor, kept everything on schedule while he was working in Seoul. Anne Davies, Song Chi-hwan, Sung Hee Suh, Ming Lo, Hein Kim, Ann Park, and Michael Hong assisted in the research and the preparation of the manuscript for publication.

Each of the contributing authors is grateful to the many individuals and organizations who were most generous in providing research materials and data. The notes to each chapter barely begin to mention all those whose cooperation was critical to the success of the research.

The contents and the conclusions of this book are the responsibility of the contributing authors and particularly the editor. They do not reflect the viewpoints of the Henry Luce Foundation, the Fulbright program, or the Asan Welfare Foundation.

Note on Romanization and Names

The McCune-Reischauer system is the accepted standard for the romanization of Korean. Also, the customary order of Korean names is family name first, followed by the personal name. The usual exceptions are proper names, such as Syngman Rhee or Seoul, which are widely known, and individuals and institutions who have indicated their own preferred romanization. Most of the Korean individuals mentioned in this book, including the contributing authors, indicated a preference for their personal romanization and Western-style name order (personal name first, family name second). The names of other persons mentioned in the book are rendered, where possible, according to the McCune-Reischauer system and in the customary order.

Abbreviations

AACSB	American Association for Collegiate Schools of Business
CCC	(U.S.) Commodity Credit Corporation
CRIK	Civil Relief in Korea
DKCL	Dow Chemical Korea Limited
ECA	(U.S.) Economic Cooperation Administration
EPB	(ROK) Economic Planning Board
FAS	(U.S.) Foreign Agricultural Service
FDI	foreign direct investment
FL	foreign license (for use of technology)
GARIOA	Government Appropriations for Relief in Occupied Areas
GTC	general trading company
IBRD	International Bank for Reconstruction and Development
ICA	(U.S.) International Cooperation Administration
ITC	(U.S.) International Trade Commission
KEBOA	Korea Export Buying Offices Association
KOFMIA	Korea Flour Mills Industrial Association
KOFOTI	Korea Federation of Textile Industries
KPCC	Korea Pacific Chemical Corporation
KTA	Korea Traders Association
LDC	less-developed country
MAF	(ROK) Ministry of Agriculture and Fisheries
MCI	(ROK) Ministry of Commerce and Industry
MFA	Multifiber Arrangement
MNC	multinational corporation
MOE	(ROK) Ministry of Education
SWAK	Spinners and Weavers Association of Korea
TA	technical assistance contract
USDA	(U.S.) Department of Agriculture
USTR	(U.S.) Trade Representative

1 Issues in the Emerging Partnership

Karl Moskowitz

In May of 1884, two years after the United States and Korea signed a treaty of amity and commerce, an American businessman named Walter Townsend arrived at the newly opened Korean treaty port of Chemulp'o, present day Inchon. Townsend, who represented an American firm in Yokohama, established his trade competing against Chinese and Japanese merchants. Korea was not an easy place to do business, and Townsend experienced numerous problems. One of his headaches was dealing with the Korean government itself; in the records we find complaints over nonperformance of contracts, failure to pay for goods, failure to enforce the law, retroactive application of new policies, and the like. Townsend pressured American diplomatic representatives in Seoul to push for satisfaction of his claims in the disputes, though this tactic was often unsuccessful. Despite his difficulties with Korean partners and the Korean government, and despite the conflicts that led eventually to Japan's seizure of Korea, Townsend flourished.[1]

In 1983, a century after Townsend's arrival, trade in goods between the United States and the Republic of Korea surpassed the $14 billion level, following a decade of rapid expansion that saw the annual totals increase from $1.4 billion in 1972 to $12.2 billion in 1982. The range of goods and services traded between the two nations broadened considerably during this period, and private business ties likewise increased in number and variety. Apparently, U.S.-Korean economic ties are flourishing. Yet many American businessmen in Korea in 1983 voiced complaints that seem to echo Townsend's difficulties: nonperformance of contracts, nonpayment for services, retroactive application of new tax rulings, contradictory government decisions, as well as new complaints about matters that had not troubled Townsend, such as inadequate recognition and protection of patents and intellectual property. They likewise sought help from the American diplomatic representatives in Seoul. Korean business interests had their own serious grievances about American trade restrictions and the actions of some American firms in Korea.

The economic relationship between the United States and Korea did not develop in a direct line from the day Walter Townsend set up

1

shop in Chemulp'o or the day the first Korean diplomatic mission to the United States in 1883 took time off for a shopping expedition in Manhattan. During the final years of the Yi dynasty more American traders joined Townsend, and others obtained concessions such as the Seoul-Inchon railroad, but they were overshadowed by the Japanese who actually bought out most American concessions long before Japan annexed Korea in 1910.

Walter Townsend stayed on after 1910, as did other American interests to which he was linked, such as the large Unsan gold mine. But Japan was in complete control, and its development of agriculture and manufacturing in Korea left little room for American participation. A few established traders such as Townsend stayed, but the only new American business presence in Korea was through the Japanese operations of large American multinationals, such as Standard Oil and Singer. The Japanese government seized American interests in Korea when the United States and Japan went to war in 1941.

The present relationship between the United States and the Republic of Korea began when Japan collapsed in August of 1945. The United States and the Soviet Union hastily agreed to divide the Korean peninsula into two zones of occupation for the purpose of accepting the surrender of Japanese forces and maintaining security until Korea's future course as an independent nation could be settled. American forces commanded by General John R. Hodge occupied their zone in September of 1945 and established a military government known by its acronym, USAMGIK.

A stepchild of the Occupation of Japan, USAMGIK's role was ambiguous from the start: it was a liberator freeing Korea from the Japanese yoke; it was an alien occupier taking all authority; it was a custodian retaining the laws and institutions of the Japanese; it was an institution builder establishing some new government offices and national military forces; it was a reformer introducing new educational policies and a limited land reform; it was a benefactor supporting Korea economically. The United States, USAMGIK, was everything, because it was the government of the southern zone of Korea.

Although there were many accomplishments during the occupation, overall progress was limited because of insurmountable economic and political problems rooted in the colonial experience and the unwanted division of the country. A satisfactory political arrangement with the Russian zone proved impossible, and the United States began to wind down its direct role. The United Nations was brought in to observe elections that led to the establishment of the independent Republic of Korea on August 15, 1948. Two years later, ongoing confrontation between North and South blew up into full-scale conventional war when North Korea attacked the South.

Despite the ambiguities and difficulties of the Military Government period and the first years of the Republic of Korea, three essential elements of the contemporary U.S.-Korea relationship were put in place in 1945. First, the American relationship has only been with the American occupation zone that became the Republic of Korea; henceforth in this book Korea will only mean the Republic of Korea, or South Korea, as it is commonly known. Second, the United States and Korea have maintained friendly relations since 1948, and the United States has assisted Korea in protecting its military security since USAMGIK created national military forces. Although a generation of commentators has blamed the withdrawal of American troops in 1949 and inadequate military and political commitment on the part of the United States for opening the door to the North Korean attack, we must remember that the United States was providing military supplies and military advisors to Korea at the time of the invasion. Third, but most important for our concern, the United States played a critical role in the Korean economy, not only as the authority deciding economic policies up to 1948, but also as the provider of massive economic aid.

Under USAMGIK, the Government Appropriations for Relief in Occupied Areas (GARIOA) program supplied more than five hundred million dollars worth of aid, principally vital commodities, but also chemical fertilizers to increase agricultural production and machinery and assistance aimed at building the economy. The primary objective of GARIOA was to prevent famine and disease, as much a military and political goal as an economic one. When Korea became independent, GARIOA was replaced by the more development-oriented Economic Cooperation Administration (ECA) program. Although still built around the supply of commodities—cotton, food, petroleum products, and fertilizer—the ECA program included infrastructure projects and technical assistance to industry. Unlike GARIOA, there was Korean participation at both the government and industry level in ECA planning.

Though nominally bilateral after the United States recognized the Republic of Korea in 1948, the relationship was actually unilateral; the United States decided, and Korea had to live with its decisions, be it the level of military support or the content and magnitude of economic assistance.

A final point about the period from 1945 to 1950 is that the uni-

lateral economic assistance relationship quickly became institutionalized and integrated into Korean government and industry. American
commodity aid stimulated the formation of associations of processors
of the relief commodities who organized themselves to manage allocation of the raw materials supplied by the GARIOA program. In 1948
the new Korean government established the Office of Supply (OS-
ROK). In Korean, OSROK's initial name was Oeja Kwalliwŏn, which
was soon changed to Oeja Ch'ongguk; both may be translated as *office
in charge of foreign materials,* because OSROK was created to manage
the acquisition and distribution of American aid commodities.[2]

The Korean War put the U.S. Army back in charge of much of
the Korean economy. The overwhelming refugee problem was met by
CRIK (Civil Relief in Korea), a UN Command program that had the
military objective of preventing unrest, famine, and disease among the
civilian population in rear areas. Even more than GARIOA, CRIK
was a military program for economic relief, not development. The
United States provided virtually all of the relief supplies distributed by
CRIK, and was likewise the mainstay of the United Nations Korea
Reconstruction Agency (UNKRA), which was established to administer the reconstruction of the wartime devastation and rebuild the
Korean economy. As the Korean War ended, the United States took
upon itself the responsibility for Korea's economic reconstruction sep-
arate from the multilateral structures of the United Nations. The UN-
KRA mission of reconstruction was taken over by the United States.

The war removed any remaining ambiguities about the American
commitment to Korea's national integrity. Solemnized after the 1953
armistice by the mutual defense treaty, the United States commitment
to Korea's military security has never wavered, though the larger foreign policy and strategic justifications for this commitment have shifted
from time to time.

Both the defense commitment and the economic commitment en-
tailed massive transfers from the United States. The details of the
various reconstruction and economic development and military assistance programs defy summary. It is sufficient to note that, for the first
decade after the Korean War, a complex of American civilian and
military programs

Paid for much of the reconstruction of war damage and the construction of new infrastructure and industrial projects.

Provided most of the Korean government's budget and shouldered
the burden of training, equipping and maintaining a large military.

Supplied Korea with vital commodities and raw materials.

Supplied Korea with most of its foreign exchange.[3]

Provided a substantial amount of technical and institutional assistance.

Some of the assistance came in the form of grants, some in the form of equipment and material, and some in the form of bulk commodities. Many programs were overlapping. For example, in 1955 Korea began to receive agricultural commodities under the PL 480 program, basically a civilian program. The commodities were sold, and the proceeds went to expenditures by the Korean government for "the common defense."[4] As one might surmise from this history, the institutionalization of the aid relationship and its integration into the Korean economy, government, and political system, begun in the USAMGIK period, grew remarkably strong and deep-rooted.

It is here that we pick up the thread of the business relationship; in 1953 American Trading Company, a firm related distantly to Walter Townsend's business, came back to Korea.[5] The American Chamber of Commerce in Korea was established the same year. American business in Korea was limited to offer agents, who bid to supply imports, mostly to the government. The other principal direct business relationship between the United States and Korea grew out of the commodity aid supplied by the United States. Raw cotton had to be processed, spun, and woven into cloth; wheat had to be milled into flour. Although the relationship between the American producers and the Korean processors was through government intermediaries, Korea became an established destination for American agricultural products. These business relationships depended upon American aid to Korea, not market forces.

Because American and Korean objectives and priorities diverged, the economic assistance relationship proved difficult. The reconstruction effort was successful, but the Korean economy made little progress toward attaining the capability to survive and grow independently, without regular injections of American aid. One problem was the integration of the aid relationship into both Korea's political and economic structure.[6] In 1960 the Korean government fell, a victim of its own corrupt and shortsighted policies. A new government emerged, but it was overthrown in 1961 by a military coup led by General Park Chung Hee.

The accession to power of the military-based government represented a fundamental turning point for postwar Korea. Park and his junta set Korea on a new course, firmly establishing economic development as the foremost national goal. An ambitious five-year economic development plan was announced, and within a few years a broad realignment of economic policies had taken effect and, supported by institutional innovations and a reformed and increasingly effective government bureaucracy, was showing positive results. The United States was supportive, helping with economic aid and cooperating closely in the economic planning process.

It is from the new policies instituted in Korea at the beginning of the 1960s that the contemporary U.S.-Korean business relationship has grown. The overall intent and effect of the economic policies was to turn outward for capital and technology, for markets, and to dismantle the elaborate, costly exchange rate and import control policies that had previously separated the Korean market from competitive world prices. These new policies opened the way for foreign investor participation in the Korean economy, and the flow of private capital and technology began almost immediately. For Korean and foreign business interests alike, the way was opened and incentives given to stimulate manufacturing for export. The new policies quickly bore fruit. On the investment side, in 1962 Chemtex became the first American investor to build in Korea; on the export side, Korean exports of cotton textiles provoked the first official trade dispute with the United States over Korean exports to the U.S. market, also in 1962.

American economic assistance remained vitally important to Korea through the late 1960s, though the essence of the aid relationship changed. One familiar aspect of the aid relationship, the provision of American agricultural commodities through the PL 480 program, expanded enormously. The last American aid went to Korea in 1975, but by this time it was an anachronism, totally overshadowed by bilateral trade that exceeded three billion dollars the same year.

Korea's economic development, its rise from the ashes of the Korean War and the morass of aid dependency, is a dramatic story that is beyond the scope of this book. The Korean development process has been studied at length, and there is extensive literature on the subject, including the contribution of American assistance.[7] The security relationship also has its share of drama, and there is a vast literature on Korean security affairs that ranges from the years preceding the Korean War up to the present.

The object of this book is rather to examine one of the fruits of Korea's growth: the private business relationship that has emerged between the United States and Korea as a result of Korea's economic development. Although most aspects of the present private sector relationship originated in the early 1960s and the policy changes that led to Korea's growth, it was only in the 1970s that the business relationship attained its contemporary dimensions. Bilateral trade began the decade at about $1 billion in 1970 and ended at the $9 billion level in

1979. Even discounting for the effects of dollar inflation on the trade figures, by the beginning of the 1980s Korea had joined the ranks of the largest trading partners of the United States.

From 1945 until the early 1970s the relationship between the United States and Korea was unilateral and asymmetrical. Despite the fiction of equality between two sovereign states, Korea was the client, surviving and then, in the 1960s, prospering with American economic support and military protection. The United States was the patron, supporting its client because of the importance of the Korea commitment to its regional and global policies. In the 1970s the relationship between the United States and Korea lost this asymmetrical, patron-client character. Economic aid finally ended, and when Korea has since received concessional terms, in its purchases of certain agricultural commodities, for example, the concessions have come not from Korea's needs, but from America's economic needs. Likewise, Korea has shouldered most of the burden of its own defense. In trade relations and, to a degree, in security, the relationship has become more symmetrical, and all indications are that this trend will continue in the future. The relationship between Korea and the United States will never be exactly equal in power or in interest; the United States is a large nation, with a large population, vast resources, a highly developed and technologically advanced economy, and security responsibilities that span the globe. Korea is not likely to become one of the top two or three trading partners of the United States, even in the distant future. But partnerships are not based on equality, they are based on mutual interests, joint long-term goals, and respect for differences.

The economic partnership, the relationship based on mutual private interests that grew so rapidly during the 1970s, has been obscured in the public mind by the domination of the security relationship. Although specialized American attention to the growth of Korea's economy and its business relationship with the United States closely parallels the actual progress of the relationship—between 1970 and 1981 the frequency of articles on the Korean economy and business affairs in *The Wall Street Journal* rose at the same rate as the growth in the current dollar value of U.S.-Korea trade—the American popular image of Korea remains dominated by memories of the Korea War, poverty, unsavory politics, and the unilateral nature of the American security commitment.[8] The Korean public mind, as reflected in the Korean press, gives priority to the security relationship, despite great public interest in Korea's economic affairs and international economic relationships.

At higher policy levels in the United States government, obsession with the security relationship seems to push everything else aside; Korea's economic success and growing U.S.-Korea trade are given dutiful mention, but there seems to be little high-level attention paid to difficulties in the trade relationship. Recent articles in American foreign affairs journals again point out serious weaknesses both in perspective and in depth among the U.S. government officials in charge of American relations with the countries Chalmers Johnson terms the *capitalist developmental* states of Asia.[9]

In Korea and, slowly, in the United States, problems in the bilateral economic relationship have attracted concern. Behind all the positive developments, behind the burgeoning trade figures, the rise of Korea's status as a trade partner, and the emergence of a real and complementary economic partnership, the past decade has not been easy on either partner. The difficulties have not been purely economic. In economic terms the relative advantage and factor endowments of the United States and Korea are highly complementary: the United States supplies Korea with agricultural commodities, machinery and capital goods, capital, and, though harder to value, services and knowledge in the form of technology and training; Korea supplies the United States with low- and medium-technology manufactured goods. The difficulties have arisen from the manner in which each nation organizes and manages its economic affairs and its economic exchange with the outside world, and from broader changes in the world economy. They are problems of political economy. Furthermore, these problems are not unique to the U.S.-Korea relationship, but reflect similar difficulties each has with other trading partners.

For the United States, rising imports from Korea have come against a background of repeated trade crises with Japan, the decline in the ability of some large American industries to compete against imports from Japan, and a pattern of dealing with the problem by the management of imports through protectionist measures. The same pattern of import management has been applied to Korean exports—at present some 46 percent of Korea's exports to the United States are under one sort of restriction or another—just as it has been applied to other countries whose exports of manufactured goods to the United States have grown rapidly.[10] Another set of continuing trade issues with Japan concerns problems of access to the Japanese domestic market; as the Korean economy prospers and matures, similar issues of American access and participation have arisen.

In the late 1970s American debate over economic relations with Japan shifted from specific complaints over certain products to a general examination of the Japanese political economy: the organization of Japan's government, business, and society, and its economic policies and relations with the outside world. This served to reflect a portion of the debate back onto the American political economy and ideas like 'industrial policy.' The industrial policy debate in the United States is far from resolved and, in any event, fundamental reorganization of the American political economic system is unlikely. What is not unlikely, however, is that the debate will eventually lead to some new forms of government-business interaction, closer government attention to the long-term evolution of industries and trade relationships, and closer government control over American technology for economic purposes as well as for security reasons.

In the meantime, there is a clear tendency in the United States to lump Korea and other high-volume Asian exporters such as Taiwan together with Japan. They are the 'new Japans,' and they appear to follow the same patterns of government-business relations and economic interaction with the outside world that have been so successful for Japan and so difficult for the United States. Even similar export product progression is identified in these countries, as the so-called new Japans move from textile products to consumer electronics to motor vehicles.[11] If the United States should enact a trade policy to deal specifically with Japan, including the retaliatory and punitive measures that have been threatened in recent years, the likelihood grows that these same measures will be applied to Korea more or less automatically, despite the fact that the actual economic and trade relationships with the United States are quite different.

One reason that Korea becomes a target is that even more than Japan, its political economic system is diametrically opposite to that of the United States. The United States has a decentralized, complex, and open political system; the same could be said of its economic system, which is not characterized by significant or effective government-business cooperation. The Korean government is highly centralized and, at least since the Yushin constitution of 1972, is not susceptible to influence by pressure groups through a competitive electoral or party process. Government supervision and control over private business activities, especially economic relations with the outside world, have been pervasive since the establishment of the Republic of Korea in 1948. Many attribute Korea's rapid economic development to the Park government's use of its close supervisory relationship with business to channel private endeavors in accordance with broader government objectives.[12]

By the late 1970s the very success of Korea's development had produced a complex economy with diverse international economic relations. Large industrial groups that dominated the manufacturing sector and produced most of Korea's exports had nurtured professional managements to high levels of expertise. These developments led to questioning of the long-term viability of close, finely tuned government guidance of economic affairs. Better to have the government step back a few paces and shift to a more open, market-oriented system was the advice heard from Korean and foreign expert alike. At the same time there was trade partner criticism that elaborate controls on imports and foreign investment were no longer necessary to protect the domestic economy and were, in fact, hampering healthy trade. A third factor that came into play was the changing nature of the foreign participation Korea desired. Increasingly, Korea sought to attract the more advanced commercial technologies, from electronics to pharmaceuticals, and, increasingly, foreign firms that had developed sophisticated proprietary technologies hesitated to enter Korea. The hesitation was due to doubts about the business environment in Korea that ranged from government-business relations to the adequacy of patent protection. One source of concern was that Korea was apparently becoming less hospitable to early foreign investors who had outlived their usefulness.[13]

Korea has a national industrial policy; the debate is over how far the government should 'liberalize,' or step back from the detailed implementation and management of that policy.[14] As in the United States, the government response so far has been characterized more by rhetoric than by meaningful action. Some measures taken in the name of liberalization, such as decreasing the authority of the once mighty Economic Planning Board, resulted not in decreased control and regulation, but decentralization of regulatory authority and control within the bureaucracy, which effectively increased red tape for foreign investors. In 1983 a number of liberalization measures were incorporated into the laws governing foreign trade and investment. Nevertheless, at the time of this writing, government-business relations and the way things work in Korea had not changed appreciably.

The time has come to separate the economic and business relationship from security affairs and from comparative economic development studies, and to focus attention on this relationship that has growing importance for the United States and continuing significance for Korea. With this idea in mind, the studies on which this book is based had three objectives. The first was historical, how we got to where we are: to describe and analyze significant elements in the contemporary partnership as they underwent the dynamic transition from the asymmetrical patron-client relationship supported by American aid to the comparatively symmetrical relationships of the present based upon private enterprise arrangements.

Unlike the particularistic aid and security relationships, private enterprise arrangements are market-based and, at least over the long term, universal, not particularistic. The second objective was to give some attention to Korea's relations with other advanced market economies to highlight unique characteristics of the U.S.-Korea business relationship, if any, and to put the American role in comparative perspective. The intention was not to undertake detailed comparisons, however, and Japan, Korea's other major trading partner, is the only country that received consistent attention and regular mention.

The third objective follows from the first: having looked backward to trace history, we turn around and peer into the future to identify elements and issues in the U.S.-Korea economic relationship that are likely to grow in importance. As with the second objective, this was met to some degree. But it was not met adequately, because there are important aspects of the contemporary relationship that we were not able to include in the studies. In the contributors' view, the third objective will be met if this book succeeds in its overall goal of stimulating more study, attention, and better-informed debate on U.S.-Korean business and economic relations.

The flow of capital and technology is an essential indicator of the character of an economic relationship. As in the aid and security relationship, the flow was in one direction until quite recently, from the United States to Korea. One component of Korea's development strategy was to attract foreign capital and technology. From the first the United States served as a major source for both.

When we think of private capital, we often think first of equity investment. Korea has always controlled foreign investment strictly, and has nearly always shown a preference for inducing foreign capital—foreign savings—as debt rather than equity. Korea's policies on foreign technology have been akin to those for capital; it controls direct foreign participation and prefers, where feasible, methods of acquiring technology that avoid foreign equity and control. Four contributors to this book examine different aspects of the investment and technology flows between the United States and Korea.

Two contributions look at Korea's experience with American investment and technology and make comparisons between its role and Japan's role. Eul Yong Park analyzes the nature of American manufacturing investments in Korea by testing different hypotheses about the characteristics of foreign investment and foreign investor behavior. One question is the relative contribution to exports of foreign investment in manufacturing. Korea's growth process has been led by expansion of the manufacturing sector and that, in turn, has been led by the expansion of manufacturing for export; foreign investors have been active in both domestic market manufacturing and in export manufacturing. Park's work helps us assess the role of American private investments and their trade behavior from the perspective of Korea's economic goals and in the broader context of MNC-LDC investment relations.

Similarly, much of Kee Young Kim's chapter on technology is devoted to a comparison of commercial technology acquired from the United States to that purchased from Japan. Kim makes his comparisons against the background of a conceptual discussion of technology and the different methods by which technology may be transferred or learned. Part of his discussion is a summary of Korean policies toward technology development that are far broader in scope than merely the inducement of commercially successful foreign technology. When a formal transfer of technology occurs, an informal process of learning and a transfer of experience must also take place in order to make it successful. Certain Korean policies have the objective of creating the human resources that can learn and absorb the experience and move on to independent technology development and application.

Both Kim and Park focus on Korea, and tend to treat American firms as entities that evince uniform attitudes and behavior. The other two contributions on investment and technology pay more attention to the varied motivations and actions of American firms in investing capital and knowledge assets (technology) in Korea. Dong Sung Cho looks at the rules. He describes the main points of the regulations and legal restrictions each nation imposes on foreign investors and on its own nationals who invest abroad, as well as the incentives that are offered. These have changed substantially and often in Korea as it adapted to new circumstances brought on by its rapid development, but the United States has also changed its regulations from time to time to meet new challenges.

Brian Levy examines the denouement of a specific investment. However, it was more than just another investment, it was Dow Chemical's Korea operation, the largest single American (and foreign) investment in Korea. In 1982 the dispute between Dow and its Korean partners in a related joint venture caused headlines in the business press and came to symbolize the complaints of some U.S. companies in Korea and the doubts of potential American investors. Levy approaches the conflict from the perspective of the petrochemical industry and Dow's global strategy rather than focusing on the Korean investment environment. Because it looks at a single investment situation, Levy's contribution highlights the private nature of the U.S.-Korean economic relationship.

These four studies on investment and technology contain a great deal of information and analysis, but there are certain questions that they were not able to address. One concerns actual government practice in implementing policies. Some Korean incentives to attract foreign investors may be written into the law, but are not automatic. In recent years numerous foreign investors have had to 'voluntarily' forgo the tax holiday that is provided as an incentive in the Foreign Capital Inducement Law as a condition of receiving the required government approval for their venture. Changes in practice may eventually be embodied in revisions of the pertinent regulations; but according to one prominent American businessman, whose personal investment experience in Korea spans the entire period of Korea's rapid economic growth, no matter how the statutes are amended, the Korean government will approve investments that meet its broader goals and reject those that do not.[15] Merely knowing the rules and responding to the incentives is not enough.

To win approval, foreign investors in certain industries must fit their operations into industry structures that have been conceived and constructed by the government, not the market. Levy demonstrates that the structural origin of the Dow conflict lay in the separation into different entities of a production sequence that is usually vertically integrated within a single firm. Yet perhaps a little 'naivete' on Dow's part may be understandable when we consider that the entire Korean petrochemical industry is structured in the same way, with different firms—often different joint ventures—occupying different positions upstream and downstream in vertical production streams for different complexes of chemicals.[16] The overall system has worked because the government has managed it and made it work by administering prices and making necessary adjustments to take care of everyone involved. When the economic conditions that determined an investment decision change drastically for the worse and when the government steps back from its managing role, discord is inevitable.

There are two dimensions of the capital and technology flow that are not covered at all, but are extremely important in the U.S.-Korea relationship. We have not looked at capital in the form of debt, although debt is the vehicle through which Korea has induced most of the foreign savings it has required. American capital markets and American banks have supplied the largest portion of the savings Korea has borrowed privately. In addition, the U.S. government finances a significant portion of American capital goods and agricultural commodity sales to Korea; a few years ago Korea became the largest customer of Eximbank, and it has always been among the largest foreign customers of the Commodity Credit Corporation.

These transactions represent more than capital flows, they represent services. Financial services that American institutions sell to Korea have been an important part of the relationship in the past, but now that Korea has more sophisticated and stronger institutions of its own, new problems have developed. Questions about restrictions on American banks, insurance companies, and other services in Korea, and on what basis they will be allowed to compete in the domestic Korean market constitute a simmering issue that might boil over with repercussions as serious as any trade dispute.

Capital and technology have flowed in one direction, but the result has been expanded bilateral trade in goods. Over the past decade the trade in goods has been more or less in balance, yet significant disputes over trade occurred. Three chapters treat different aspects of the trade relationship. Ku-Hyun Jung examines the Korea-U.S. trade channel, the private institutional structures by which goods manufactured in Korea are transferred from the producers in Korea to the purchasers in the United States. Jung shows that rapidly increasing trade volume and changing product composition, among other factors, have worked a transformation of the trade channel. The result is that certain categories of Korean firms and American firms have captured larger shares of the trade volume from intermediaries that formerly dominated the channel, such as the Japanese general trading companies.

John Odell's research concerns trade disputes between the U.S. government and Korean government over Korean exports to the American market. The focus is not on the private sector, but on how the two governments handle trade conflicts. Odell analyzes thirteen major disputes over the period from 1962 to 1981 that were the subject of official negotiations between Washington and Seoul. Included in the analysis is consideration of the elements that cause private sector complaints to turn into official disputes, as well as attention to factors that influence the relative outcomes of different negotiations. Of interest is Odell's informative description of how each government actually goes about the process of disputing with another over private sector relations.

The contribution by the editor looks at the other side of Odell's coin: relations between industry groups in the United States and Korea. Trade disputes occur because of antagonistic relationships between competing national industries. Yet certain industries in the United States and Korea have established close ties that work to protect mutually beneficial trade. The ties that are strongest and most deeply rooted on both sides are those founded on long-standing producer-consumer relationships, the most important of which date back to American agricultural commodity aid to Korea prior to the Korean War. Instead of provoking the conflicts that Odell examines, these industry relationships bring political pressure to bear on both governments to preserve the special market ties that have developed.

We are lacking an analysis of the United States to Korea trade channel. Also, we have not examined the problem of access to the Korean market for American products. Demands for access to the Korean market and differences over treatment of American business within the Korean domestic market are often discussed by the two governments. However, the problem is access itself, not the quantity permitted, as in the case of disputes over Korean exports to the American market, and these demands are unlikely to become official disputes unless they reach levels of tension where retaliatory actions may be threatened. Questions of American access and participation in the Korean market are comparatively recent, however, and arise because Korea's economy has grown to the point where it represents an important potential market that, in the American view, no longer needs to be protected so tightly. There are indications, including recent public statements from U.S. officials, that these problems are heating up into a serious bilateral issue.

The final chapter by Hak Chong Lee opens up consideration of another dimension of private sector relations: business organization, culture, and practice. Lee reviews the development of business and management education in Korea and shows how critical changes were introduced from the United States in the late 1950s that shaped the subsequent course of management education, both in formal teaching and in faculty relations with the business world. Lee's work reflects back on the importance of the human element in technology stressed by Kim, in this case the human organization aspect of technology. In business schools, as in other institutions ranging from science laboratories to military academies, we may identify points of strong American influence, although it is impossible to delineate or quantify the actual effects of this influence. What is clear, however, is that one result of the program Lee describes is a new generation of Korean businessmen and managers who are professionally trained and better able to understand and do business with their American counterparts.

The list of questions we would like to ask of U.S.-Korean business relations goes on and on. There are two important dimensions of the relationship that bear mention, though the mention is in the form of a combined disclaimer and apology for not addressing them. Both relate to the 'special relationship' between Korea and the United States since 1945 and how it has affected the development of private sector economic relations between the two nations.

First, there is a very important complex of business ties that are part of the security relationship. These ties include direct arms sales to Korea; technology licenses for Korean production of military equipment; training and service contracts; and, for certain products, direct competition between American and third country suppliers. Moreover, military-related commercial transactions and Korean exports of certain goods manufactured under restricted license have been the subject of disputes between the two partners that have had more commercial than military implications. Nevertheless, the military relationship and everything it involves is governed by the political and military objectives of the alliance as dictated by the security situation on and around the Korean peninsula, not market forces.

The second question is broad enough to warrant a tome of its own: how has the special relationship in security, aid, and diplomatic affairs influenced the development of private sector economic relations between the United States and Korea? In other words, how much of the present private business relationship is natural, that is, how much can be explained by Korea's independent economic development and universal market forces, and how much can be better explained by the particularistic security and aid relationships dating back to 1945?

This question is really a set of complex historical issues, but there are certain basic points that should be kept in mind. The first is that if markets are information structures, we must remember that the security and the aid/diplomatic relationships were the principal avenues of communication between the United States and Korea until the 1970s. Investment missions of American businessmen from the early 1960s through the 1970s were often led by prominent personages who had ties to these establishments. At certain points the support, even if only implied, of these establishments must have influenced decisions. They also played a role in getting the principals together, as through the investment missions, for example. For another example, American military procurement in Korea and the contracts for construction and supply of American and Korean forces in Vietnam are often cited as key factors in the rise to international prominence of the Korean construction industry.

The one concrete example treated in our study is the private sector alliances that developed in the agricultural commodity trade as a consequence of the aid relationship. This example reminds us that the information flow is in two directions. It is likely that Korea gained information and insights about the American market and the workings of American government programs, ranging from CCC to GSP, that it has been able to employ advantageously because of experience and ties cultivated through these older relationships. It would certainly appear that Korea has been able to make better use of these programs than many other developing countries.

The interplay between security, assistance, close diplomatic support, and the private sector has not been ignored. The Koreagate investigations, the Pak Tong-sŏn affair, and the related rice scandals emphasized the negative possibilities.[17] This happened just as the U.S.-Korea trade relationship began to take on real importance for the United States, and the increasing symmetricality of the partnership became visible with the first major Korean investments in the United States. Again, the influence of the security and aid ties are not part of the present so much as they are part of the past and the historical development of U.S.-Korean business relations in the 1960s and 1970s. In the 1980s the military and diplomatic alliance will not weaken, but it will probably have little new influence on the future development of U.S.-Korean economic relations.

When the first centennial of the establishment of U.S.-Korean diplomatic relations was observed in 1982, the contemporary relationship was often termed a partnership. President Reagan emphasized the theme of partnership when he visited Korea in 1983. As the preparation of this book nears completion in the spring of 1984, one hundred years after Walter Townsend arrived in Chemulp'o, we too are struck by the broad partnership that has emerged in private business relations between the United States and Korea. The potential for the continued development of mutually beneficial trade, investment, and technology ties between the United States and Korea is very strong. The potential for trade conflict and friction to undermine these ties is also very strong and has increased noticeably in the past few years. The title of this book is meant to reflect the change in the relationship that has been most gratifying for both parties—the transformation of the United States from Korea's patron to Korea's partner. The future course of the partnership will depend on the manner in which the two nations address the problems that arise between them.

2

An Analysis of the Trade Behavior of American and Japanese Manufacturing Firms in Korea

Eul Yong Park

According to the studies of host country policy toward foreign direct investment (hereafter FDI) in developing countries, host governments generally try to achieve multiple economic objectives through FDI.[1] For instance, FDI, along with foreign loans, has been an important means of closing the gap between investment and domestic savings. Host governments also aim at increasing GNP and employment, as well as acquiring skills, technology, and management know-how, including foreign marketing. Among the many objectives, an increasing number of advanced developing countries appear to regard access to advanced technology and foreign markets (exports) as the primary goals of FDI. The traditional literature on FDI, especially empirical studies, shows the conflicting motives of multinationals and host governments in technology transfer and export trade.[2] On the export trade issue, it is argued that an investor's main motivation for FDI is to sell in the local market rather than to export. Studies maintain that multinationals generally invest in host countries to overcome trade barriers and other barriers, such as transportation cost, that make the export of their products into the host country less efficient than local production.

Although trade barriers often play an important role as an incentive to make FDI in developing countries, increasing evidence suggests that trade liberalization does not necessarily reduce FDI when other factors are favorable. In some cases, FDI tends to increase in host countries that have liberalized their foreign trade regime.[3]

This seemingly contradictory result is due to the fact that there are two different types of FDI. The first is investment projects associated with import substitution/infant industries. In this case, trade liberalization is likely to reduce the FDI flow because the import-substituting industry may not be able to compete successfully with imports. The second type of FDI is to exploit the comparative advantages of a host country and realize gains from economies of scale, specialization, and trade. Evidence indicates that this second type of FDI in developing

19

countries grew significantly in the 1970s.[4] The share of world trade conducted by multinational companies has been increasing, and the share of exports in the total sales of foreign firms in developing countries has also been increasing.[5] For this second type of FDI, trade liberalization and FDI would be correlated positively. The reduction of the cost of communication and transportation, and increasing competition among firms in the industrial countries seem to lead firms to search for the most efficient production locations.

Trade Theory and Industrial Organization Theory

Foreign investment and trade behavior of multinational firms are generally explained by two different bodies of theory: international trade theories and industrial organization theories.[6] The two bodies of theory try to explain why foreign firms invest and produce in foreign countries rather than serve the market by export. If export and capital flows (FDI) are not perfect substitutes because of transportation cost and differences in technology that may justify local production, then why do foreign firms rather than local firms invest to produce, despite the many disadvantages foreign firms have vis-à-vis local firms.

One key assumption neoclassical trade theory makes is the immobility of factors of production, an assumption that is not realistic. Several economists have explored trade theories by relaxing this assumption and allowing capital to be mobile and labor immobile.[7] In general, substitution between trade and capital movements would not be perfect because of the transportation costs and differences in the production functions and immobile factors in two different countries. When capital is allowed to move relatively freely, the assumption of differences in production function becomes important in the determination of production location and trade. Production location will be determined primarily by the relative endowment (and hence real cost) of relatively immobile factors: unskilled and skilled labor and other resources (land, for example) and infrastructure such as services, assuming that other factors are allowed to move.

Location theory and product life cycle theory also provide ways to explain further the location of production and trade patterns. The location theory considers the cost of transporting products as a key determinant of production location and trade pattern. It also takes into account locational factors in the differences of information costs. The product life cycle theory, originally developed by Vernon and others, relates the maturing process of production technology to production costs as the determinant of production location.[8] The theory suggests that as the demand for a new product increases and its production technology matures, competition will develop and the cost of production becomes an important determinant of production location. The possibility of FDI occurs at this point to reduce production and marketing costs by using cheap factors of production and locations closer to markets.

Scholars of industrial organization questioned how multinational firms could compete with local firms because of the many disadvantages the multinationals have as foreign firms. Their studies showed that multinational firms often have certain ownership advantages in FDI which compensate for their disadvantages as foreign firms.[9] The advantages specific to ownership include appropriate firm size and proprietary advantages such as new technology, management and marketing skills, access to markets, and access to raw materials and other intermediate goods. The presence of some of these advantages is a necessary condition for FDI. Without them, newly entering multinational firms would not be able to compete with existing firms in host countries that know the local economy and investment environment better. Specifically, the ownership advantages frequently associated with FDI are[10]

Firm size: this relates to the industries for which economies of scale or product diversification is important

Technology-based advantages, including trademarks, patents, and others

Management-related advantages, production management, marketing, and other organizational advantages

Exclusive or favored access to factor inputs, capital, labor, natural resources, and information, as well as the ability to obtain them on favorable terms

Exclusive or favored access to product markets

Government protection

The host country should have some location advantages to attract FDI. They include market size and growth rate, performance of existing foreign firms, low input costs such as labor, raw materials, energy and land, low transport and communication costs, and other costs related to economic distances between hosts and home countries. These factors include differences in language and customs, legal, financial and commercial practices and institutions, predictable economic policies and political stability, favorable investment environment, and favorable attitudes of policy planners and economic policy elites. These factors are identified by firms as significant in their decision-making process on foreign investment.[11]

Investment Pattern and Trade Behavior

The review of FDI in Korea in manufacturing reveals interesting characteristics.[12] First, FDI has never been a significant source of foreign capital. Since the early 1960s the share of FDI in total annual capital imports rarely exceeded 10 percent. This means that Korea preferred foreign resources in unpackaged form, that is, capital, technology, and management, when necessary, separately rather than in the packaged form of FDI. Second, most FDI were made in the form of joint ventures with local partners rather than in the form of wholly owned subsidiaries. In 1980 only 16 percent of the foreign firms in manufacturing were owned entirely by foreign parents. This is quite different from typical FDI patterns in other countries, in which wholly owned ventures predominate.

Third, Japan and the United States are the most prominent home countries of foreign affiliates in Korea. As of 1980, 53 percent of the total investment in terms of value came from Japan (74 percent in terms of number of firms) and 23 percent from the United States (15 percent of firms). Japan and the United States are also the most important trading partners and sources of foreign technology, suggesting that all these economic transactions are related. Fourth, FDI is concentrated in a few industries. They are either in labor-intensive sectors like textiles and apparel, electronics, musical instruments and toys, or in capital-intensive sectors such as chemicals, petroleum refining, and machinery. For example, nearly 20 percent of the total number of investment projects is in the electrical and electronics category.

Finally, the average size of investment was very small. About 68 percent of the investment projects were for less than $300 thousand and only 15 percent were for amounts greater than $1 million as of the end of 1978. This reflects the fact that a significant number of foreign investments were in small, highly mobile types of manufacturing operations in labor-intensive industries.

The main objectives of FDI are to substitute for imports in the local market of a host country and to reduce the costs of production for export by utilizing the host country's immobile factors. In the first case, some factors exist that make import substitution necessary, such as import barriers, transportation costs, and service considerations. In the second case, inexpensive labor or natural resources such as energy

Table 2–1
Number and Value of Foreign Investment by Industry and Country (1978)
($US 1,000,000)

Industry Sector	Japan		United States		Others		Total	
	Number	Value	Number	Value	Number	Value	Number	Value
Food	33	8.5	11	5.1	4	1.6	48	15.2
Textiles	106	103.7	8	3.8	8	9.1	122	116.6
Wood and paper	13	1.7	2	1.7	1	0.5	16	3.9
Chemicals	68	127.4	22	130.1	15	49.9	105	307.4
Metal and nonmetal minerals	57	40.5	3	4.5	3	7.1	63	52.1
Machinery	295	163.4	47	69.3	22	34.0	364	266.7
General machinery	64	26.9	6	8.1	2	5.1	72	40.1
Electronics and electrical machinery	157	88.8	23	26.8	8	21.9	188	137.5
Transportation equipment	13	17.3	3	25.9	1	0.7	17	43.9
Fabricated metals	31	21.8	10	6.8	3	3.0	44	31.6
Precision machinery	30	8.6	4	1.7	8	3.3	43	13.6
Toys, miscellaneous	45	10.3	4	0.6	—	—	49	10.9
Grand total	617	455.5	97	215.1	53	102.2	767	772.8

Source: Economic Planning Board, *Foreign Direct Investment Special Survey,* 1979.

are examples of immobile factors that foreign investors seek in order to reduce production costs.

The two different types of FDI, import substitution and export base, are not mutually exclusive in a host country with a relatively large domestic market and export growth policy. In the case of Korea, we frequently notice that import substitution products whose manufacturing processes can be divided between labor-intensive, and technology- and capital-intensive processes, become export products relatively soon after they are produced locally for the first time.[13] Producers simply import those components that require technology and capital-intensive processing for the manufacturing and then add value based on labor-intensive processing. Meanwhile, the producers increase domestic content gradually as the level of technology and competitive situations change.

Both domestic-market-oriented and export-oriented FDIs were made in Korea. But a large number of FDIs were of the latter type. This is partly due to Korean government policies to encourage export-oriented foreign investment. As already noted, FDIs are concentrated in certain industries, such as electronics and electric machinery, textiles and apparel, musical instruments and toys, chemicals, and machinery. Except for the last two, an important characteristic of the industries in which FDIs are concentrated is relatively high labor intensity. It suggests that a principal reason to invest in Korea was labor. The survey of foreign investors' motivations revealed that cheap labor was the most important reason for almost all industries. In the early 1970s, when many of these investments were made, the wage differential between Korea and the United States and Japan ranged as high as one to ten.[14] Even if one discounts the differences in productivity, the real wage differential was very large. The second motivation of FDI was local sales of the product. This motivation is strong for the chemicals, basic metals, general machinery, and transportation equipment industries.

We would expect that the import and export behavior of import-substitution-oriented FDI and export-oriented FDI would be significantly different. The FDI decision and trade behavior of foreign firms are mostly determined in the planning stage and therefore are not likely to change suddenly. Table 2-2 shows the export behavior of foreign firms in 1978. Some industries, such as textiles, apparel, electronics, toys and musical instruments (miscellaneous) have very high ratios of exports to total sales. This is partly the result of government policy which allowed only export-oriented FDI in labor-intensive industries in which the technology gap between foreign firms and domestic firms is not large. The government policy was motivated by the

Table 2–2
Export Share of Sales and Industry Share[a] of Foreign Firms by Industry and by Home Country (1978)
(in percent)

Industry Sector	Japan		United States		Other Countries		Total	
	Export Share	Industry Share	Export Share	Industry Share	Export Share	Industry Share	Export Share	Industry Share
Food	54	7	51	6	100	4	56	6
Textiles and apparel	73	15	98	1	93	3	76	7
Wood and paper	70	2	18	0.4	5	8	27	2
Chemicals	50	18	8	75	50	38	17	50
(excluding petroleum)	(50)	(18)	(34)	(11)	(50)	(38)	(44)	(16)
Metal and nonmetal minerals	33	11	22	1	11	16	26	6
Machinery	61	46	45	16	39	29	54	28
General Machinery	29	5	99	0.5	10	17	26	4
Electronics and electrical machinery	66	33	92	7	93	9	74	16
Transportation equipment	32	4	3	8	—	—	10	6
Miscellaneous	97	2	99	—	31	2	82	1
Grand total	58	100	18	100	40	100	35	100
(excluding petroleum)	(58)		(44)		(40)		(51)	
Total sales in billions of won	1293		1888		402		3583	

Source: Calculated by the author from Economic Planning Board, *Foreign Direct Investment Special Survey*, 1979.

[a]Industry share is the share of total sales by the FDI from one home country. It indicates the weight of an industry in FDI from that country.

notion that Korea would not gain much from this kind of FDI except foreign market access, and therefore wanted to restrict local sales.

The export intensity of industries such as petroleum products, transportation equipment, general machinery, and certain chemical products are fairly low, only about 10 to 25 percent, because they are basically intended for the domestic market. All of these industries are capital- and technology-intensive. When we compare the data for 1975 with that for 1978, we find that the export intensity pattern in those two years is very similar, indicating that changes in market orientation did not occur.[15]

Table 2-3 shows the import trade pattern of foreign firms. We find that the shares of imported raw materials and intermediate inputs are high across all sectors except for food products. The fact that, except for petroleum refining, the share of imported raw materials is higher in export-oriented investments is seen by comparing the export-intensity and import-intensity figures from tables 2-2 and 2-3. These facts confirm the hypothesis that utilization of inexpensive labor is an important objective of foreign investments in Korea, and that foreign firms appear to have special access to foreign markets for imports and exports through their parent companies. It is interesting to see that, even for the textile and apparel industry, linkage with domestic industry was small.

The most interesting fact, however, is that the import intensity of FDI in manufacturing has declined between 1975 and 1978. When we exclude petroleum, import share declined from 67 percent in 1975 to 54 percent in 1978. The linkage has been growing between foreign firms and domestic industry. The decline of the import share is especially noticeable in textiles and apparel (81 percent to 63 percent), electrical machinery and electronics (73 percent to 63 percent), transportation equipment (52 percent to 37 percent), and miscellaneous industries (74 percent to 54 percent). The increase in linkage can be explained by a rapid increase in competitiveness in the price and quality of domestic components and materials, some of which are produced locally by foreign firms. In particular, foreign firms were involved in backward linkage in the electronics industry as the volume of local demand grew significantly.

Comparisons of Investment Patterns and Trade Behavior of American and Japanese Firms

Do all foreign firms behave similarly under the same host country environment and respond similarly to the same host country policies?

Table 2–3
Changes in the Share of Imports in the Raw Material and Intermediate Inputs Used by Foreign Firms in Korea between 1975 and 1978

(in percent)

	Japan		United States		Other Countries		Total	
	1975	1978	1975	1978	1975	1978	1975	1978
Food	14	34	22	20	0	0	19	21
Textiles and apparel	85	65	87	63	35	53	81	63
Wood and paper	42	48	69	63	57	64	56	60
Chemicals	77	61	94	94	61	69	92	91
(excluding petroleum)	(77)	(61)	(65)	(58)	(61)	(69)	(69)	(61)
Metal and nonmetal minerals	72	62	28	21	87	45	74	58
Machinery	67	58	85	52	64	62	71	56
General machinery	61	52	100	99	66	67	68	64
Electronics and electrical machinery	66	56	91	86	71	64	73	63
Transport equipment	25	41	56	37	0	0	52	37
Miscellaneous	77	55	44	41	60	53	74	54
Grand total	69	58	92	84	62	57	85	75
(excluding petroleum)	(69)	(58)	(65)	(48)	(62)	(57)	(67)	(54)

Source: Calculated by the author from Economic Planning Board, *Foreign Direct Investment Special Survey*, 1979.

In the Korean case we would like to compare the behavior of the American and Japanese FDI, because they are the two most prominent home countries for foreign firms in Korea. In general, determinants of FDI include factors relating to the firm, the industry, and the home and host countries. Certain competitive advantages which foreign firms need to compete in overseas production will be related to the home country environment, such as the size of the domestic market, relative factor intensity, and level of development of technology. It is quite conceivable, for instance, that firms from a large developed country and those from a small developing country may have different competitive advantages.

After noticing differences in the American and Japanese foreign investment patterns in the 1960s and in the early 1970s, Kojima proposed the hypothesis that Japanese FDI is fundamentally different from American FDI.[16] He noted that the Japanese firms are typically small and medium-sized firms in relatively labor-intensive sectors, whereas the American firms are typically large, oligopolistic firms with differentiated products and advanced technology. Kojima maintained that Japanese investment in developing countries is in sectors in which host countries have comparative advantages, and therefore Japanese FDI augments the exports of the host countries. American investment, on the other hand, is concentrated in the capital- and technology-intensive sectors and import-substitution-type projects, for which host countries do not have comparative advantages. Such investments will replace foreign trade, but will not increase exports. Kojima's argument implies that the Japanese type of investment is better from the host country and global welfare point of view.

Some differences are apparent in the Korean case. First, Japanese investments are more numerous than American investments. By 1980, for example, 47 percent of the total foreign investments came from Japan and 29 percent from the United States.[17] Korea is one of the few countries in which FDI from Japan is greater than that from the United States, which has been by far the largest foreign investor in the world. Several factors appear to explain this. Korea's need for foreign savings during the 1960s and 1970s was met mostly by loans rather than FDI. The small size of the Korean market, physical distance, and restrictive government policies toward foreign direct investment all worked against large American investment. Japanese firms, which were just beginning to make FDIs, found Korea in the late 1960s and early 1970s quite attractive because of the abundant inexpensive labor. Because of their physical and cultural proximity, Japanese entrepreneurs knew Korea much better than American businessmen.

FDI is generally made in the countries that investors know best.

In the case of the United States, foreign investment began with Canada, Mexico, Europe, and Latin America, in that order, before extending to other regions of the world. Second, the Japanese need for foreign production locations for their declining labor-intensive industries matched nicely with Korean policies aimed at promoting exports in labor-intensive sectors. Japanese firms did not insist on establishing wholly owned subsidiaries; instead they were willing to undertake joint venture operations with Korean firms, which was also consistent with Korean government policy direction in the 1970s. Third, Korean entrepreneurs were familiar with Japan and therefore preferred Japanese partners over American partners because of better communication. Koreans also found that technology imported from Japanese firms was more appropriate for the Korean situation in such crucial matters as savings of space, energy and material. There are more similarities between the basic factor endowments of Korea and Japan than there are between Korea and the United States.

Although there were fewer American investments in Korea than Japanese, the average size of investment and sales was larger than the Japanese investments. The differences in size of investment and sales between the American and Japanese FDIs is closely related to the industry sectors in which each country's firms have concentrated their FDI. American FDI dominated the capital- and technology-intensive industries such as petroleum refining, chemicals, and transport equipment, which require large capital investment and scale of production to achieve scale economies. The Japanese investments, on the other hand, were strong in the labor-intensive sectors such as textiles and electronics, mostly in assembly operations, which would not require large capital investment because of the labor-intensive production processes.

The difference in investment concentration by sector between American and Japanese firms also explains in large part why the Japanese firms are more export-oriented and the American firms are more domestic-market-oriented. Japanese firms' FDI in the labor-intensive sectors in which Korea had comparative advantages led them to export more. Many American FDIs were in import-substitution type industries, which were not able to export competitively. When we compare American and Japanese firms in the same industry, we find that most of the differences in their trade behavior disappears.

For instance, American firms in the electronics sector exported 93 percent of their total sales in 1978, which is even higher than the export share of Japanese firms in the same industry (66 percent). In the case of chemicals, the export share was 34 percent for the U.S. firms and 50 percent for Japanese firms in 1978, if we exclude petroleum refining.

In Korea, therefore, investment patterns and trade behavior of FDI at the firm level are determined by the policies of the Korean government, the characteristics of the industry, and the firm and the industry-specific advantages of the foreign firms, rather than simply by differences in home country. This finding shows that, irrespective of their home country origin, foreign firms behave similarly in the same environment and respond similarly to host country policies.

Since the apparent differences between American and Japanese firms' investment and trade behavior appears to be closely related to the differences in the sectors in which each country has predominantly invested, the question is why do such differences in FDI concentration by industry occur? The answer should be traced to the competitive advantages that American and Japanese firms possess that cause them to invest in foreign countries, because without those advantages, FDI would not occur.

It is easy to understand why U.S. firms have dominant positions in petroleum refining, petrochemicals, and transport equipment. These are the industries in which American industry has dominated in terms of technology and market share. The American presence in the semiconductor industry is likewise explainable. What kinds of competitive advantages do Japanese firms have in the labor-intensive sectors, such as textiles, that enables them to make FDI in Korea? Until the late 1960s Japan had comparative advantages in these sectors and their exports were very large. Japanese firms began to lose competitiveness in the late 1960s and early 1970s because of labor shortages and sharp rises in wages. Japan still had competitive advantages in export marketing and production technology. With those advantages they came to Korea, where they could get cheap labor. With some training of Korean workers, the Japanese could fully utilize their existing competitive advantages in foreign market access and production skills (design, quality) of exportable products.

The import trade behavior of American and Japanese FDI will tell us the extent of their linkages with domestic industry. The import share of the total raw material inputs for all American FDI was 84 percent in 1978, whereas the same share for Japanese FDI was 58 percent. This result appears to indicate that, despite the American FDIs' domestic market orientation, their linkage with other domestic industries is weaker than the Japanese. However, we find that this result is misleading because of petroleum refining. If we exclude refining, we find the import share for American firms' FDI is reduced to 48 percent, which is lower than the Japanese share. Therefore, domestic market orientation and higher domestic linkage seems to hold true.

Observation of individual industries further confirms the fact that export propensity and import propensity are positively correlated. For instance, the import share of raw materials in American electronics and electrical machinery firms (86 percent in 1978) is much higher than the Japanese firms (56 percent). But the export share of American firms (93 percent) was also much higher than the Japanese share (66 percent). During the three-year period from 1975 to 1978, the import share declined for both Japanese and American firms. But the share of the American firms declined more than the share of the Japanese firms. This difference seems to be related to the fact that in export-oriented industry, in which Japanese firms are more numerous than American firms, the dependence on imports of Japanese components is continuing, or even growing in the case of transport equipment.

In conclusion, we see that the data confirm a simplified form of the Kojima hypothesis. Furthermore, we see that the differences in what Kojima and we have observed are mainly due to the difference in the level of development of Japan and the United States in the late 1960s and early 1970s, from which the home country competitive advantages were derived. This means that as the level of development and market structure of the two countries become more alike, the differences which Kojima observed will tend to disappear.

Government Policy Toward FDI

The distinct patterns of FDI in Korea are largely a result of the government policy toward foreign investment. In the early 1960s the government tried to attract FDI as a means of industrialization. However, the small size of the domestic market and the low export base of the economy did not attract much investment until the late 1960s, when a number of Japanese and American firms invested in labor-intensive industries. Investment oriented to the domestic market also began to grow. In 1973 the government adopted a new policy that had much more restrictive entry conditions and performance requirements.[18] In principle, wholly owned subsidiaries were not allowed unless they exported all production or brought in desired new technology. For FDI in those industries in which Korea had comparative advantages, exports were routinely required as a condition of entry. By 1978 more than one-half of all FDI projects had some kind of export requirement. Unless it was in the export sector or an import-substitution investment that the government desired, FDI was not encouraged.

Integrating export promotion into Korea's policy on FDI led to the establishment of an FDI pattern significantly different from the typical pattern of industrializing countries: tightly controlled, wholly owned subsidiaries producing goods for the domestic market of the host country. The restrictive regime adopted by Korea and the rapid increase in real wages in the latter 1970s slowed FDI inflow; the lack of an efficient promotion policy to compete with other host countries, such as Singapore and Ireland, may have been another factor.[19] Since 1980 the government has begun to liberalize its FDI policies for reasons discussed in detail in chapters 3 and 5. Export requirements have been abolished in principle, and the government has opened more industries to FDI. For many industries, local participation is no longer required. It is yet to be seen how these changes will influence FDI flow into Korea.

An Analysis of Export Propensity

To understand the export characteristics and behavior of manufacturing FDI in Korea we tested data from a survey conducted by the Economic Planning Board in 1979. The data base contained 397 samples, representing 85 percent of FDI over $300,000, and 35 percent of FDI under $300,000. One limitation was that there was only data on subsidiaries, not on parent firms. Hence, we could not relate parent firm variables with subsidiary behavior. To test some of the hypotheses we have discussed, we ran a multiple regression analysis of the entire sample and some subsamples. The hypotheses and variables are defined as follows:[20]

Hypotheses and Variables

1. The dependent variable is EP: Export Propensity, defined as exports/total sales.
2. Factor Intensity: We hypothesize that variables relating to factor intensity, especially labor intensity, will be closely related to EP: positively to labor intensity and negatively to capital intensity.

   KI: Capital Intensity—fixed assets/value added
   LI: Labor Intensity—total labor/value added
   LK: Labor Capital Ratio—total labor/ capital
3. Imported Raw Materials: We hypothesize that the propensity to import raw materials will be positively associated with EP, because what foreign firms sought in Korea was mainly labor-intensive processing and Korea does not restrict imports of raw materials

for exports. IM: Import Propensity of Raw Materials—imported raw materials/ total raw materials used.

4. We hypothesize that FDI with high EP use simple technologies and unskilled labor, and will be concentrated in sectors with low technology gaps between Korea and the industrial countries. The proxy for labor skill is WG: Average Wage—total wage/ total labor. The proxy for the technology gap is TI: Technology Transfer (dummy).

5. We hypothesize that the share of foreign equity will be positively related to EP, because high export shares reduce the need for a Korean partner both in practical terms and also according to Korean government policy. SF: Share of Foreign Equity—foreign investment/ total equity.

6. We tested Kojima's hypothesis that the home country of FDI is significantly related to EP. CC: Home Country (dummy).

7. We hypothesize that Korea's export requirement policy for FDI was effective. EC: Export Requirement (dummy).

The results of the regression analysis are reported in tables 2-4 and 2-5. The results for the factor intensity hypotheses show that labor intensity was the most significant variable explaining the export propensity of FDI. The sign of the coefficient is positive and statistically significant. In most equations capital intensity carried negative coefficients, but the results were not statistically significant. The coefficients for labor/capital ratio are positive and statistically significant. These results confirm that the comparative advantage that attracted FDI to Korea was labor.

The second important variable is the share of imports in total raw materials used by FDI. Our results show that import propensity is closely associated with export propensity, and that high exports by manufacturing FDI were supported by high shares of imported raw materials and components. Again, this confirms that FDI were using Korean labor to process imported raw materials and intermediate goods.

We thought that the share of foreign equity would be positively related to export propensity, because when the export share of production is high, the need for a local partner is reduced. In the case of Korea, the policies on FDI support this. Our results show that the share of foreign equity is positively associated with export propensity.

We hypothesized that industries with high export propensity use simple production technology with unskilled labor and will be concentrated in the sectors in which technology gaps between Korea and industrial countries are small. We used two proxies, contract for tech-

Table 2–4
Regression Analysis of Export Propensity

						Independent Variables							
		Constant	LI	KI	LK	IM	SF	EC	TI	WG	CC	R^2	F
Total samples	(1)	-0.06	0.65 (40.7)*	-0.002 (0.02)		0.25 (32.5)*	0.21 (10.0)*	0.25 (22.6)*	-0.20 (26.8)*			0.4150	43.7*
												0.4116	20.2*
Foreign investment													
LT. $300,000	(2)	-0.08	0.52 (12.2)*	-0.007 (1.61)		0.23 (13.7)*	0.23 (4.0)**	0.36 (20.4)*	-0.18 (7.4)*			0.4116	20.2*
GE. $300,000	(3)	-0.03	0.72 (23.0)*	N.S.		0.28 (17.5)*	0.22 (5.2)**	0.16 (5.2)**	-0.22 (17.5)*			0.4295	23.8*
Share of foreign investment													
LT. 50%	(4)	-0.29	0.64 (14.4)*	0.15 (1.2)		0.16 (5.1)**	0.19 (5.1)**					0.2816	10.8*
GE. 50%	(5)	-0.24	0.92 (33.3)*	-0.03 (0.71)		0.32 (31.2)*	0.35 (26.4)*					0.4697	30.4*
Assets (Wŏn billions)													
LT. W 1	(6)	-0.1	0.47 (10.8)*	-0.03 (5.4)**		0.22 (14.4)*	0.29 (10.2)**	0.41 (20.1)*	-0.17 (6.8)*			0.4001	21.0*
GE. W 1	(7)	-0.005	0.72 (20.7)*	N.S.		0.30 (18.1)*	0.15 (2.1)	0.17 (6.8)*	-0.22 (18.0)*			0.3955	19.0*

*indicates the level of significance at 1%; **indicates the level of significance at 5%.

Note:

1. In the case of regression equations (4) and (5), TI was omitted because the correlation efficient between TI and EC was high ($r^2 = 0.65$).
2. Figures in parentheses represent F statistics.
3. N.S. means the coefficient was close to zero and not significant.

Table 2–5
Regression Analysis of Export Propensity

	Constant	LI	KI	LK	IM	SF	EC	TI	WG	CC	R^{-2}	F
								Independent Variables				
Total samples												
(1)	54.4			0.015	0.29			−30.28	−0.03	7.02	0.2519	27.8*
				(2.7)*	(6.3)*			(−7.3)*	(2.1)**	(1.66)		
(2)	49.2	0.0154**	−0.002		0.31*			−30.0*	−0.23	10.57**	0.2352	23.51*
	(10.1)	(2.2)**	(−0.11)		(6.8)*			(−7.3)*	(−1.6)	(2.56)**		

Note: 1. *t* statistics are in parentheses.

2. *indicates the level of significance at 1%; ** indicates the level of significance at 5%.

nology transfer (dummy) and average wage, to measure technology gap and level of labor skill, respectively. The results confirm that export intensity is negatively correlated with technology and skill intensity.

Does the home country make a significant difference in explaining FDI export propensity as Kojima's hypothesis maintains? Equations (1) and (2) in table 2-5 show some positive and statistically significant correlation that seems to confirm that Japanese FDIs in Korea tend to export more than American FDIs, but the association is weak. The same regressions with subsamples did not show significant differences between Japanese and American and other FDI. Finally, the results for the dummy variable for government export requirement were positive, as expected.

Conclusion

Our overall comparison of the trade behavior of American and Japanese FDI in Korea tends to support Kojima's hypothesis. American FDIs are strongly represented in domestic-oriented, capital-intensive industries, whereas Japanese FDIs are concentrated in export-oriented, labor-intensive industries. However, the difference is relative; there are Japanese investments in the domestic-oriented chemical industry and many American investments in the export-oriented electronics industry. It is the petroleum refining industry that caused most of the differences in the aggregate analysis because of its total import dependency and domestic orientation. If we exclude petroleum, the overall differences between American and Japanese FDI narrow greatly. When we compare the behavior of American and Japanese FDI in the same industry, we find that firms behave the same irrespective of home country.

The apparent differences between American and Japanese FDI in the aggregate data that support the Kojima hypothesis were due to the differences in FDI distribution among industries, and do not hold within a specific industry. This suggests strongly that the FDI behavior of firms in the same industry will be similar in the same host country environment. Therefore, the success of host governments in achieving economic development objectives through FDI will depend on the ability of the host country to create and maintain the the proper environment, including both factor advantages and government policies, to attract the appropriate type of FDI, regardless of country of origin.

Korean government policy encouraged export-oriented FDI and differentiated between export-oriented FDI and domestic-market FDI, although the general policy approach tended to be restrictive. Despite the limited participation of FDI in manufacturing, the Korean government was generally successful in attaining its objectives because FDI contributed to the growth in Korea's exports during the 1960s and 1970s.[21] Growth in total exports contributed directly to increases in real GNP and in employment.

Other common host country objectives, such as acquiring technology and increasing linkages with domestic industry (growth of related domestic industries) were not achieved as successfully by export-oriented FDI. Export-oriented FDIs were typically low-technology, relatively unskilled operations (even in the high technology industries) that came to Korea because of low labor costs. The percentage of imported raw materials, components, and capital goods was high, so linkages with domestic industries were limited, although domestic linkage did increase significantly over time. The development of international market links and trade channels was limited in comparison to other advanced developing countries (see chapter 6).

However, the relative lack of success in meeting these other objectives through FDI has drawn notice only recently, as Korea's labor cost advantage declined sharply in the late 1970s and as Korea's economic strategy shifted emphasis to higher technology industries.[22] New export-oriented FDI declined sharply and many existing FDI left Korea for other locations that had cheaper labor, while the acquisition of higher technology FDI and even total annual FDI fell far short of Korea's objectives in the early 1980s.[23] To attain its new FDI objectives, Korea recently changed its policies on FDI, as is discussed in detail in chapters 3 and 5. Whether the new policies will be successful in attaining Korea's revised FDI objectives remains to be seen.

3

Incentives and Restraints: Government Regulation of Direct Investments between Korea and the United States

Dong Sung Cho

The history of modern nations has been one of continuous enlargement of government functions.[1] Today one cannot understand any nation's business and economy without considering the government's role in relation to business.

In Korea the government has been at the hub of economic growth for the past twenty years. The impact of governmental planning and control functions on Korean business and economy can hardly be exaggerated. But the use of the term Korea, Inc. by journalists to suggest tightly knit, supportive relations between business and government may be misleading. The Korean government has influenced Korean business not only as a benevolent supporter but also as an obstructive regulator. Indeed, Korean government regulation is perhaps more obstructive than supportive of business. In many cases red tape, in the form of directives, warnings, and administrative reservations of discretionary power, has discouraged entrepreneurial businessmen, especially in smaller companies, from realizing attractive opportunities.[2]

The general image of the American government's liberal attitude toward business may also be an oversimplification. Whereas independent local government does not exist in Korea, the United States government hierarchy is comprised of federal, state, and various subordinate local governments. Although the federal government in general stays out of individual business activities, each of the fifty states and thousands of local governments actively exercises various administrative controls to encourage the growth of local economies or to preserve their resources.

As a means of exploring government-business relations in the United States and Korea, we will examine bilateral direct investments between the two countries, with particular attention to (1) the balance between each government's supportive and regulatory roles; (2) the degree of government influence on such investments; and (3) changes in government attitudes toward such investments.

Four Basic Models of Government-Business Relations

Various external institutions, including stockholders, labor unions, consumers, government, and social organizations, affect the management of business enterprises. Because it can directly control various aspects of management through its public power, government is perhaps the most important of these institutions.[3]

Most scholars have emphasized the coercive element of government's role in relation to business. A. Elkins and D. Callaghan stressed the impact of government policies and regulations on the managerial decision process as a means to guard fair competition, to regulate price and market entry, and to promote social welfare.[4] Murray L. Weidenbaum pointed out the role of government, especially in the United States, in regulating the relations between consumers and producers, employees and employers, and society and private companies over matters such as pollution.[5] F. Luthans, R. Hodgetts, and K. Thompson also emphasized the regulatory aspects of government-business relations and suggested a need for business influence to reduce the hidden cost of such regulation.[6]

Few have emphasized government's ability to support business, though government itself has actively preached such a beneficent role. The Johnson administration in the mid-1960s stressed the importance of partnership between government and business in order to cope with the difficulties facing the American economy.[7] Specifically, it pointed out the government's role in creating and maintaining a stable economic environment to facilitate business activities.

These two views have been synthesized by George A. Steiner, who acknowledges government's dual role. On the one hand, government supports business activities as a maker and guide of economic plans, as well as a source of financing. On the other, it functions as the guardian of social welfare and the controller and redistributor of resources.[8] In Thomas C. Schelling's *black box* model, government executes its policies in order to direct business to fulfill its social responsibilities satisfactorily. He argues that a balance should be maintained between the voluntarism of business and the coercion of government.[9] Milton Friedman sees government as fundamentally a rulemaker and umpire, and considers the roles of enforcer and paternalistic guardian as supplementary.[10] While Friedman's model is based on the government of a developed country, Leroy P. Jones and Il Sakong have described the role of government in the developing economy of Korea as that of a rule-maker intervening actively in business affairs through direct commands and the manipulation of the various discretionary and nondiscretionary measures at its disposal.[11] Four fundamental models of business-government relations can be defined in terms of the strength of government's regulatory and supportive roles, as shown schematically in figure 3-1. The four models—constitutionalism, paternalism, liberalism, and mercantilism—are theoretical, but historical examples are easily found. In the West we observe a progression from mercantilism through liberalism and constitutionalism to paternalism.

Government first became substantially involved in business in sixteenth-century Europe, when the economy was regarded as the foundation of political sovereignty and the source of the military strength of a nation. Therefore, the task of the *mercantilist* government was to support, to strengthen, and to encourage the business sector.

With the Industrial Revolution, *liberal* governments began to abjure their active involvement with business in favor of a capitalistic laissez-faire market system. One result was the gradual formation of very large corporations, which established barriers to discourage the entry of potential competitors. The *constitutional* pattern of government-business relations emerged in the late nineteenth-century United States as a reaction to the monopolistic exploitations of big business. Antitrust laws were passed, regulatory agencies established, and criminal sanctions were applied to business transgressions. The final transition, to the *paternalistic* model, took place as the government supplemented its regulatory activities with supportive policies. During the depression of the 1930s, for example, the United States government adopted several incentive programs to stimulate business. Now government was taking the initiative in its relations with business through various administrative mechanisms.

Governments and Foreign Direct Investment

Foreign direct investment has both positive and negative effects on the economies of both the host and the home countries. Consequently both governments generally attempt to control the investment as well as the investor. Some characteristic supportive and regulatory measures by

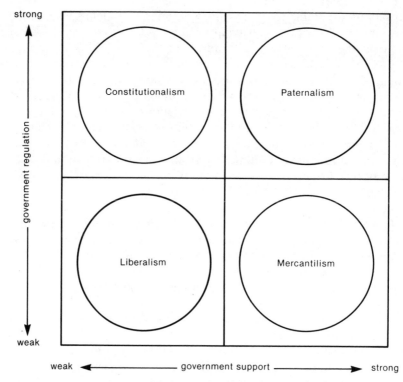

Figure 3–1. Four Models of Government-Business Relations

the home government are risk insurance, financial assistance, or restrictions on capital outflow. Typical host government incentives are tax concessions, guarantees on remittances, and local infrastructure support, while typical regulations restrict entry and limit ownership control. Governments on both sides of an international investment try to use it as a means to strengthen their respective economies, but each reserves the ultimate power to protect domestic sources of economic strength or to maintain independence from foreign domination.[12]

Korean Government Policies toward Foreign Direct Investment

Korean companies first began to invest outside the country in the early 1960s. Government policies on outward direct investment since then can be divided into four periods:[13]

First period: Formation of the base
Early 1960s to 1975

Second period: Establishment of the system
1975 to 1978

| Third period:
1978 to 1981 | Strengthening of investment
control |
| Fourth period:
1981 to the present | Liberalization |

In the first stage, which lasted until 1975, government did not sys-
tematically regulate direct investment abroad, although it instituted
articles concerning outward direct investment within the Foreign Exchange Control Decree in December 1968. Only a small number of
direct investments were made by Korean companies in this period.
The second period began with the Foreign Investment Permission and
Control Decree of April 1975, which specified the criteria for foreign
investment. Minority ownership was not to be permitted in principle,
for example. Investment in certain categories of business, including
recreational facilities, restaurants, and jewelry trading, was prohibited,
and investors were required to file periodic reports.

In the third period the Korean government tightened its regulatory
controls, fearing that the economic boom that had begun in 1975 might
encourage unwise private investments abroad. In October 1978 a new
government decree on foreign investment increased the minimum paid-
in capital of companies investing abroad, required at least three years
of experience in the same industry, and stiffened other requirements.
The government also reserved the right to approve individual cases of
investment abroad and classified industries abroad into three categories: prohibited, restricted, and promoted.[14]

The prosperity of the Korean economy was short-lived, however,
and by 1979 Korean firms were wracked by numerous troubles, such
as the increasingly protective trade policies of developed countries and
the increasingly nationalistic controls on their resources by developing
countries. Accordingly, the government decided to emphasize overseas
investment by Korean companies. The new Foreign Exchange Control
Decree of July 1981 drastically lowered the minimum conditions of
overseas investments. Now only one year's industry experience was
required instead of three; investment permission was to be granted by
the Bank of Korea instead of the Ministry of Finance; and prohibitions
against outward direct investment in certain countries and in certain
industries were eliminated.[15]

The current system regulating outward direct investment is much
more permissive than in the past. Korean investors abroad are offered
a variety of incentives.[16] The government offers them foreign risk insurance against expropriation, war losses, and the inability to repatriate
profits. Financial assistance is also provided. The Export-Import Bank
of Korea and other commercial banks may loan up to 70 percent of

the total capital needed by Korean investors abroad. In addition, the Korea Mining Promotion Corporation subsidizes the initial costs for feasibility studies of potential resource development investments abroad. Tax incentives include credits and tax reductions on losses incurred from investment abroad. In addition, the government has entered into international agreements on taxation and reciprocal protection that facilitate direct investment abroad.

The Korean government still controls outward investments that might jeopardize Korea's diplomatic relations with other countries, damage national prestige, or create ill effects on the economy. The Bank of Korea is empowered to monitor the performance and activities of Korean investors abroad and to cancel the investment permit under the following conditions:

infringement of Korean laws and regulations controlling foreign exchange

failure to repatriate profits without proper justification, or failure to repatriate profits for five years or more

cessation of business for more than one year

accumulation of losses greater than the original capital invested

failure to meet the conditions attached to the initial investment permission

failure to take appropriate remedies after warning, or suspension of the title for business, or other restrictive measures

In 1957 the U.S. government instituted the Development Loan Fund based on the Foreign Assistance Act in order to substitute loans for grants-in-aid previously provided to underdeveloped countries, including Korea.[17] Since then, Korean government policies toward direct investment by foreign entities have progressed through six distinct stages:[18]

First period: 1957 to 1962	Establishment of the system
Second period: 1962 to 1965	Active promotion
Third period: 1966 to 1969	Loan-first, investment-second policy
Fourth period: 1969 to 1972	Institution of incentives

Fifth period: Imposition of restraints
1973 to 1981

Sixth period: Liberalization
1981 to the present

Early attempts to institute a system to promote inward direct investment finally resulted in the Foreign Capital Inducement Law of January 1, 1960, which provided foreign investors in Korea with tax incentives and investment guarantees, while imposing certain conditions such as limits on dividend repatriation. The law was fundamentally very similar to the present one.[19] But the Student Revolution of April 19, 1960, and the military coup d'état of May 16, 1961 were more than enough to frighten potential foreign investors away from Korea.

The law was revised in 1962 to enable the newly established Economic Planning Board (EPB) to coordinate and promote the inducement of foreign loans and investment in Korea as part of its overall economic planning mission. Since the level of domestic savings was so low, the government required a substantial inflow of foreign capital to accomplish the investments planned. A steady stream of foreign capital was attracted to Korea starting in 1962, and Gulf Oil Corporation initiated a new era of active foreign participation with an investment of $5 million in Korea Oil Corporation in 1963.[20]

In 1966 the investment law and regulations on foreign loans were incorporated into a new Foreign Capital Inducement Law. Together with a declaration of a general policy for the rationalization of foreign investment management in 1967, the 1966 law emphasized promotion of foreign loans as a means of securing the capital needed for investments critical to the growth of the Korean economy. Direct investment's share of the total foreign capital attracted to Korea fell from 34 percent to only 7 percent in 1966, while public loans captured 40 percent and commercial loans 53 percent, respectively.[21]

The loan-first, investment-second structure of the law resulted in mounting pressures on the government to pay loan principal and interest. In response to this problem, in 1969 the government started to regulate the quality of loans, while reemphasizing foreign investment, by declaring a policy to encourage foreign investment and the successful development of foreign-invested enterprises.[22] Also, the government established the Masan Free Trade Zone in 1970 in order to attract foreign capital. This change in policy resulted in a surge of direct investment. In 1970 direct investment represented 11.7 percent ($65.2 million) of the total capital inflow, up from 2.2 percent ($12.7 million) in 1969.[23]

As the robust growth of its economy made Korea attractive for investment, the government gained bargaining power over competing foreign investors. In 1973 the EPB issued a general guideline which imposed a number of restrictions on foreign investors. The guideline set a maximum of 50 percent equity participation in principle, specified the industries eligible for foreign investment, and imposed various other conditions, such as minimum investment size.[24]

In 1981 as part of a government reorganization program aimed at increasing efficiency and coordination between the government and the business sector, the responsibility for handling foreign investment affairs was transferred from the EPB to the Ministry of Finance. The number of industrial sectors eligible for foreign investment was expanded to 521 out of the 855 in the Korean Standard Industrial Classification. In 56 sectors, 100 percent investment is permitted, while up to 50 percent investment is allowed in the others. The government plans to allow foreign investments in all 855 industrial sectors by the end of the 1980s.[25]

The current system offers a variety of incentives to foreign investors. The Foreign Capital Inducement Law guarantees repatriation of capital, remittance of profits, royalties, principal and interest of a loan, and payment for imported capital goods. Similarly, government laws and decrees guarantee the properties owned and operated by foreign invested enterprises against expropriation, except in the case of national emergencies. A number of tax exemptions are offered. Tax laws provide that foreign-invested enterprises are to be exempt from corporate taxes, income taxes (on unincorporated enterprises), property taxes, and property acquisition taxes for the first five years; for the next three years, taxation is to be at only half the standard rate. No taxes are imposed on dividends or the distribution of profits accruing from the shares owned by foreign nationals for the first five years. Royalties or fees for technical assistance are not taxed for the first five years and then taxed only 50 percent of the normal rate for the ensuing three years. Finally, foreign investors are assured, in principle, of equal treatment with Korean nationals.

At the same time, the Korean government regulates foreign investors in several ways. Entry controls bar foreign investors from 334 industrial sectors that are vital to national security or not considered appropriate for foreign participation. These sectors include such businesses as newspaper publishing, broadcasting, telecommunications, real estate, and tobacco and ginseng manufacturing. In addition, the minimum investment is set at $100,000. Ownership control may limit the maximum share of foreign participation to 50 percent depending on profitability, contribution to technology transfer, and other factors.

The government also imposes certain management controls. Foreign investors cannot make up a larger proportion of the board of directors than their share of stock ownership. In the case of 50 percent ownership, directors representing foreign investors cannot, in principle, have veto power.

In addition to these restraints, the government has the power to approve or disapprove individual applications for foreign investment. Each case is reviewed to assess its economic and technological feasibility and desirability.

Policies of the United States Government toward
Foreign Direct Investment

Since it would be virtually impossible to examine all the control mechanisms exercised by various state and local governments, this review of United States government-business relations will be mainly geared toward the federal level. This should in no way imply that the federal government is the only source of government influence on business.

Before World War II, following the principle of freedom in international trade and investment, the American government assumed a laissez-faire attitude toward outward direct investment. After the war, however, investment abroad was actively encouraged as a means of assisting European reconstruction and creating export markets for American industry. In the 1950s foreign investment by American companies was seen as a way to alleviate the dollar shortage of foreign countries and to keep them from falling under communist influence.[26]

This supportive investment policy, together with the growing economic power of Western Europe and Japan, led to deficits in the U.S. balance of payments in the 1960s. The government revised its tax code in 1962 to abolish tax havens used by American companies and in 1965 initiated a voluntary restraint program to curb the flow of U.S. investment abroad.[27] In 1968 a mandatory ceiling was imposed on foreign direct investment by any company. Labor and protectionist groups argued that foreign direct investment by U.S. companies was hurting domestic employment and GNP growth.

The Overseas Private Investment Corporation (OPIC), created in 1971, offers American foreign investors comprehensive insurance coverage against the political risks of expropriation, confiscation, war, revolution, insurrection, and nonconvertibility of profits and capital.

OPIC also offers financing, 50 percent subsidies on the cost of investment surveys abroad, and other incentives.[28] In addition, the federal government allows credits (recently reduced) against taxes paid to foreign countries, and has entered into various international agreements to protect ownership and management by U.S. companies.

The major premise of American policy on foreign direct investment has been that free market forces should determine the direction of capital flows throughout the world to maximize economic efficiency. Thus, foreign investors have generally been freely admitted and treated on a basis of equality with domestic investors in their U.S. operations. Over time, however, certain restrictions have been imposed.[29]

The Sherman Act of 1890 and the Clayton Act of 1914 significantly reduced the freedom previously enjoyed by business. For example, foreign investors were now expressly barred from acquiring stocks or assets of U.S. corporations if the effect might substantially lessen competition or tend to create monopoly. In 1917 the Trading with the Enemy Act empowered the President to control the property of foreign nationals in time of war or national emergency.

Other restrictions apply to specific industries. The federal government restricts foreign investment in the maritime and aviation industries, and state laws, while not prohibiting foreign ownership of railroads, may have an inhibiting effect. The Mineral Leasing Act of 1920 excludes foreigners from the development of coal, oil, and natural gas on federally owned land and bars them from acquiring interests in leases through stock ownership in American corporations unless their home country grants like privileges to American citizens. In banking, state laws may prohibit a foreign bank from conducting commercial banking operations. Foreigners may not acquire hydroelectric power facilities nor, under the Atomic Energy Act of 1954, may they be issued licenses for the operation of atomic energy utilization or production facilities.

Finally, in the wake of the 1973 oil crisis, fears grew that oil-rich Arab countries might initiate a massive takeover of U.S. companies. An interagency Committee on Foreign Investment in the United States was established in 1975 to monitor the impact of inward direct investment and to coordinate the implementation of policies regarding foreign investment.

On the positive side, individual state governments provide out-of-state investors, including foreign investors, with various incentives such as financing, tax concessions, building of infrastructure facilities, and training of personnel. Since foreign investors can choose where to invest, local government incentives tend to outweigh restraints in making direct investment decisions.

**Bilateral Direct Investment between Korea and the
United States**

Economic relations between Korea and the United States date back to
1882 when the two governments signed the Treaty of Peace, Amity,
Commerce, and Navigation. However, the last twenty years have been
perhaps the most significant, since it was during that period that the
two countries established a bilateral relationship in political, social,
and cultural matters as well. An understanding of the fourth and fifth
periods of table 3-1 may provide us with a basis for predicting the
likely future patterns of the two countries' overall relationship.

U.S. investment in Korea began in 1962 when Chemtex brought
in $1.4 million to build a plant for manufacturing filament nylon yarn
as a fifty-fifty joint venture with Kolon. Since then, 154 investment
projects have been implemented by Americans with a total investment
of $418 million currently outstanding (table 3-2). The United States is
the second largest investor in Korea, with 29 percent of the total inward
direct investment currently outstanding. Japan has invested $772 mil-
lion in 625 projects. In the period since 1981, however, the United
States has been the largest investor, representing more than half the
total investment from overseas.

Gulf Oil Corporation's 1963 investment in Korea Oil Corporation
provides us with a vivid example of Korean economic conditions and
government attitudes during that period. The Korean economy was
not in a position to attract foreign investors because of the 1960 student
revolution and the 1961 military coup. The government approached
several major oil companies to negotiate a joint venture for an oil
refinery. It sought an investment of $20 million together with oil refin-
ing technology and a supply of crude. At that time Gulf Oil was anxious
to find a stable outlet for its excessive supply of high-sulphur crude
from Kuwait, which most oil-importing developed countries did not
want. Not realizing Gulf's motivations, the Korean government was
happy to strike a deal with a reputable oil major and extended a variety
of incentives, such as an unconditional guarantee against expropriation, guarantee on remittance of profits and capital, tax exemptions,
and an exclusive right to supply crude to the joint venture. Later, when
Gulf's ownership of Korea Oil Corporation increased to 50 percent, it
was granted veto power.

Although Gulf was subject to a number of restrictive measures,
such as the limitation on foreign ownership of stock, its participation
in Korea Oil Corporation enabled it to control a secure market for its
crude, while minimizing its capital risk. Thanks to active government
support and vigorous Korean economic growth, Gulf's investment of

Table 3–1
History of Economic Relations between Korea and the United States[a]

Criterion	First Period (1882–1908)	Second Period (1908–1945)	Third Period (1945–1961)	Fourth Period (1962–1972)	Fifth Period (1972–)
Characteristics	Mammonist and hermit kingdom	Relations abandoned	Military foothold versus economic benefits	Reciprocity of economic benefits	Progress on an equal basis
Korea's interest	U.S. presence as counterbalance against Japanese	No expectation	Dependence on U.S. for economic survival	Utilization of American capital and market	Deep-rooted economic cooperation
United States' interest	Pursuit of bonanza	Recognition of Japanese suzerainty	Aid on security grounds	Benefits derived from trade and investment	Recognition of Korea as equal partner
Initiator	U.S. businessmen	=	U.S. government	Korean government and U.S. businessmen	Korean businessmen and U.S. businessmen
Trade pattern	Korea ← U.S.	=	Korea ← U.S.	Korea ↔ U.S.	Korea ↔ U.S.
Investment pattern	Korea ← U.S.	=		Korea ← U.S.	Korea ↔ U.S.
Size of relation	Small	=	Medium	Large	Very large
Overall economic relation	Unilateral and asymmetric	=	Unilateral and asymmetric	Bilateral and asymmetric	Bilateral and symmetric

[a]Excerpted from Exhibit 1, with a minor revision, of my paper "From Unilateral Asymmetry to Bilateral Symmetry: Retrospect of the Economic Relationship between Korea and the Unites States 1882–1981," which was presented to the Centennial Conference of Korea-U.S. Relationship, Honolulu, May 1982.

Table 3–2
U.S. Direct Investment in Korea (currently outstanding as of March 31, 1983)

Year	62-66	67-71	72-76	77	78	79	80	81	82	Total
Number of projects	9	34	37	9	10	10	14	12	19	154
Amount [A] ($million)	21.9	12.4	67.9	14.6	26.6	35.5	46.2	85.2	107.6	418.0
Total foreign investment in Korea [B] ($million)	23.0	72.7	565.2	65.9	128.4	107.3	140.8	145.3	187.8	1436.4
[A/B]	95%	16%	12%	22%	20%	32%	33%	58%	57%	29%

Source: Oegugin t'uja in'ga hyŏnhwang, Ministry of Finance, (March 1983), 2.

$4.8 million in 1963 generated a handsome $3.5 million in the following year in the form of profits from crude sales, transportation, and dividends from Korea Oil Corporation operations. In 1965 this figure rose to $6.6 million, and it continued to grow.[30]

The U.S. government gave Gulf an ordinary package of support, such as risk insurance against expropriation and restriction on repatriation of dividends and capital, and foreign tax credits. Gulf management was said to have declined the diplomatic support of the United States government. On the regulatory side, the most dramatic instance of government involvement was the federal indictment of Gulf for its political contribution to President Park, which resulted in the firing of then chairman Robert Dorsey in 1975. In addition, Gulf Oil was regulated by several clauses of the Antitrust Act as well as the Boycott Clause, which prohibited the Korean joint venture from transactions with certain countries. Diplomatic considerations were also a factor on at least one occasion. In 1973 Gulf Oil and Zapata Exploration Company were jointly exploring potential crude reserves in the Yellow Sea. Anxious not to provoke a boundary dispute between China and Korea, the State Department put pressure on Gulf and persuaded the company to give up its operation while it was in the middle of drilling a hole.[31]

Over the years the Korean government has gradually shifted from discretionary to nondiscretionary intervention and from direct control over individual projects to prior guidelines on a general basis. Accordingly, the government's role as supporter and regulator gradually declined in the 1970s, and private enterprises came to assume the central role in dealing with foreign investors, from the initiation of contacts through the negotiation, consummation, and implementation of the investment project. A good illustration is the joint venture between Samsung Electronics and Corning Glass Works of the United States.

In 1973 Samsung Electronics was already one of the world's largest assemblers of television sets, but it wanted to integrate backward by manufacturing the glass bulbs for the Braun tubes, which constituted a significant portion of total cost. Corning Glass Works agreed to be a partner for the plant. The joint venture proceeded smoothly and subsequently provided Samsung Electronics with cost reductions, quality improvements, standardization of product, assurance of parts supply, and above all, a substantial increase in profits.

Corning Glass Works received the Korean government's support in the form of tax exemptions and arbitration on labor disputes. At the same time it was subject to requirements to employ local labor, restrictions on management control, and control of dividend remittance. In contrast to the Gulf Oil situation, the government was not directly involved in every aspect of business. Thus Corning Glass was able to overcome these restraints successfully by coordinating with Samsung Electronics. In time, all the American personnel were replaced with well-trained and capable local management, and Corning Glass willingly decided to reinvest in Korea all the profits generated from the joint venture.[32]

The first case of Korean investment in the United States began in 1972 when Samsong Industrial Company, a deep-sea fishery company, invested $10,000 to establish a marketing subsidiary in Los Angeles. Between then and June 1982, there were 134 cases of Korean investment in the United States, as shown in table 3-3. At the end of the period, the total amount of investment outstanding was $48.6 million, or 19 percent of the outstanding total Korean investment abroad. The United States has been the leading offshore investment site for Koreans.

Until the mid-1970s, Korean investment in the United States was mainly oriented toward local marketing as an extension of export promotion activities. The first case of natural resources development abroad by Korea was the $54 million investment project by Pohang Iron Steel Company (POSCO) in Tanoma Coal Mine, Pennsylvania, which changed the general attitude of Korean businessmen toward foreign investment. This venture, which began in 1976, was wholly owned and operated by POSCO as part of its long-term plan to secure a supply of raw materials needed in its steel plant. The Korean government provided various incentives for this project, such as the joint survey of prospective coal mines by the Ministry of Commerce and Industry (MCI), Korea Mining Promotion Corporation, and POSCO. The Exim Bank of Korea and Korea Mining Promotion Corporation supplied all the required capital, which was composed of $11 million in owner's equity and $43 million in long-term debt. To avoid United States taxation at the source on interest and dividends, the actual investment was made by Tanoma Coal Company, a paper company set up by POSCO in the Netherlands Antilles.[33]

Another type of Korean investment in the United States began in 1981, when Gold Star Electric Company established a local manufacturing subsidiary in Huntsville, Alabama, with the goal of circumventing growing U.S. trade barriers against color TVs imported from Korea. The Korean government did not intervene as either supporter or regulator in this project, which was 100 percent owned and operated by Gold Star management. Minister Suh of MCI visited the plant site once, and the governor of Alabama reciprocated by visiting government officials in Korea. However, American authorities, especially at the state and local levels, were heavily involved in the project. The city of Huntsville issued industrial revenue bonds in order to provide

Table 3–3
Korean Direct Investment in the United States
(currently outstanding as of June 30, 1982)

Year	59–71	72–76	77	78	79	80	81	82.6	Total
Number of projects	—	32	19	38	8	13	14	10	134
Amount [A] ($million)	—	3.4	4.4	12.1	7.4	4.4	5.6	11.3	48.6
Total Korean foreign investment [B] ($million)	14.3	49.6	17.8	43.4	22.8	21.1	40.1	42.8	251.8
[A/B]	—	7%	25%	28%	33%	21%	14%	26%	19%

Source: Uri nara ŭi haeoe t'uja, Bank of Korea (August 1982).

Table 3–4
Government Incentives and Restraints in Four Cases

	U.S. Investment in Korea		Korean Investment in the U.S.	
	Gulf Oil	Corning Glass	POSCO	Gold Star
Year	1963	1973	1976	1981
Ownership	25% → 50%	50%	100%	100%
Korean government	*as host government*	*as host government*	*as home government*	*as home government*
incentive	various guarantees tax exemptions	tax exemptions arbitration of labor disputes	joint survey financing	diplomatic support
restraint	ownership control	employment of local labor control on dividend remittance	—	—
U.S. Government[a]	*as home government*	*as home government*	*as host government*	*as host government*
incentive	risk insurance tax credit (F)	risk insurance tax credit (F)	—	financing (L) tax and tariff exemption (S) labor training (S)
restraint	diplomatic pressure (F) antitrust regulation (F) boycott clause (F) code of conduct (F)	—	—	—

[a]The definition of U.S. government includes not only federal government (F), but also state (S) and local (L) government.

a $5.5 million loan to Gold Star's American subsidiary, while the State Department of Alabama granted exemptions from property taxes and transaction taxes for products shipped out of state from the bonded factory and agreed to provide a training program for local laborers.[34]

Hypotheses about the Roles of the Korean and U.S. Governments

We have reviewed the policies and practices of both the American and Korean governments, and we have derived three broad hypotheses about each government's practices:

1. Both governments maintain a balance between incentives and re-straints. However, neither the Korean nor American government belongs to the classic mercantile or constitutional model.
2. The Korean government exerts more control over foreign invest-ment as both supporter and regulator. Thus Korea conforms more to the paternalistic model than the U.S. government, while the United States is closer to the liberal model.
3. The policies of the Korean and American governments toward foreign direct investment have been converging.

We attempted to test these hypotheses by assessing managers' perceptions of the practices of both governments. A questionnaire was sent to companies that have invested capital cross-nationally between the two countries and were still operating actively in the other country as of February 1, 1983. Questionnaires went out to 78 Korean and 76 American companies; answers came back from 29 Korean and 22 American companies.[35] Although the rate of return was low, statistical tests show that the sample collected can be considered representative of the industry composition of cross-national investments between Ko-rea and the United States at the 5 percent level of significance.

To insure that the perspectives of the firms represented in the sample were similar, we compared the motives for investment of the Korean and American firms. Of the Korean companies that have in-vested in the United States, 76 percent were motivated primarily by a desire to expand foreign markets, while 17 percent wanted to secure raw materials, and 7 percent wanted to overcome stagnation in the Korean market. American companies invested in Korea to expand foreign markets (77 percent), to secure raw materials (9 percent), and to take advantage of lower factor costs (9 percent). The motivations and perspectives of the two response groups can be considered homogeneous at the 5 percent level of significance.

Before analyzing the results, we must stress the limitations of the survey data. First, the sample is too small to warrant any broad conclusions. In addition, there is probably some structural bias in the respondents' answers, which is inevitable because subjective perceptions are involved. Finally, respondents in the sample groups were not truly comparable. Because the research was conducted in Korea alone, Korean companies investing in the United States were represented by Korean managers at their domestic headquarters who participated in the investment decision, while American companies investing in Korea were represented by resident American managers, most of whom probably did not participate in the original investment decision. Comparable data from American company headquarters or managers of Korean subsidiaries in the United States might support different conclusions.

Responses to the questions testing the first hypothesis indicate that both Korean and American managers sense little difference between the impacts of the incentives and the restraints established by the Korean government. However, while Korean managers see little difference in the effectiveness of the incentives and restraints of the American government, American managers perceive their government's incentives to be more helpful than its restraints are restrictive.

These results show that the managers do not perceive that the Korean and U.S. governments fit the mercantile or the constitutional model, except that the U.S. government's role toward outward direct investment is more supportive than regulatory. This anomaly probably reflects the impact of OPIC, because the American managers, who appreciated the incentives provided by their government to invest in Korea, attached great importance to the foreign risk insurance program.

The same procedure was used to test the second hypothesis. The questionnaire response data regarding this hypothesis lead to the observation that, in general, the managers think that the incentives and restraints employed by the Korean government on both outward and inward direct investments affect business more than those of the American government, except that the American government's incentives on outward direct investment are as helpful as those of the Korean government, if not more helpful. Thus it appears that the Korean government is more paternalistic than the U.S. government, except in the case of the U.S. government's incentives on outward direct investment. Apparently the managers believe that the Korean government lacks a structural support comparable to that provided by OPIC.

The third hypothesis postulated that the United States and Korean governments have been changing their policies in ways that tend to reduce the differences between the two. A test of this hypothesis requires a longitudinal data base. Thus the questionnaire data used to test the first and second hypotheses, which reflected perceptions as of a particular time (February 1983) were not suitable. However, the review of the historical trends and the case studies of direct investment provide substantial evidence that both governments have changed their policies over time as described in the hypothesis, although the pace of change has been much faster in Korea than in the United States. In particular, the four case studies illustrate the liberalization of the Korean government's control over business, as private enterprise has begun to replace the Korean government as the initiator of economic relations with the United States.

The two diagrams in figure 3-2 illustrate Korean and United States government attitudes toward outward and inward direct investment. The strength of each government's regulatory and supportive efforts is measured on the basis of the managers' perceptions reported in the survey questionnaires. For both outward and inward investments, the Korean government is found in the upper right-hand paternalistic quadrant of the matrix. The United States government, in contrast, appears to fit the liberal model, except for its support of outward direct investment.

Conclusion

We have reviewed the history of incentives and restraints by the Korean and American governments on both outward and inward direct investments. We reviewed the performance of direct investment between Korea and the United States during the past two decades and examined four cases to illustrate the workings of government policies in bilateral direct investment. Finally, we tested our hypotheses against the perceptions of managers from Korean companies with capital investments in the United States and American companies with capital investments in Korea.

This review suggests several conclusions. First, the Korean government has adopted a paternalistic attitude toward foreign direct investment. It has provided strong support to both outward and inward direct investment, while maintaining equally strong regulatory controls. This attitude is a reflection of the Korean government's role as formulator and executor of national economic development plans that required substantial inflows of foreign capital without sacrificing economic independence.

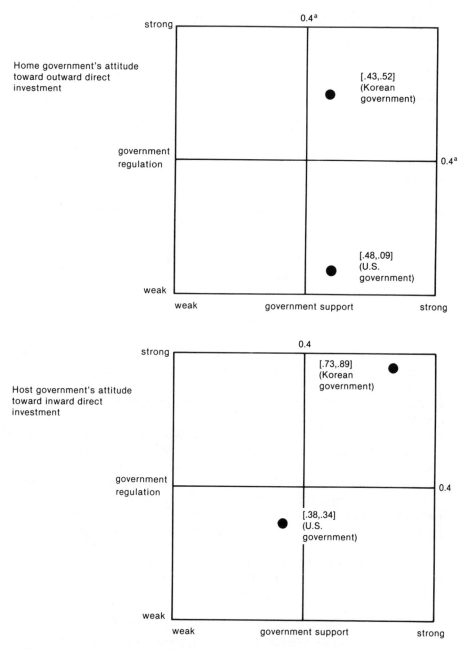

Figure 3–2. United States and Korean Government Regulation and Support of Investment Abroad

The U.S. government, in contrast, has adopted a liberal attitude toward foreign direct investment. With one exception, it has not provided incentives or restraints of any significance to outward or inward direct investment. The U.S. government has provided substantial support through OPIC's risk insurance program for outward direct investment. The Korean government has not provided Korean companies with equally effective support.

Although empirical tests of this hypothesis were not possible, we noted some evidence that the Korean government's role as supporter and regulator of foreign direct investment has decreased recently, while the control of the United States government over foreign direct investment has gradually increased over the past several decades. This shift in the American government's role, however, does not mean that it is moving toward the paternalistic model. We can see that the Korean government has become more liberal, allowing private enterprise to take the initiative. This shift parallels the process of economic growth which has transformed Korea from a passive recipient of economic aid from the United States into an equal partner in a mutually beneficial two-way economic relationship.

These conclusions may contribute to a basic understanding of government-business relations, especially in the Korean economy. Korea has never really been 'Korea, Inc.' Instead, Korea is moving in the direction of a privately led, relatively open liberal economy. This change can be seen in a series of recent policy shifts such as private ownership of commercial banks, import liberalization, and reduction in emergency financing to rescue bankrupt companies.

Before jumping blindly onto the liberalization bandwagon, however, policymakers should understand what the policies on foreign direct investment have been, and more importantly, how they have been perceived by businessmen who have made investment decisions. Businessmen should also understand the past development of the government policy on foreign direct investment as well as the likely directions in the future before they make any decisions related to a foreign investment. After all, it is the businessmen who should benefit from the government-business relations; thus it is their responsibility to make the most of the government policies and systems.

4 The Perils of Partnership: Dow in Korea

Brian Levy

Many Koreans are deeply ambivalent about foreign investment. Although the country has long been reluctant to open its doors to multinational firms, rapid economic development has created new pressures to permit their entry. The economy has begun to expand into technologically more complex sectors of industries; the technology in these sectors sometimes is controlled by multinational firms that are reluctant to supply their special knowledge to outsiders.[1] As one way to gain access to technology, the government has loosened restrictions on foreign investment in Korea; most investments have taken the form of joint ventures between multinational and Korean firms, but on occasion foreign companies have been permitted to set up wholly owned subsidiaries.[2]

The chemicals industry is one important example of an emerging industry in Korea that has attracted substantial foreign investment. In the late 1960s the Korean government began to encourage chemicals production. In 1973 the country's Ulsan Petrochemical Complex came on stream, to be followed in 1979 by the Yeochun Petrochemical Complex.[3] By 1978 foreign investment in chemicals and petroleum refining accounted for almost 40 percent of the value of the entire stock of foreign investment in South Korea.[4]

Dow Chemical Company's investments in the 1970s made it the single largest foreign investor, both in the chemicals industry and in the Korean economy as a whole. But Dow's involvement in South Korea was short-lived; in 1982 it pulled out of the country altogether. What were the reasons for Dow's discontent with its Korean investment? Are there wider lessons to be learned about the role of foreign investment in Korea? These questions are the subject of this study.

The Dow Connection

Before the Second World War the Dow Chemical Company was a "comparatively simple, thriving business, built and run by a single, resourceful, hardheaded family."[5] By 1959 it had outgrown its small-town Midwestern roots to become the third largest chemical company in the United States.[6] Although for much of the 1950s it thought of the export business merely as a sideline, and in 1957 exports accounted for only 8 percent of company sales, this inward orientation shifted rapidly.[7] By 1966 the company had "completed the framework of an organization designed for worldwide operations."[8] In 1979, for the first time, sales from overseas operations exceeded revenues from United States sales.

Dow's expansion into manufacturing abroad first touched South Korea in 1968 when the company invested $7 million in a joint venture, the Korea Pacific Chemical Corporation (KPCC), which was to produce vinyl chloride monomer (VCM). The plant came on stream in 1974 and was soon described as "a real jewel" by Dow's president for the Pacific region.[9] By 1976 Dow had announced a major new investment in a chlorine/caustic soda/ethylene dichloride plant to be run by a wholly owned subsidiary, the Dow Chemical Korea Limited (DKCL); Dow's new commitment was to total about $140 million.

But this time things did not go smoothly. Problems with Dow's joint venture partners in KPCC (which was slated to be the user of a substantial portion of the new plant's output) began soon after DKCL began production in 1979. By 1982 Dow officials had begun to hurl insults publicly: "These people haven't run a garage; they have no industrial experience. . . . it's like being partners with cotton wool," the president of Dow Pacific said of his Korean joint venture partners.[10] "We're not interested in investing five cents more in South Korea until the present problem is solved. . . . [and I] would advise investors who haven't already invested in South Korea that they ought to consider the situation very carefully," said the chairman of Dow following a meeting with Korea's President.[11] Finally, in October 1982, Dow agreed to sell out to a consortium of Korean firms for $60 million, taking a loss of about $100 million.

What went wrong? This study explores the question by focusing on the industrial economics underlying Dow's South Korean venture. Two topics appear especially relevant: the linkages between Dow's wholly owned upstream operation (DKCL) and the jointly controlled downstream firm (KPCC), and shifts in the strategic objectives of Dow as a result of changes in the structure of the world chemicals industry. But before addressing these topics, we must explore the forces that led Dow to make a major investment in the Korean chlor-alkali industry in the first place.

Dow's Expansion: The Role of Chlorine

As we shall see later, there are some special reasons why Dow chose Korea as a major investment location. However, the forces that lay at the root of the Korean investment were essentially those that led the company to undertake its general expansion abroad and to give the production of chlorine a major role in that expansion.

Chlorine production has long been important to Dow's business strategy. Produced jointly with caustic soda via the electrolysis of a salt solution, chlorine became the company's major product shortly after the first plant went into operation in 1897 atop Michigan's massive underground brine deposits.[12] Even in 1952, after the company had diversified extensively and was producing about 600 different chemical products, chlorine was described as "*the* Dow raw material—supplied almost like power to nearly all plant groups.[13] In 1975 chlorine, its coproducts, and major intermediate derivatives accounted for about 20 percent of total Dow sales.[14]

Chlorine's share in total Dow profits cannot be estimated as readily, but the structure of the chlorine market and Dow's position in that market suggest that for much of the company's lifetime the commodity's profit contribution exceeded its contribution to sales. Between 1950 and 1974 U.S. chlorine capacity rose at an average of over 7 percent per annum. Throughout this period (and perhaps dating back to the 1930s) Dow had been far and away the leading producer. In 1957 Dow accounted for 30 percent of chlorine production; in 1967 its market share was a little above 32 percent; and between 1967 and 1975 "Dow increased its share of capacity substantially.[15] Between 1957 and 1980 Dow's capacity was consistently at least twice that of its nearest rival.[16]

Given the large share in production of the market leader, it is not surprising to find that chlorine is one of the more highly concentrated sectors of industry in the United States. Between 1963 and 1975 the capacity share of the four largest chlorine producers rose from 54 to 64 percent; the average level of concentration in the chemical industry in these years was 40 and 46 percent.[17] As of 1977, an industry with a four-firm concentration ratio in excess of 60 percent was among the 20 percent most concentrated sectors of manufacturing in the United States.[18]

The existence of a high level of concentration in any one industry is not prima facie evidence that higher than normal profits are being earned. In principle, the threat of entry (rather than a dilution of concentration via actual entry) is sufficient to induce sellers to price at competitive levels. Thus, if we are to uncover the extent to which chlorine historically has been an important source of profit for Dow, we need to examine the barriers to entry into chlorine production.

A tradition of mutual forbearance among chemical companies appears to be one important deterrent to entry. Rapid rates of innovation and the continual emergence of new chemical markets throughout the twentieth century raised the specter of rampant instability as chemical companies jockeyed with one another for position. At the same time, however, the industry was dominated by "a relatively small number of giant companies . . . meeting each other in one market after another."[19] The obvious resolution to these opposing forces was negotiated coordination. This coordination reached its apogee between the First and Second World Wars when world chemical markets were divided up among the three giant companies of the time: Germany's I.G. Farben, Britain's Imperial Chemicals Industry, and the United States firm, Du Pont. Stocking and Watkins characterized the relationship between two of these firms:

> Both companies gave heed to strategic considerations favoring some kind of understanding . . . Both realized the hazards of seriously antagonizing each other and, above all, the folly of upsetting the market. This was the nature of their gentleman's agreement: They would co-operate wherever possible, and in any event they would act like gentlemen.[20]

After the Second World War, competition intensified as a result of the breakup of I.G. Farben, an antitrust conviction against Du Pont, and the rapid growth of other chemical companies, such as Dow. Nonetheless, as Scherer notes, "competition among chemical makers continues to have a mild quality."[21]

Turning to barriers to entry that are specific to the chlorine industry: at almost $100 million the capital requirements for a new chlorine-caustic soda plant are a large, but not overwhelming obstacle for a determined new entrant such as an oil company.[22] As for technology, even though Dow claims some special technical advantages which it refuses to supply to other companies, widespread licensing by other leading firms has made the requisite skills readily available. The most important barrier to entry results from the interaction of large minimum efficient scale and a limited merchant market for chlorine. The costs per unit of production for a plant of 1,000 tons per day are more than 20 percent below the equivalent costs for a plant with a capacity of only 600 tons per day.[23] While in 1975, 1,000 tons per day amounted to only 3 percent of chlorine capacity, no more than 41 percent of chlorine produced in the United States was sold on open markets, with the remainder used by producers in their own operations downstream. This pattern of partial integration turns out to be especially important for the present study. As a result, the output of an efficient-size chlorine plant will supply 8 percent or more of the merchant market. In the face of a relatively inelastic demand by industrial users, "a potential entrant faces the likelihood that its entry will have a substantial depressing effect on price as existing sellers lower their prices to protect market positions."[24]

The combination of mutual forbearance, diseconomies of small scale, and a limited merchant market imply that the restraining influence of potential new entrants on the pricing policies of chlorine producers is likely to be limited, and chlorine production is likely to be highly profitable. Indeed, in 1975 the return on capital of new chlorine-caustic soda facilities was estimated to be about 22 percent, 11 percent above the comparable return on all the operations of diversified chemical (and other) manufacturers that also produce chlorine, and 14.5 percent above the average return to capital for all United States manufacturing.[25]

What are the implications of this market structure for our analysis of Dow's business strategy? One possibility is that for a long period of time Dow took advantage of its leadership position and the apparently minimal threat of the entry of new competitors to price chlorine in such a way as to reap upstream most of the potential profits available in the vertically integrated chain of chlorine-based products. While this would amount to little more than a bookkeeping operation within Dow, its external implication is that Dow could use its upstream market power to increase its own profitability at the expense of its customers (and competitors) downstream. But even if the characterization of entry barriers and estimates of profits are overstated, there is little doubt that Dow's position as market leader with the largest cumulative volume of production (and thus experience, and, if the learning curve is to be believed, cost advantages) and the largest average plant size in the industry made the production of chlorine a highly profitable line of business for the company.[26] Dow's ongoing investments to maintain its market share as the demand for chlorine expanded points clearly to the importance of chlorine to the company's strategy.

All of this helps to explain another feature of Dow's strategy that is especially important for this study: Even though Dow was generally quite willing to take on foreign partners once it went abroad, it was insistent that all of its overseas chlorine-caustic soda plants were to be wholly owned subsidiaries. This insistence is hardly surprising considering the important place chlorine occupied in the company's strategy, as suggested here.

As noted earlier, in 1975 chlorine-based products accounted for only 20 percent of total Dow sales; it would be wrong to describe chlorine as the centerpiece of Dow's post World War II strategy. Nonetheless chlorine is an important example of that strategy. As *Fortune* magazine put it, "the bulk of Dow's production is what the trade calls 'upstream' . . . Du Pont is a 'downstream' company that

buys the kinds of basic commodities Dow produces.[27] Along with
chlorine and caustic soda, other basic materials in which Dow has
substantial upstream investments include bromine and ethylene as well
the metal magnesium. In 1979 almost 70 percent of Dow's revenues
came from these basic chemicals and their intermediate derivatives
which were supplied primarily to other chemical companies.[28]

As Dow has demonstrated, a company that specializes in upstream
chemicals can be highly profitable as long as the markets for these
chemicals are growing rapidly and the company can expand its share
in these markets. But once the growth in demand begins to slow and
the company has moved from upstart entrant to market leader, the
potential for further profits is limited. As early as 1962 Dow had reached
such an impasse. In that year's annual report the company president
noted plaintively that "the [United States] chemical industry has become a most strenuous testing ground. New competitors almost out-
number our long-time competitors. Whenever we look up, it seems
one more brand-new competitor comes charging at us. In this testing
we have seen markets shifted, prices beaten down, profit margins pressured. And it still goes on."[29]

At first it seemed that Dow's response would be to emphasize
innovation and move into more specialized chemicals markets downstream. The president said, "We have a depth of knowledge, patiently
home-grown, that reaches from research to market for each of our
businesses. Drawing on this knowledge and developing it further, we
will find continuing profitable growth and fresh opportunities."[30] Instead
Dow chose to replicate its American strategy in foreign markets: "For
some materials, foreign economic and industrial trends largely parallel
U.S. conditions. . . . Our practice is to enter international markets
with export materials and then, when local production will result in
substantial sales increases at acceptable profit levels, to establish plants
in or near major consumption areas."[31] The share of Dow's capital
expenditures made abroad rose from 21 percent in 1967 to a still un-
equaled high of 55 percent only four years later.[32] As in the United
States, basic chemicals were emphasized. In a 1980 report Dow listed
wholly and partly owned facilities at seventy-nine locations in twenty-
eight foreign countries. It described six of these (all wholly owned) as
"major production plants"; five facilities—two in Canada, and one
each in West Germany, Brazil, and South Korea—had the production
of chlorine and caustic soda as their base.[33]

Investment abroad only postponed the need for Dow to reevaluate
its emphasis on upstream production. By the late 1970s structural
changes in the world chemical industry were pressing Dow to move
increasingly to a downstream orientation. But we are getting ahead of

the analysis. Before detailing these pressures we must conclude this section by examining briefly the specific reasons for Dow's investment in Korea and then analyze in some detail the conflicts surrounding that investment.

Although Dow had placed a high priority on expanding its Pacific operations, it is likely that in the early 1970s it had little intention of locating a chlorine-caustic soda plant in South Korea. In late 1973 Dow approached the Japanese Ministry of International Trade and Industry (MITI) with a plan to build a wholly owned plant capable of producing 360,000 tons of chlorine and caustic soda per annum. Dow's bid gained highly visible status as an early test of MITI's purported liberalization of Japan's restrictive foreign investment code; the liberalization apparently permitted, for the first time, 100 percent foreign ownership of new ventures in the chemical industry, among others. The application was not accepted, in large part as a result of pressure from Japanese caustic soda producers who were themselves feeling pressure to shift to a more environmentally sound production process, and feared that they would be unable to meet Dow's competition while making these major new investments.[34]

After it became apparent that this bid would be turned down, plans to build a new plant in Korea began to surface. As the bid in Japan reveals, Dow had made a clear decision to set up a major chlorine-caustic soda production unit in the Pacific region; its earlier Korean plant had come on stream and seemed to be a great success, so given the Japanese disappointment, Korea seemed the obvious alternative for a major investment. What Dow did not foresee, however, was that by building a new wholly owned plant it was setting itself up for conflict with its downstream Korean joint venture partners.

Upstream Versus Downstream

Dow's new investment in Korea produced chlorine and caustic soda in approximately equal amounts. The bulk of the caustic soda went directly to export markets and so played little role in the conflict between Dow and its Korean partners. By contrast, all of the chlorine was used downstream within Korea itself in the plants of the joint-venture KPCC; these plants react the chlorine with ethylene (procured from another company) to produce ethylene dichloride (EDC), which is further processed into vinyl chloride monomer (VCM) before being sold to other Korean firms (which use the VCM to produce various plastic products). (Here the terms *upstream* and *downstream* are now being used in a different sense than before. They refer to the relative position in the specific production processes of the DKCL and KPCC. In terms of the usage earlier—where these terms were used in relation to the chemical industry as a whole—the KPCC would itself be defined as an upstream operation.) The transactions along this chain hold the key to the conflict between Dow and its Korean antagonists.

In general, the price at which an upstream plant sells its chlorine to the downstream user determines how the profits or, as has been the case in Korea since 1979, losses from the production and sale of VCM are to be distributed. For any given price of VCM, the higher the price of chlorine charged to the downstream plant, the larger the share of profits that gets taken upstream. If the earlier characterization of Dow's strategy is accurate, then it is likely that the company fully intended to price chlorine so as to take a disproportionate share of its Korean profits in its wholly owned upstream plant. What Dow did not expect was that its joint venture partners downstream would balk at this distribution of profits and challenge the chlorine pricing policy.[35]

The local partners thought they could improve the profitability of the downstream operation by importing their raw materials at a lower price than Dow was willing to offer, given the high cost of electricity in Korea.[36] These additional profits would, of course, come at the cost of enormous losses for the upstream plant because it would have no ready market downstream, but these losses would be borne solely by Dow. Dow's response to this challenge, and to persistent losses both upstream and downstream that together amounted to $60 million over two years, was to propose a merger of the upstream and downstream operations. Dow claimed that the merger would save $20 million over five years by eliminating some duplication of activities by the two companies. Such a merger also implied that Dow's Korean partners, who would become minority stockholders in the merged venture, would obtain a share of profits, or share the burden of losses, in direct proportion to their share of total equity. When the local partners objected to the merger proposal, Dow claimed that they "do not understand the chemical business."[37] It is obvious that the actions of the local partners were a far cry from the 'gentleman's agreements' that had governed the chemical industry in earlier days. What is less clear is whether the import plans of the Korean KPCC directors could in fact provide the gains to the KPCC that were claimed. To clarify this issue, we need to examine the international organization of the chlorine-EDC-VCM production chain.

Ideally, the KPCC would have sought to import chlorine in place of its purchases from the DKCL. But chlorine is corrosive, explosive, and poisonous, and as a result, expensive to transport.[38] International chlorine trade is almost nonexistent.[39] The KPCC's intention was to import EDC to convert to VCM, even though this would imply leaving idle their own EDC capacity. Though still limited, international trade is more prevalent in EDC than in chlorine. In 1979 the United States accounted for 90 percent of total world exports; these exports amounted to only 9.6 percent of total United States production.[40] So an examination of EDC in the United States production chain helps provide a clearer picture of the availability of EDC exports.

The United States market for EDC is more highly concentrated and the degree of vertical integration far higher than the market for chlorine. As in chlorine, Dow is the leading firm with one third of the market, but the remaining firms also have large market shares. In the latter part of the 1970s, the largest four firms accounted for 71 percent, and the largest seven for 92 percent, of total EDC capacity in the United States.[41] One implication of this high level of concentration is that not only were the potential sources of EDC imports open to the KPCC limited in volume and location, very few companies apart from Dow were in a position to provide supplies.

The fragility of the international market appears even greater once the effects of vertical integration are considered. In 1979, 88 percent of all United States EDC production was used in the producers' own downstream plants (almost all for the production of VCM).[42] In general, upstream producers that are part of a vertically integrated firm give first priority to their own downstream operations. As a result, for products where vertical integration is as extensive as EDC, the character of the open market varies widely with the level of demand for the downstream product.

In times of economic slowdown, upstream producers are likely to have surplus capacity on their hands even after they have met the demand of their downstream affiliates. They are likely to be willing to use this surplus capacity to supply independent buyers as long as they are paid a price in excess of (or perhaps only equal to) the short-run increments to the cost of the additional production and the costs of transportation. In times of economic boom, however, the position is very different. Internal demand alone is likely to suffice to keep the upstream firm operating at full capacity. Independent buyers seeking to purchase the upstream product would have to offer a price that at the least covered all upstream production costs (including capital costs), as well as the costs to the integrated downstream affiliate of foregoing some supply to which it had a prior claim.[43] Thus, independent buyers of products that are largely supplied through vertically integrated channels are likely to face widely fluctuating prices. In times of surplus, the price in the open, residual market may amount to little more than the short-run variable costs of additional production; when supply is tight the price will be in excess even of long-run production costs.[44]

The international market serves as a residual outlet for EDC. The volume of EDC (and VCM) exports from the United States generally has moved in inverse proportion to domestic demand: the higher the domestic demand, the lower the volume of exports.[45] The KPCC's claim that it could import EDC at a price below Dow's Korean production costs came at a time of glut. If the analysis above is correct, then the advantages of imports were short-term only.[46] In the long run, once United States demand expanded and the market tightened, the relative cost disadvantages of domestic Korean production would diminish.[47] But by then, were KPCC to implement an import strategy, the upstream Korean plant might have been forced to close down.

Explaining the Behavior

The import strategy proposed for the KPCC by Dow's Korean partners does not seem to take into account the way international EDC trade was organized. Although it is possible that, as Dow claimed, the proposal of this strategy was a result of the Korean partner's failure to understand the chemical industry, there might well be other, more cogent reasons why the Koreans took the approach they did.

In the absence of any alternative source of chlorine, the relationship between DKCL and the KPCC was one of bilateral monopoly. At stake was the distribution of the fixed pool of revenues that accrued from the sale of VCM. Given the failure of Dow and its local partners to agree on an appropriate distribution of these revenues, there was only one strategy for the local partners to adopt if they were to turn the balance of bargaining in their favor: threaten to take action that would cost Dow far more than would an agreement to reduce the price of chlorine. If the threat could be made credible despite being inordinately costly to the KPCC as well as Dow, so much the better.[48] However, once Dow responded to the threat, not by capitulation but with a counterproposal of its own, it became inevitable that the Korean government would step in as arbiter.

Dow's public insults foreclosed the possibility of compromise, leaving the government with only two options: support Dow's bid for a merger or arrange for local firms to take over its Korean operations. Aside from the impact of a takeover on other potential foreign investors, there was little reason for the government to side with Dow.[49] Dow did not possess any special technical skills that were unavailable elsewhere and without which the plant could not function. It was not bringing in from abroad any raw materials which were not available in Korea; it was not providing access to overseas markets that would otherwise be closed to a Korean-based operation.[50] Under these circumstances it is hardly surprising that faced with the choice of caving in to a foreign firm or extending national control over the chemical industry, the Korean government chose the latter course of action.

Even given the provocation of its local partners, it remains to be explained why Dow, which must have realized that there was little standing in the way of a local takeover, fueled the conflict with its public insults, thereby foreclosing the possibility of eventual compromise. Once again the answer appears to lie in part in the structure of the international market.

By early 1982 dominance by United States firms (most notably Dow) of the export market for EDC seemed set for a rapid decline. The United States share of world exports was predicted to fall precipitously from 90 percent in 1979 to 29 percent by 1985 and a paltry 10 percent in 1990. Canada, with a predicted 44 percent of the market in 1990, the Middle East, and Mexico to a lesser extent were slated to become the dominant EDC exporters.[51]

The combination of low-priced natural gas and lowered barriers to entry provided the impetus for these predicted shifts in the global pattern of production. Natural gas was for a long time simply flared as a valueless byproduct of crude oil extraction; as energy prices rose, oil-producing countries began to consider the possibility of converting it into a marketable product. One alternative was to set up petrochemical plants which, using the natural gas as feedstock, could produce basic petrochemicals for sale on world markets. This is not the place to explore the barriers to entry into petrochemical production in any detail. It must suffice to note the existence of vast oil revenues, an explosion of international lending, the presence of construction and engineering companies willing to build new petrochemical plants anywhere in the world, and vendors of technology willing to sell the skills needed for many of these plants. These factors, combined with the willingness of multinational firms to undertake joint ventures with private firms or state-owned enterprises in energy surplus countries, made it possible for a host of new petrochemical producers to enter the industry. One common product of these new petrochemical ventures was ethylene, the value of which could be increased further by reacting it with chlorine to produce EDC and VCM for sale on the international market.[52] As of 1979 the cost of ethylene made up 40 percent of the total costs of VCM production, so EDC and VCM producers with access to low cost natural gas had, potentially, a major cost advantage over producers elsewhere.[53]

The projections just outlined might imply that the Korean partners not only understood the organization of international EDC trade but also were unusually prescient in devising a strategy consistent with emerging global trends. But this seems doubtful. There is no available evidence that the proposed KPCC strategy was based on a careful analysis of international trends; even though the geographical locus of EDC exports appeared to be shifting rapidly, it did not follow that an open international market would emerge. Indeed Japan, which earlier had decided to rely increasingly on imports of EDC and VCM rather than local production, took steps to maintain a vertically integrated structure, though now on an international scale. Japanese chemical companies took equity in a new 300,000 ton per annum EDC plant in Alberta, Canada, and they also attempted to become partners in a proposed EDC-VCM venture in Indonesia.[54]

The projected shift in the international EDC market did, however, have some important implications for Dow. Even if some of the new ventures were organized on a vertically integrated basis, an increase in the number of suppliers would inevitably add to the opportunity of downstream users to shop around for new, lower priced sources of EDC. Nor was it only on the supply side that trends were looking bleak. The growth of demand also was predicted to slow; energy price rises of the 1970s increased the relative price of petroleum-based products, including plastics, and encouraged substitution away from them. Moreover, government restrictions aimed at limiting the environmental damage associated with the production and use of plastics seemed likely to result in further cutbacks in demand. Plastics had become a mature product with a demand growth not much in excess of the overall rate of increase in the level of economic activity.[55]

Once again, although we have focused here on petrochemical products that have chlorine as a major input, the emerging trends in fact indicated widespread problems in Dow's strategy of emphasizing basic chemicals upstream. Aside from shifts on the international front, the growth of demand for basic chemicals in the United States fell from 8 percent per annum in the early 1970s to only 2 percent per year a decade later.[56] Dow's move abroad in the early 1960s and subsequent investments in energy supplies had helped postpone the time when it would have to redirect its upstream orientation. But by the end of the 1970s, a reevaluation of strategy could no longer be delayed.

Dow's move downstream began in 1978. In 1981 the company president spelled out the implications of this shift: "Longer range, the nature of Dow's business is changing rapidly. We intend to maintain our position as a world leader in basic chemicals and plastics, but much of our future growth will come from specialized products and services which can grow more rapidly and generate a better return."[57] Estimates of the source of Dow's profits give some indications of the magnitude of the proposed shift: In 1982 specialty chemicals accounted for only 37 percent of total profits; yet Dow's president promised that by 1990 about 60 percent of profits would come from specialty products and services.[58]

Since the company had already borrowed heavily to finance its overseas expansion, one way for Dow to raise additional capital for its move downstream was to sell some of its existing assets. Some sales were of United States properties. But in 1982 alone Dow withdrew from five major basic chemicals projects abroad. Two of these—in Argentina and Saudi Arabia—had been slated to produce ethylene and some of its derivatives downstream (though not those that used chlorine as a major input); two more—in South Korea and Yugoslavia—were geared to produce chlorine and its downstream derivatives; and the fifth was a long-time Japanese joint venture that produced a host of basic chemical products.[59]

This is the context in which to interpret Dow's behavior in the conflict with its Korean partners. The Korean investments no longer were part of the main thrust of Dow's strategy. If they could provide a continual stream of profits, that was all to the good. But if their profitability was limited, and they were to be a source of continual conflict, then it would be better to be rid of them; indeed, any capital Dow received in compensation for its withdrawal would be especially useful at a time of company reorientation of strategic direction. Dow, then, had little incentive to search for compromise. The primary goal was a clearcut resolution of the Korean entanglements. Whether Dow would still be active in Korea after this resolution seems to have been of only secondary importance.

Some Larger Implications

There are a number of larger issues that emerge from an analysis of the history of Dow's investments in Korea. The first has to do with the way in which these investments were organized. As is by now wellknown from experience the world over, the likelihood of conflict between joint venture partners is unusually high if one of these partners also is the supplier of some critical input.[60] Dow's offer to merge its wholly owned chlorine-producing company with the chlorine-using

KPCC joint venture might have resolved this organizational impasse, but the offer came too late. The conflict had already escalated beyond the possibility of compromise. The Dow experience is a reminder, especially in countries such as Korea where there is a strong predisposition in favor of some local participation, that all participants in joint ventures must structure their enterprises to minimize the likelihood of conflict among the partners.

The need to take such care is especially great if the actions of the KPCC partners are characteristic of the behavior of Korean partners in joint ventures. In many developing countries local participants in joint ventures are content to take on the role of sleeping partners sharing any profits that are made. That was not the role the KPCC partners took on for themselves. This study has not explored the reasons why the Korean partners adopted an adversarial stance toward Dow. If their behavior was symptomatic of a general ambivalence towards foreign investment within Korea, joint ventures between Korean and multinational firms are likely to experience continuing internal conflict.

Perhaps the clearest implication of the present study is that Dow's behavior cannot be explained by focusing only on its relationship with its local partners and the Korean authorities. As has been shown, Dow's eventual decision to withdraw was consistent with larger shifts in the company's strategic orientation. As such, it is a reaffirmation of the truism that the decisions of multinational firms are based on global considerations rather than the national development strategies of the particular countries in which their subsidiaries happen to be located. American firms have been committed partners in Korea's economic growth, but benevolence has never been the sole motivation of multinational firms in Korea.

Whether or not foreign investments can make a positive contribution to national development in Korea and elsewhere depends on the extent to which national goals are consistent with the global strategies of individual multinational firms. Sometimes there will be a close correspondence between the two sets of goals; at other times, as with Dow in the early 1980s, there will not. No standard generalization will substitute for a careful examination of the merits of particular proposals for inviting multinationals to become partners in promoting Korean economic development.

5 American Technology and Korea's Technological Development

Kee Young Kim

Over the past two decades Korea has achieved remarkable success in industrialization. The exploitation of technology is central to the industrialization process. How Korea's technological capability evolved in the process of industrial development has not received much attention. As in other developing countries, the ultimate source of technology for Korea has been the advanced countries, principally the United States and Japan.

Following Dahlman and Westphal, technology is defined broadly as a set of processes that transform inputs into product, together with the social arrangements that structure the activities that support or carry out these transformations; technological mastery is the command and comprehension of technological knowledge that enables a firm or a country to use the knowledge and apply it effectively.[1] The achievement of advancing levels of technological mastery depends on many factors: indigenous efforts to develop and apply technology, the stage of technology development reflected in a country's industrial structure, government policies that support technological efforts, and the availability of human resources.

The United States has contributed to Korea's technological development in two ways. It has been a source of technological knowledge (information): Aside from its practical uses in industry, this imported knowledge has substituted for indigenous efforts at technology development. Second, the United States has been the principal overseas location of the training of human resources that Korea has utilized in its technological efforts. The main concern of this chapter is to assess the role of American technology in Korea's technological development at different stages of its rapid industrialization. The questions we attempt to answer are what sorts of technologies Korea has acquired from the United States and what have been the mechanisms and characteristics of the transfers of American technology to Korea. Inevitably, this approach focuses on formal technology transfer agreements that can be captured statistically and analyzed. Nevertheless, we will pay due attention to the development of human resources and the

indirect methods of technology transfer that are so crucial to the
achievement of technological mastery.

The Modes of Technology Transfer

There are two sources of commercially useful technology: technology
developed domestically and technology developed in a foreign country
which may be transferred. In the case of technology from another
country, the process of assimilation assumes critical importance. From
a national standpoint as well as that of the firm, decisions about importing technology must take into account both the level of sophistication of the technology and the availability of people able to assimilate
the technology. These factors influence the choice of the mode preferred for a particular transfer.

The best known methods of transfer are contractual business relationships. Foreign direct investment (FDI) is the mode when technology is brought into a country by a foreign investor. Foreign licensing
(FL) is when a firm purchases the right to use a technology from its
foreign owner. A firm may purchase technical assistance (TA) in order
to gain expertise in using a technology.

Technology is also transferred through modes that are informal.
Business deals such as turnkey contracts, machinery purchases, and
raw material imports often are accompanied by technology transfers.
The seller may provide the client with instructions in the use of the
product, thus eliminating the necessity of obtaining the knowledge
through formal arrangements. Similarly, a firm may acquire technology
from its clients. Foreign buyers' designs and product specifications,
along with quality inspections, provide manufacturers with new ideas
and mastery of processes which would otherwise have to be obtained
through FDI, FL, or TA.

Regardless of the mode of transfer, the attitudes of the foreign
specialists involved in a particular transfer have a great effect on the
teaching and transfer process. Success in transfering technology often
depends on understanding the conditions of the local industry and the
various problems faced by the local engineers who are learning the
technology.[2]

An important route for the acquisition of technology is through
human resources. Employees sent abroad for training will return with
critical background knowledge that can speed up the assimilation process. University-level teaching and research in basic sciences and engineering likewise produces people with appropriate advanced training.
In addition, people who have absorbed specialized knowledge during

their careers may be hired for their experience in working with a given technology. Finally, a company may bring in outside specialists to provide on-the-job training and to work with its employees.

While transfer of technology through human resources may be diffuse and indirect, the practical experience of how a technology actually works, including the supporting human organization, that is transferred through this mode is often crucial to the success of formal technology transfers or domestic technology development projects.

Korea's Technology Acquisition Policies

Korea's economic development began in the early 1960s. During the periods of the first five-year plan (1962-1966), the second five-year plan (1967-1971), and the third five-year plan (1972-1976), Korea achieved annual growth rates averaging over 10 percent. At the beginning of the process, Korea was technologically undeveloped and capital-poor. These two realities conditioned Korea's policies toward the acquisition and inducement of technology from abroad.

During the first two plan periods Korea needed two different types of industrial technology. Key industries such as fertilizer, petroleum refining, and cement were necessary to build infrastructure and provide basic inputs. These industries required high levels of both technology and capital. At the other extreme, Korea wanted to promote labor-intensive light industries in order to increase employment and to produce exports for foreign markets.

Both types of technology were induced. Key industries were built with the participation of foreign capital and technology, mostly through the FDI mode. Simple technologies were acquired for the development of labor-intensive export industries. These simpler techniques were induced in various ways, but the informal modes were of particular importance, as foreign buyers brought in product and market information. Much of the high rate of growth during the first three periods (1962-1976) may be attributed to labor, not technology.[3]

In the early 1970s policy emphasis turned to the development of heavy and chemical industries. This was an import-substitution policy based on the concept that these new industries would be sufficiently large and efficient to compete internationally. Foreign capital and technology played crucial roles in the establishment of these industries. In industries such as petrochemicals, transfers of complex technology packages occurred through the FDI mode, which served as the primary means of acquisition of these new technologies. The need to improve production efficiency and quality in light manufacturing and assembly industries, which were the largest employers, also received attention. Production efficiency and product quality were improved mainly through the FL and informal modes.

In the late 1970s, inflation, rising labor costs, and rising costs of imported raw materials due to factors such as the second oil shock, undermined Korea's strategy. The heavy industries, which are intensive in capital, technology, and energy requirements, were increasingly burdensome, while their international competitiveness was thrown into doubt. Meanwhile, Korea's light industries were losing their competitive edge because of rising labor costs that were outstripping gains in productivity. The need to improve production efficiency in existing facilities to offset rising production costs and upgrade product quality became even more critical.

Korea's Technology Policies for the 1980s

Faced with structural problems revealed by the 1979 oil shock and the changing world competitive environment, declining cost advantages in key growth and export industries, and growing difficulties in obtaining advanced technology from abroad, the Korean government undertook a fundamental policy reevaluation. The result was a reorientation of overall policy objectives to stress the development of high technology industries for the 1980s. Supporting this strategy was a comprehensive technology policy that emphasized the development of domestic capabilities as well as the inducement of advanced technologies. The effect was to raise technological development to a national goal; this was symbolized by the institution of the Expanded Technology Promotion Meetings by President Chun in 1981. The meetings are comparable to the export promotion meetings that President Park initiated in the 1960s to focus national attention on the goal of expanding exports.

However, unlike exports, technology development and transfer are complex processes that are difficult to measure. The new technology policy has several elements, some of which actually date back to the 1960s. One element is aimed at strengthening the human resource base that supports technological development. There is increased support for education and research in the basic sciences and for sending students abroad for advanced scientific and technical training. This element is not new; in 1967 the government established the Ministry of Science and Technology and in 1973 the National Council for Science and Technology was founded in order to enhance scientific development and communication among government and private research centers.

Government-supported research institutes that originally appeared in the latter 1960s, such as the Korea Institute of Science and Technology (KIST, now called KAIST) established with American help in 1966, conduct research and train graduate students. New institutes specializing in such industrial technologies as electronics were founded during the 1970s; the new technology policy aids these institutes. A recent addition to the manpower development policy is to encourage the repatriation of technical and scientific specialists who are living abroad. Former emigrants who return to Korea not only have up-to-date knowledge of their professions, but also those who worked in industry before repatriating have personal experience in the application of technologies—the informal knowledge that is often crucial to the successful assimilation of a technology. The 1982-86 plan sets a target of 80,000 technical specialists, out of whom it hopes to recruit 5,000 from abroad.

The new policy stresses the rationalization of resource allocation for technology development, principally by the encouragement of R&D in private industry, where it is closest to actual application and market information. There are incentives for firms to establish research facilities. The R&D promotion policy also encourages firms to establish research facilities in overseas locations where advanced technologies are centered and to undertake R&D efforts in joint ventures for foreign firms. An important policy element that relates to R&D and to the goal of private firm initiative instead of government direction is the loosening of government controls on technology imports. Firms now have more freedom to acquire technologies abroad according to their own strategies.

The third major policy element is new. This is the application of planning concepts to achieve an integrated approach to technology development. One aspect is the increased support for science education, basic research, advanced training abroad, and for the repatriation of experienced specialists. None of these activities constitutes a transfer or direct development of a technology, but they are necessary to lay the foundation for both the absorption and the independent development of advanced commercial technologies in Korea. Another aspect is the identification of strategic base technologies to be obtained by acquisition from abroad and by independent development.[4] Still another aspect is balance: Korea cannot depend on success in one or two strategic technologies, but must achieve balanced progress in upgrading technological skills across diverse industries. In addition to lessening risk by diversification, this reflects the fundamental assumption of the new technology strategy: that Korea has the human resources that will enable it to absorb and apply foreign technologies as well as develop its own applications. Another feature of the balanced approach is that Korea is not abandoning the industries she has already built up; in these industries, the stress will continue to be on reducing costs and raising quality.

Although Korea's current level of technology—Korea's competency level—lags far behind the advanced nations, Korean firms have recently achieved signal successes in independent development of sophisticated technologies. One example is the synthesis of interferon by a research team at Cheil Sugar Company.

The Contribution of Technology from the United States

Technology transfers occur through various modes. Other analytical tests reveal the typological characteristics of the acquired technologies, and these tests can help us illuminate the characteristics of the U.S. technologies that have been transferred to Korea and differentiate them from technologies transferred from other countries. One test is Woodward's framework for relating types of production to the level of organizational complexity of the firm: unit and small batch are the lowest level; large batch and mass production are the middle level; and continuous process systems are the highest level.[5] For the purposes of this study, the value of Woodward's scheme is that it relates level of technology to the economies of scale of production systems. Another test for measuring the sophistication of imported technology comes from Wells' intermediate technology hypothesis, which emphasizes the level of technological attainment of the technology importing company and its ability to absorb imported technology.[6] One can measure the gap between the technology-providing country and the technology-receiving country by using price per contract or elapsed time between introduction and production. A third test is the technology-market relationship. It asks if a technology was imported by a firm for the domestic market or for export production, particularly export to a specific country. A fourth test is to classify technologies as product technology or process technology, according to the system developed by Abernathy and Utterback.[7] Kojima's work, which compared the characteristics of Japanese and American foreign investments, gives us a fifth test. According to Kojima, U.S. firms tend to transfer their technology piece by piece in the form of patents alone, while Japanese firms tend to transfer packages that include not only the specific knowledge, but also the accumulated experience of the development process that produced the knowledge.[8]

FDI, FL, and TA are the modes that are easy to capture and

analyze statistically because they are recorded by contract. Tables 5-1 and 5-2 and figures 5-1 and 5-2 show the historical trends in FDI and FL transfer from the United States, both as a percentage of all such transfers and specifically in comparison to Japan over the two decades from 1961 to 1981. The data show that the frequency of technology transfer through both FDI and FL has increased dramatically over time. Also worthy of note is that in the most recent period the trend has been for FDI to decrease and FL to increase, although FL is already far greater than FDI. Up to 1980 the United States accounted for about 24 percent of FDI and FL in comparison to about 57 percent for Japan. However, Japan's share has declined in recent years, whereas the shares of the United States and other countries have risen. The United States also accounted for 24 percent of all TA agreements up to 1981, the same as its FDI and FL share. Though Japan has dominated FDI, FL, and TA in terms of number of contracts, the United States has dominated in total value and value per contract.

Reliable figures are impossible to collect for the less formal modes of technology transfer, though one can make some observations. Technical know-how that comes from foreign suppliers of machinery or materials will come predominantly from Korea's main suppliers of these goods: Japan, the United States, and European countries, in that order. Technical information that comes from foreign buyers, conversely, should follow Korea's export markets. Here again, the United States and Japan loom largest, but the proportion of such technical know-

Table 5–1
Trends in FDI and FL (number of cases)

FDI and FL	1962–71 (10 yrs.)		1972–76 (5 yrs.)		1977–80 (4 yrs.)	
FL	266	(84%)	349	(80%)	898	(92%)
FDI	52	(16%)	85	(20%)	76	(8%)
FDI by Source	1962–71 (10 yrs.)		1972–76 (5 yrs.)		1977–80 (4 yrs.)	
Japan	191	(72%)	219	(63%)	484	(54%)
U.S.	50	(19%)	75	(21%)	205	(23%)
Others	25	(9%)	55	(16%)	209	(23%)
FL by Source	1962–71 (10 yrs.)		1972–76 (5 yrs.)		1977–80 (4 yrs.)	
Japan	23	(44%)	61	(72%)	36	(47%)
U.S.	24	(46%)	15	(18%)	22	(29%)
Others	5	(10%)	9	(10%)	18	(22%)

Source: Economic Planning Board, *Current Status of Technology Imports.*

Table 5–2
TA by Source[a]

	1968–71 (4 yrs)		1972–76 (5 yrs)		1977–82 (6 yrs)		Total	
U.S.	14	(15.1%)	38	(18.5%)	182	(26.9%)	234	(24.0%)
	12,136	(72.2%)	7,674	(41.5%)	29,527	(39.7%)	49,338	(45.0%)
Japan	64	(68.8%)	118	(57.6%)	327	(48.4%)	509	(52.3%)
	3,133	(18.7%)	5,984	(32.3%)	22,917	(30.8%)	32,035	(29.3%)
W. Germany	5	(5.4%)	13	(6.3%)	45	(6.7%)	63	(6.5%)
	704	(4.2%)	659	(3.6%)	3,616	(4.9%)	4,980	(4.5%)
Others	10	(10.7%)	36	(17.6%)	122	(18.0%)	168	(17.2%)
	823	(4.9%)	4,177	(22.6%)	18,238	(24.6%)	23,239	(21.2%)
Total	93	(100%)	205	(100%)	676	(100%)	974	(100%)
	16,798	(100%)	18,496	(100%)	74,299	(100%)	109,594	(100%)

Source: Economic Planning Board, *Current Status of Technology Imports.*
[a](upper line: cases; lower line: US$1,000)

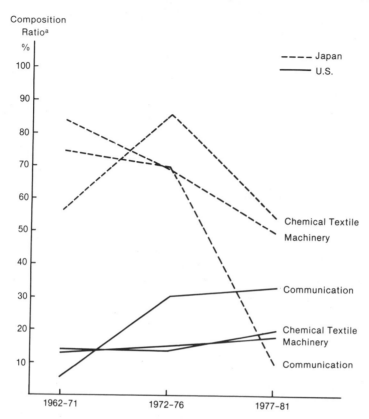

Source: Economic Planning Board, *Current Status of Technology and Imports.*
[a]Ratio is the proportion of technology imports from the U.S. and Japan out of the total imports in each sector.

Figure 5–1. Combined FDI and FL in Selected Sectors

how from the United States is probably larger. The most indirect and diffuse mode, that of education abroad and the return of expatriates who have studied and worked abroad, is undoubtedly dominated by the United States.

How can we explain these statistics and trends? One point is that Korea did not normalize relations with Japan until 1965, so Japan was not a major factor in the first five-year plan period. Second, because of Korea's bitter experiences with foreign domination and Japanese colonialism, Korea has closely regulated FDI. In the period 1967-71 the FDI permitted in Korea amounted to 4 percent of GNP, while the figure was 34 percent in Brazil and 32 percent in Taiwan; for 1972-76 the figures were 8 percent, 23 percent, and 13 percent, respectively.[9] This is one reason for the small percentage of technology transfer

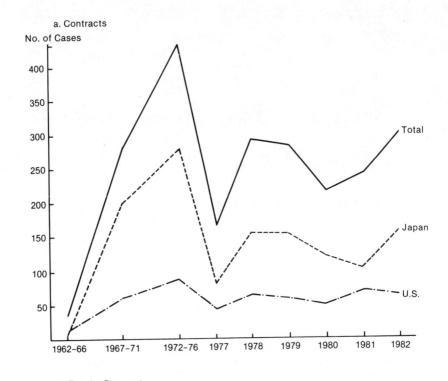

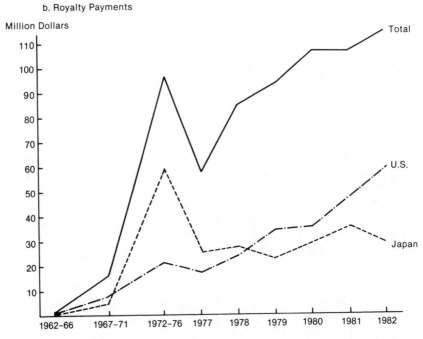

Figure 5–2. FDI and FL from the United States and Japan

through FDI. Similar considerations of security from domination lay behind Korea's policy of diversifying its international economic relations, including technological relations. This helps explain why technology transfer from sources other than the United States and Japan has increased, although Japan and the United States still dominate Korea's technological relations as well as its trade relations.

Specific patterns of technology transfer differ from one industry to another, as is seen in figure 5-1. At the industry level the patterns of technology transfer result from the interplay of government policies and the competitive strategies of individual firms. Nevertheless, we can propose a pattern that should hold across different industries. First, Korean firms will seek FDI at the initial stage of the transfer of a new technology in order to induce the technology and, especially in the 1961-76 period, to induce the capital necessary to implement the technology. This tendency is strongest in industry sectors designated by the government; in some cases the FDI decision, including the selection of both Korean and foreign partners in joint ventures, is a government decision, not a firm decision.[10] Both the government and the firm desire to have the foreign technology provider bring in the technology and be committed to the success of the project through equity participation.

Once a Korean industry achieves mastery over a technology, however, further development of that technology through technology transfer is likely to be through the FL and TA modes. The textile industry and the electronics industry, both of which have been developed as important industries in Korea, represent the two extremes. In the textile industry, Korea had achieved a certain level of technological mastery even before rapid economic development began. Consequently, formal technology transfers have been almost entirely through FL and TA, besides numerous informal transfers from suppliers and buyers. In the electronics industry, by contrast, cases of FDI are significant. In fact, the pattern of initial introduction by FDI and subsequent development through FL has been repeated several times as completely new electronics technologies have been introduced. Recently, a major technology transfer through FDI was in sophisticated semiconductor and integrated circuit production technology. The government played a key role because of the importance of the technology for national security and economic development.[11]

In order to study the actual patterns of technology transfer, we interviewed Korean firms in three broad industry sectors: electronics and electrical goods, machinery, oil refining and chemicals. The electronics and electrical goods sector includes electric appliances, electrical equipment, components, instruments, and telecommunications; the machinery sector includes machine tools, automobiles, and shipbuilding; the oil refining and chemicals sector includes refining, petrochemicals, and chemicals. These sector groupings follow the industrial classification scheme employed by the Korean government. Some seventy firms were interviewed, and these included almost all the firms that had introduced foreign technology.

First, who imports U.S. technology? What are the characteristics of the companies in terms of size, target markets, and type of products? Korean law distinguishes companies that employ 300 or fewer people from firms that employ more than 300, and classifies the former as *small and medium* companies. Large firms have accounted for about 80 percent of the FDI and FL transfers from the United States in the firms surveyed, almost the same as the proportion from third countries other than Japan. In contrast, close to 40 percent of the transfers from Japan have been induced by firms in the small-to-medium category. Obviously, scale of production and company size depend on the characteristics of an industry, but we can say that FDI and FL transfers from the United States tend to go to larger firms.

We can analyze imported technologies by looking at the target market of the firm that imports the technology. Companies that desire to export to a particular foreign market are likely to import the product technology from that country. Product technology from the target market embodies technical knowledge that is specific to that market and allows firms to avoid the costs and risks of modifying product technologies different from the ones prevailing in the target market. Firms oriented toward the domestic market will seek product technologies that have characteristics preferred in the domestic market, and the country of origin will not be so important.

Table 5-3 isolates the data for the electronics and electrical goods industry. It shows clearly the relationship between the country of origin of the technology and the target market of the company importing the technology. The American market has been the most important market for the companies that export, and they have sought to obtain technology that fits the requirements of the American market. Conversely, even though the Japanese market has been more difficult for Korean exports to penetrate, Korean companies importing product technology for the domestic market are likely, because of similarities in Japanese and Korean tastes, to import technology that has been accepted in the Japanese market. Survey results for all three sectors confirm what we found for the electronics and electrical goods sector.[12]

In table 5-4 the production processes of the firms in the survey are analyzed according to Woodward's scheme. The majority of the firms importing technology from the United States employ mass production and continuous process production, whereas the firms importing Japanese technology were concentrated in the small batch type of pro-

Table 5–3
Target Markets and Sources of Technology for the Electronics and Electrical Equipment Sector

	Domestic	Export
U.S.	1	11
Japan	6	6

Source: Survey data.

Table 5–4
Sources of Technology according to Woodward's Analysis of Technological Complexity

	U.S.	Japan	Total
Small batch	9	21	30
Mass production	14	12	26
Process production	11	7	18

Source: Survey data.

duction. The American technologies are more sophisticated and complex, and fit large-scale systems better than Japanese technologies. Figures on R&D expenditures obtained during the survey support this observation because they show that the companies introducing technology from the United States spend higher percentages of sales on R&D. In other words, these firms are more technology-intensive.

The question of the sophistication of technologies acquired from abroad is complex and depends on the particular industry, but based on Wells' work we can apply some tests to indicate the gap between the imported technology and the level of Korean technology. If we take price as a proxy for the gap and assume that the higher the price, the more sophisticated and recent the technology, then table 5-5 shows that the average contract price of U.S. technology has been more than double the average for Japanese technology. The difference is greatest for the most recent five-year period, but the trend has been for the price of American technology to rise steadily.

Another proxy for the gap is the time required to absorb a technology and implement production, then to modify it to meet domestic or foreign market requirements, and finally to develop new products based on the imported technology. The survey results in table 5–6 show that at each stage the average time required for American technology was significantly longer than for Japanese technology.

During the survey, the respondent companies were asked about their perceptions of the level of U.S. technology compared to the level

Table 5–5
A Comparison of Average per Contract Prices for FDI and FL by Source
(Unit: $1,000)

	1962–71 *(10 yrs.)*	1972–76 *(5 yrs.)*	1977–81 *(5 yrs.)*	1962–81 *(20 yrs.)*
U.S.	113.1	236.2	528.8	406.0
Japan	23.6	209.4	222.2	181.2
W. Germany	257.5	432.9	200.2	238.9

Source: Economic Planning Board, *Current Status of Technology Imports.*

Table 5–6
Time Requirements for Different Stages of Technology Absorption
(Unit: month)

	Implementation	*Modification*	*New Product Development*
U.S.	42.6	38.3	48.7
Japan	28.0	28.0	31.3

Source: Survey data.

of Japanese technology. Twenty-nine of thirty-three respondents who had imported U.S. technology thought that the American technology was more advanced than that of other countries, whereas twenty of thirty-seven respondents who had imported Japanese technology thought that Japan did not provide technologies as advanced as those provided by other nations. Although these are opinions that are not quantifiable in the same way as price and time gaps, they tend to confirm the figures. The fact that the Japanese technology might be older and semiobsolete would mean that it would be cheaper and also perhaps easier to transfer and assimilate because the gap would be narrower.

Technology may be classified as product technology or process technology. Seventeen of thirty U.S. technology imports covered by the survey were product technologies, ten were process technologies, and three were both. However, all ten of the process technologies were in oil refining and chemicals, a sector in which most technology transfer is done in packaged process systems rather than individual products or 'pieces.' Product technologies are probably more dominant overall than our survey results indicate. A recent study showed that the United States has provided more product than process technologies, and that the same was true of Japan.[13] According to the same study, Korean firms aiming at the domestic market tended to import product technologies first, and then later import process technologies in order to reduce production costs for competitive reasons.

Another way of analyzing technology is to classify it into three levels of ascending technological development. Assembly of imported knockdown kits into final products is the lowest level of capability in any industry. The next level is when important components are locally fabricated. The highest level is achieved when a country has the ability to produce base and feedstock materials. Table 5-7 shows how the composition of U.S. technology induced by the electronics and electrical goods industry in the period from 1972 to 1980 has been shifting from the first level up to the third.

Kojima has argued that American firms transfer technology by the patent or 'piece' alone, while Japanese firms transfer packages that include accumulated technology development experience. According to the respondent companies, of thirty-nine transfers from the United States, twenty-three were comprehensive packages, whereas twenty-three out of forty-six transfers from Japan were in packages. Thus, the results of the survey contradict rather than support Kojima's view for these three sectors.

Finally, our survey asked the respondent firms about how the firms

Table 5–7
U.S. Technology in the Electronics and
Electrical Equipment Sector

Type of Technology	1972–76 (5 yrs.)	1977–80 (4 yrs.)
Assembly	12	16
Components fabrication	4	15
Material production	3	8

Source: Survey data.

Table 5–8
Information Sources of Technology

Sources	U.S.	Japan
Suppliers of raw material, parts, machinery		
Foreign	23	27
Domestic	4	5
Customers		
Local agent	15	6
Foreign agent	2	8
Local consumer	11	22
Foreign consumer	9	11
Overseas branch of technology importing firm	18	22
Joint venture partner	10	9
Technology (patent) owners	12	12
Information		
Foreign	9	4
Organization		
Domestic	13	5
Korean government	5	5
University research centers	6	5
International trade fairs	7	9

Source: Survey data.

received information on foreign technology, who in the firms was influential in the decision to obtain a particular technology, and how the firms evaluated the performance of the technology they had induced. Table 5-8 shows the distribution of different sources of significant information about American and Japanese technology. There are few differences, though the fact that domestic consumers have been a major source of information about Japanese technology supports our finding that Japanese technologies have been preferred by firms oriented to the domestic market. As for the decision to import a specific technology, in the case of U.S. technologies the engineering and R&D departments were more influential, while in firms importing Japanese technology, marketing people have exercised more influence. Again, these tendencies are consistent both with the data that show that U.S. technology induced into Korea has been more sophisticated and the survey data about market orientation. Responses to the query about performance indicated that American technology had been of significant help in the development of new products, while Japanese technology had contributed to reduced production costs and improved quality.

Hyundai Motor Company

A case study of the development of an important product at Hyundai Motor Company (HMC) will enable us to see how the patterns of technology transfer and development actually work at the firm level. HMC was founded in 1967 by the Hyundai group. Its first operation was the assembly of the Cortina passenger car, based on FL and assembly agreements with Ford. HMC started at the first stage of assembling imported knockdown components to make automobiles.

The Long-Range Auto Industry Promotion Plan adopted by the Korean government in 1974 motivated automobile companies to upgrade their technology to the level required to produce their own car models. Immediately, HMC commenced construction of integrated automobile manufacturing facilities. From 1974 to 1976 HMC acquired technologies for engine block design, transmissions, and rear axles from Japan; factory construction and layout and internal combustion engine systems from England; and car designs from Italy. The experience that allowed HMC to absorb these technologies was gained through the FL and TA from Ford. In 1976 HMC began production of its own automobile model, the Pony. About 90 percent of the parts were manufactured in Korea. Eighteen technology transfers, mostly in the TA mode, took place before the Pony's introduction.

In 1979 HMC turned to its next phase of technological development, in part because of incentives provided by the government's machinery export promotion policy.[14] To produce automobiles for export, HMC needed to meet quality standards required by the major car markets. To meet American safety and pollution standards, HMC licensed more than thirty different technologies from Japan, England, and the United States.[15] Even as HMC developed the Pony and improved its quality, the assembling contract with Ford was maintained to continue producing middle-sized cars for the domestic market.

The next phase of technological development had three objectives. The first was intended to develop a middle-sized car of a higher quality than the Pony for domestic sale by 1983, while still maintaining the Ford assembly contract. The second was the expansion of Pony production capacity from 100,000 to 300,000 units. The expansion of production capacity is being carried out by a joint venture between HMC and Mitsubishi Motors of Japan. The long-term objective of the joint venture is the third goal: the design and production of a world car aimed at major export markets.

Figure 5–3 presents HMC's technology imports over the past sixteen years. The first technologies from the United States provided the initial concepts of how to make an automobile; HMC's first FL agreement was signed with Ford in 1968 and provided for Ford to help HMC lay out assembly lines, select tools, and teach the workers how to assemble automobiles. More recently, HMC has imported advanced American automobile technology in order to improve upon the technology imports from sources such as Japan and England, and the advances made by its own R&D. HMC's approach is that it goes to several sources to obtain technology, rather than relying only on a single source. This means that it will sometimes go to two different sources for the same type of technology. Recent examples are technologies for emission control, universal joints, and brake systems. HMC obtained the fundamental concepts from an American firm, but then turned to a Japanese firm for help in practical assimilation and efficient production.

In 1979 HMC established its own R&D center for product development and production process development. Its technology acquisition programs expanded beyond FL and TA to include informal consulting arrangements with foreign specialists. HMC's experience using specialists from Japanese companies is that the Japanese engineers have more understanding of the situations confronting HMC than do American specialists. One reason seems to be that the Japanese specialists personally experienced the whole series of development stages that the Japanese industry went through from the backward 1950s to the technically advanced present. Thus they know the prob-

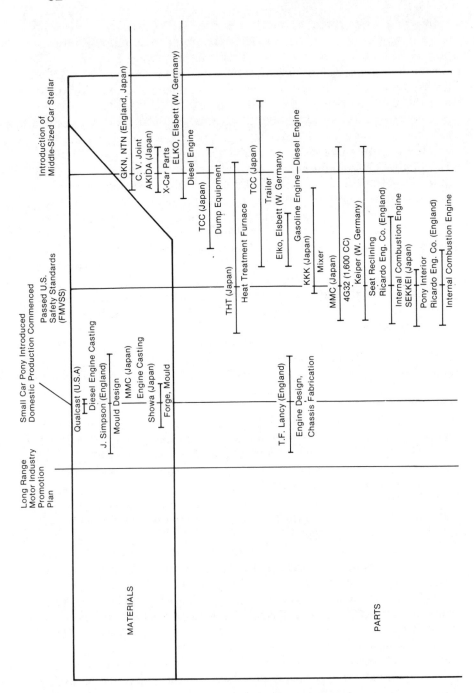

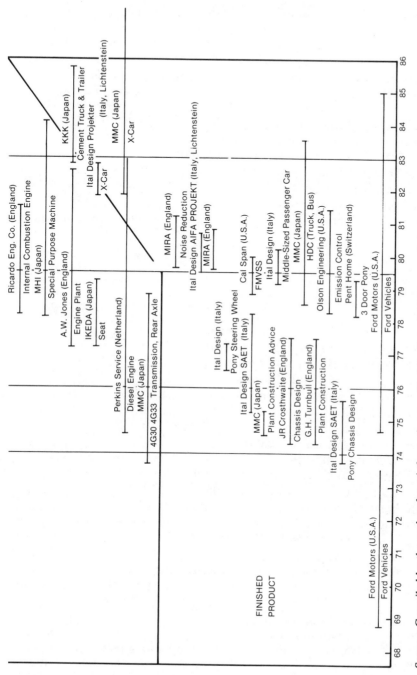

Source: Compiled by the author from information provided by Hyundai Motors and the Economic Planning Board.

Figure 5–3. Hyundai Motor Company's Technology Imports

lems that HMC encounters as it assimilates technical expertise and
achieves higher levels of production, and they can be of more help to
HMC engineers and managers in solving the problems. In contrast,
American engineers have not experienced the early stages of industry
development and cannot readily comprehend these problems.

HMC restricted its technology imports to TA and FL modes of
transfer, avoiding joint ventures (FDI) in order to preserve its independence. In March 1982, however, HMC entered into a joint venture
with the giant Mitsubishi Motor Company of Japan, the first FDI in
which HMC has participated. At the same time HMC began to increase
its R&D expenditures, which were planned to be 5 percent of sales in
1983. Recent reports of exploratory talks with Chrysler, which already
has an established relationship with Mitsubishi, indicate that HMC may
be on the threshold of achieving its technology goals and its export
goals.[16]

Perspectives on the Future

Technological relations between Korea and the United States have
changed periodically as Korea's economy, industrial structure, and level
of technological mastery developed rapidly, and as Korea's policies on
technology acquisition and development were modified in response to
changing conditions and objectives.

In the first period the United States was the source of technology
and capital (FDI) for many key industries, and it was also the source
of informal transfers of product and market information from buyers.
After Korea normalized relations with Japan in 1965, Japan quickly
surpassed the United States as a source of technology, although the
most sophisticated and advanced technologies continued to come from
the United States. However, from the mid-1970s technology imports
from Japan declined relative to imports from the United States and
other countries. This was due to changing economic conditions, the
increasing sophistication of the technology sought by Korea, and also
government policies on foreign investment and technology imports.

The motivation for American firms to transfer technology to Korea
varies from case to case. We can say that for technology transferred
as part of domestic-oriented FDI, the key factor has been the incentives offered by the government's foreign investment policies. For export-oriented transfers, the incentives have been a combination of
government policy incentives and also comparative factor advantages,
as discussed in detail in chapter 2. In recent years, however, transfer
motivations have become more complex, because many transfers by

FDI and FL in the heavy and chemical industries in the latter 1970s were apparently made because of both domestic and international market opportunities.

Korea's new technology policies for the future, which aim at acquiring and developing high technologies with commercial applications, require new forms of technological relations with the advanced nations. Computers, industrial materials, biotechnology, and the like are leading technologies in which the United States, Japan, and other countries are competing face to face. These technologies are in flux, guarded closely by the firms developing them and by increasingly protectionist national technology policies.

Korea hopes to enter into joint ventures with foreign firms in which joint R&D for the development of product applications suitable for the market in Korea and other advanced developing nations is a major objective of the joint ventures. However, there may be serious obstacles to realizing these hopes. One is Korea's business and regulatory environment. The concern of foreign firms about inadequate legal protection for their proprietary technology has become a serious problem in recent years. Government restrictions on the entry of joint ventures into activities not allowed in the original FDI approval, along with the well-established fact that FDI ventures in all host countries tend to be less innovative than native firms, make expectations about entrepreneurial R&D activities by joint ventures in Korea questionable until the Korean business environment becomes more attractive for such ventures.

Instead of FDI in Korea, the more likely pattern is Korean FDI in the advanced countries where the leading technologies are under development. In the past year there have been several cases of Korean firms establishing research centers in Silicon Valley in California and investing in R&D projects with American biotechnology firms.

More than anything, Korea will have to rely increasingly on its own technology development efforts. The foreign contributions will be indirect: the advanced training of scientists and engineers, basic scientific research, and information from foreign suppliers of equipment and materials. We may cite Sunkyong's development of high quality videotape as an example. Rebuffed when it sought to purchase videotape manufacturing technology from foreign manufacturers, Sunkyong succeeded in developing the product using its own R&D staff, available scientific knowledge, and information from the suppliers of production equipment and chemicals, who were also the suppliers for Japanese manufacturers of videotape. In 1980, when Sunkyong commenced production, Korea became the fourth country in the world after the United States, Japan, and West Germany to develop this advanced technology.

The United States has always been the leading source of human resources for Korea, both in advanced formal training and also immigrant specialists with practical work experience who repatriate back to Korea. Recent Korean investments abroad in technology development have been almost exclusively in the United States. Although international competition in new technology development may become even more heated in the future, the recent trend for the United States to grow even more important to Korea as a source of technology information is certain to continue. But the benefits are not to Korea alone, because Korean investment in American R&D ventures, the training of human resources in the United States, and possible joint R&D ventures in Korea will also contribute to American technology development and the development of applications for advanced U.S. technologies in international markets.

6 Trade Channel Evolution between Korea and the United States

Ku-Hyun Jung

The United States is the world's largest market. It has huge purchasing power. American importers and large retail chains take advantage of U.S. market power in bargaining with foreign suppliers. American buyers, operating with a global outlook in purchasing, go around the world to locate the most favorable suppliers in terms of price, quality, and delivery. Besides having access to the world's largest market, American buyers are also well informed about demand and supply conditions, technology and taste shifts, and changing comparative advantage structures in the world market.

Foreign suppliers, especially those in less developed countries, are in a disadvantageous position in terms of access to the U.S. market and information. Aware of this weakness on their part, many LDCs have attempted to increase their influence in the trade channel. Korea, in the last decade, attempted to increase its channel involvement by setting up bigger and better trading houses. The Korean government initiated the general trading company designation system in 1975 with the objective, among others, of increasing the involvement of Korean companies in the external trade channel. The export trade channel is defined here as a structure of intermediaries involved in the process of making a product available for foreign end-users and consumers. One can hypothesize that the export trade channnel evolves over time under the influence of several environmental variables. These variables are increases in trade volume, change in product composition, and the imposition of import restrictions. These variables, together with channel-member factors, are assumed to affect changes in channel member roles and functions, as shown in figure 6-1. These changes in turn are assumed to affect the channel performance. In this study, channel performance is viewed mainly from the position of the exporting country. As the relative power of its suppliers and national trading companies increases compared to that of buyers, we can expect the exporting country to gain a higher degree of control, faster growth in exports, and more stable export earnings.

In analyzing channel structure and change between Korea and the United States, we must answer these questions:[1]

1. Who are the intermediaries involved in the trade between Korean manufacturers and U.S. end-users, and what functions do they perform?
2. Has the channel changed in the last decade? If so, what factors have contributed to this change?
3. Have changes in channel structure influenced the performance of the channel? How has it affected the trade performance of the Korean export products in the U.S. market?

The time frame of this chapter is essentially limited to the twelve-year period from 1970 to 1981. The analysis focuses only on Korea's export channel, and the products studied are the ones that have accounted for relatively large shares of Korea's total exports to the United States. Here, however, we can not be too specific because the basic unit of analysis of this research is the individual channel member. When a single channel member handles many different kinds of products, all these products are naturally included in the analysis. Nevertheless, clothing, footwear, consumer electronics, industrial equipment, and iron and steel products will be the products most frequently mentioned.

Enviromental Changes in the Trade Relationship

The comparative advantage theory of trade tells us that international trade is conducted on the basis of the comparative cost advantages of

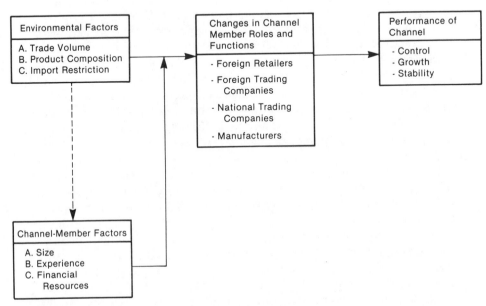

Figure 6–1. A Model of Trade Channel Evolution

different countries. Cost advantage, however, is only one factor that determines international trade flows. There are many different intermediaries involved between a manufacturer and a foreign end-user. This intermediary structure—the trade channel—is also an important factor that influences a nation's international competitiveness.

It was with this in mind that the United States Congress passed the Export Trading Company Act in 1980. The act specifically aims to establish export channels for small and medium-sized manufacturers. It recognizes that the export performance of small manufacturers depends as much on the availability and performance of export channels as on the competitiveness of the products they make. The United States is not alone in looking at export channels as a possible approach to improving less-than-satisfactory export performance. Korea started its own version of an export trading company act, the general trading company designation system, in 1975. The Korean version was apparently inspired by the success of Japanese general trading companies (GTC), at least up to that time. Many other developing countries have also not failed to connect Japan's export success with her GTCs.[2]

The Korean general trading company (KGTC) system was started by the government to achieve the following objectives:[3]

increase export marketing efforts, especially for heavy industry products, and to third-world countries

provide a better export channel for medium and small manufacturers

increase the size of exporters in order to achieve economies of scale

shift some of the export assistance burden of the government to large business groups

Heavier involvement by Korean exporters in overseas markets was viewed by the government as a desirable step to improve the export performance of the country. There are currently nine private KGTCs and one semipublic KGTC, the latter specializing in arranging exports for small manufacturers.

The volume of trade between Korea and the United States has increased steadily over the last twelve years. Korean exports to the United States, which started at a low of $370 million in 1970, increased every year to reach $5,660 million in 1981. (All dollars in this chapter are current United States dollars unless specified otherwise.) Although the percentage of Korea's exports going to the United States has decreased from 47.3 percent in 1970 to 26.6 percent in 1981, the United States remains the biggest market for Korean products. American exports to Korea have also increased steadily, from $580 million in 1970

to $6,049 million in 1981. In 1981 the United States was the second
largest supplier of products to Korea, next to Japan. In 1982 the United
States regained the position of the largest exporter to Korea by exporting $5,956 million, or 24.6 percent of Korea's total imports, while
Korean exports to the United States were $6,243 million, or 28.6 per-
cent of total exports. In the total trade volume including exports and
imports in 1981, the United States was the second largest trading partner of Korea, while Korea was the ninth largest trading partner of the
United States. The increase in the overall volume has resulted in the
increase of export volume of individual exporters. The 1981 exports to
the United States by individual KGTCs shown in table 6-1 ranged from
$38 million to $491 million. Within eighteen broad product categories,
there were three companies that exported more than $100 million of
one product line; this increase in trade volume should have made it
feasible to set up marketing outposts in the United States. Table 6-2
shows that the number of subsidiaries of Korean companies increased
from 34 in 1976 to 94 in 1980. In other words, sixty new subsidiaries
were established in the four-year period from 1977 to 1980. Most of
these subsidiaries were set up for trading.

The Korea Traders Association uses a product classification scheme
in which products are grouped into twenty-six broad product categories. From 1970 to 1981, six product categories out of twenty-six
have consistently accounted for more than 80 percent of Korean exports to the United States. In order of importance, these are clothing,
machinery, metal products, footwear, miscellaneous manufactured articles (miscellaneous products include wigs, toys, travel goods, furni-

Table 6–1
Exports to the United States by KGTCs (1981)
($ million)

	Total Exports	*U.S.A.*	*Share of the U.S.* *out of Total*
Daewoo	1,904	491	25.8
Hyundai	1.724	176	10.2
Samsung	1,607	327	20.4
Kukje	844	355	42.1
Hyosung	788	188	23.8
Ssangyong	758	71	9.4
Bando	622	197	31.7
Sunkyong	585	119	20.3
Kumho	189	38	20.3
GTC total	8,905	1,952	21.9
Korea total	21,074	5,580	26.5

Source: Kukje Corporation, *Chonghap sangsa ŭi kinŭng kwa silch'e* (Seoul: 1982), 156.

Table 6–2
Korean Companies in the United States

	Subsidiaries	Branches	Offices	Total
1976	34	—	392 —	426
1977	62	35	352	449
1978	84	71	332	487
1979	87	81	380	548
1980	94	119	470	683

Source: Adapted from Korea Traders Association, *Haeoe chisa unyŏng hyŏnhwang kwa hwal-sŏnghwa pangan* (Seoul: 1981), 53.

ture and plastic goods), and wood products. However, over this period, the relative shares of these products have changed rather significantly.

As we see in table 6-3, three product categories have gained significantly, while three have lost. The gainers are footwear, metal products, and machinery; the losers are clothing, wood products, and miscellaneous products. If we regroup the products into light manufactures and heavy manufactures, we can see that the share of heavy products increased from 17.2 percent in the 1970-72 period to 43.7 percent in the 1979-81 period. The gain has come at the cost of light manufactures, whose share decreased in the same period from 80.0 percent to 52.1 percent.

The major contributors to the higher share for the category of heavy products include iron and steel products, electronics (All electronics goods, both consumer and industrial ones, are considered "heavy" goods in Korea), and transportation equipment (mainly ships). This shift in product composition reflects the efforts guided by Korean economic planners to diversify into more capital- and technology-intensive products in the last decade. As the share of industrial products and consumer durables increases, one can hypothesize about the nature of changes in the export channel. First, industrial products have short distribution channels and relatively few buyers. At the same time, the omnipotent market control of American mass merchandisers is not present in these product markets. As a result, exporters are required to get more deeply involved in the industrial product export channel. Second, in consumer electronics and also in capital equipment, after-sale service requirements oblige manufacturers to establish some sort of service facilities in foreign markets, which, in turn, stimulates them to establish marketing arms in those markets.

Many major products that Korea exports to the United States are under various types of import restrictions. The oldest and most significant is the bilateral import quota on textile products under the provision of the Multi-Fiber Agreement. This restriction has been in effect

Table 6–3
Changing Shares of Major Export Products (percentages)

3-year Average Share	Light Manufactures				Heavy Manufactures	
	Clothing	Footwear	Wood Products	Misc. Products	Metal Products	Machinery
1970–1972	34.2	4.9	19.9	15.9	6.2	10.5
1979–1981	23.2	9.4	3.5	9.6	14.6	25.6
Gain or loss	−11.0	+4.5	−16.4	−6.3	+8.4	+15.1

Source: Calculated from Kukje Corporation, *Chonghap sangsa ŭi kinŭng kwa silch'e* (Seoul: 1982), 168–169.

Percentages are out of total exports to the U.S.

since 1971. Other important products under import restriction include iron and steel products under the trigger price mechanism.

The Korea Trade Promotion Corporation (KOTRA) keeps statistics on Korea's exports to major markets that are under various types of import restrictions (table 6-4). The table shows that the share of exports to the United States under import restrictions reached as high as 50 percent in 1980. The table also shows comparable figures for Korean exports to Japan and the EC 9 countries. The reason why the share decreased for the United States in 1981 was because the orderly marketing arrangement (OMA) was lifted for nonrubber footwear in June 1981.

It is not clear how import restrictions affect the export channel. Because the quotas are mainly allocated on the basis of previous export performance, restrictions definitely favor established exporters over new entrants. How would an established exporter react to the imposition of a new quota? It will partly depend on how restrictive the quota is in terms of the exporter's production capacity. If it is so restrictive as to reduce seriously his capacity utilization rate, the exporting manufacturer may be forced to take actions to counteract the quota. He may follow a market diversification strategy or may attempt to bypass the quota by moving production locations to foreign countries. On the other hand, if the quota is not so restrictive and enables the maintenance of at least the export level of previous years, the established exporter will not feel too threatened. Instead, he will be able to reap the benefits of being a selected supplier. His position is comparable to that of a successful cartel member. As long as demand remains strong, he will feel little pressure to take independent measures to penetrate the foreign market. If we follow the logic of this analysis, import restrictions tend to favor the established channel members, thus limiting the possibility of channel switching and changes. This may be what has happened in the case of textile products.

Major Channel Members

There are three types of intermediaries involved between Korean manufacturers and American end-users. Because manufacturers and end-users themselves may also perform channel functions, there are actually five types of actors in the Korea-United States trade channel. We will briefly describe each type and the functions they perform. The actual channel adopted could be any combination of manufacturers and end-users with zero, one, or more middlemen in between. This is depicted in figure 6-2. According to this schematic diagram, there can

Table 6–4
Share of Exports under Import Restrictions Out of Total Exports
(*$ million*)

	U.S.A.		Japan		EC 9 Countries	
	Exports	*Percentage under restrictions*	*Exports*	*Share*	*Exports*	*Share*
1976	2,492	37.5	1,801	14.5	1,150	31.6
1977	3,118	34.1	2,148	18.9	1,192	27.4
1978	4,058	39.5	2,627	26.3	1,850	33.2
1979	4,378	44.7	3,353	18.9	2,333	45.9
1980	4,606	50.4	3,039	28.1	2,887	47.8
1981	5,560	44.3	3,444	20.3	2,686	51.6

Source: Adapted from Korea Trade Promotion Corporation, *Chuyoguk ŭi suip kyuje hyŏnhwang* (Seoul: 1982), 196.

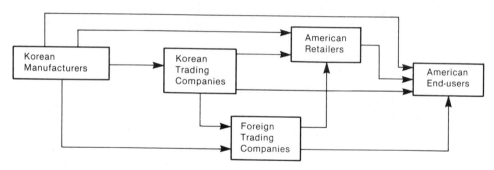

Figure 6–2. Broad Types of Channel Members

Table 6–5
U.S.-Related Party Imports as Percentage of Total Imports
from Asian NICS (1977)

	S. Korea	Hong Kong	Taiwan	Singapore
Textiles	5.5	4.9	13.1	4.3
Nonelectrical Machinery	64.2	68.5	19.3	90.5
Electric machinery	67.3	43.4	58.1	97.0
Clothing	7.1	3.4	1.2	0.5
Footwear	1.8	3.6	3.1	0.0
Scientific instruments	12.1	30.4	67.1	85.3
Total manufacturing	19.7	18.1	20.5	83.3

Source: OECD, *North/South Technology Transfer: The Adjustments Ahead* (Paris: 1981), 60.

be eight different channels, although the actual number of middlemen involved in a specific transaction could be more than three.

In this discussion we do not include intracorporate transactions. It is estimated that about 20 percent of Korean exports to the United States is between related parties, meaning American parents importing from manufacturing subsidiaries located in Korea. Table 6-5 shows that, except for machinery, intramultinational corporation (MNC) trade accounts for a small percentage of total exports from Korea. The ratio is especially low in consumer products.

The functions performed in the trade channel are grouped into three types:

Transactional functions
   1. Negotiation
   2. Contracting
   3. Export documentation
Facilitating functions

    4. Promotion
    5. Information/Research
    6. Financing
    7. Risk taking
Mechanical functions
    8. Shipping
    9. Warehousing
    10. Quality control

Manufacturers

Some large Korean manufacturers have set up marketing subsidiaries in the United States in order to market their own products. The Bank of Korea reports that 103 direct investment projects had been approved and implemented as of the end of 1981.[4] The total amount of investment was $32.6 million. Of the trade subsidiaries reported, the author counted thirty-one parent companies that are manufacturing companies. Not all of these thirty-one subsidiaries were established to import the parent's products; some were set up to procure raw materials. Twenty-one subsidiaries were recorded as having imports from their parents.

    Efforts by Korean manufacturers to become directly involved in the United States market really started around 1976-1977, as can be seen in table 6-6. This move was separate from efforts of KGTCs to set up their own marketing arms. Although the number of marketing subsidiaries of manufacturing companies is not very large, this type of channel accounts for a significant level of exports. The Bank of Korea data shows that the total exports to these subsidiaries by the parents amounted to $744 million in 1981.[5] These manufacturers, as well as their subsidiaries, perform most of the three categories of channel functions listed above. Three major product lines represent about 80 percent of the total exports using this direct channel: electronics, tires, and steel products.

    The author visited three of these importing subsidiaries in October 1981. Their lines of business were consumer electronics, automobile tires, and pipe products. The consumer electronics manufacturer is one of the three largest electronics companies in Korea. Its American subsidiary was established in 1978. Its products, mostly black-and-white and color TVs, are marketed under its own brand to more than one thousand retail stores. The sales of the subsidiary reached $100 million in 1981, and the subsidiary was ranked nineteenth in color TV sales with a 0.75 percent share of the United States market in that year. The

Table 6–6
Dates of Approval for Korean Trading Subsidiaries in the United States

Years	KGTCs	Other Trading Companies	Manufacturers	Total
1973–1975	5	1	3	9
1976–1978	9	19	18	46
1979–1981	5	8	11	24
Total	19	28	32	79
Total number of expatriates as of the end of 1981	200	92	94	386

Source: Classified from Bank of Korea, *Haeoe t'uja hyŏnhwang* (Seoul: 1982), 120–135.

subsidiary's sales figure does not include the parent's direct exports to large retail stores such as Montgomery Ward and K-Mart.

The steel product subsidiary was also set up in 1978. It sells directly to local 'warehouses,' which are wholesalers selling directly to end-users or fabricators. The subsidiary had sales of $30 million in 1981; this sales figure does not include the exports of the parent to other American importers. In 1981 the parent's total exports to the United States was $101 million. The tire subsidiary was set up in 1981; its parent company belongs to a business group that includes a KGTC. Until the establishment of the manufacturer's subsidiary, the tire exports had been handled by the KGTC. The subsidiary expected its tire sales in the United States to reach $60 million in 1981.

Korean Trading Companies

The definition of *Korean trading company* is not clearcut. KGTCs may be considered a subset of the much more numerous trading companies. Only the largest nine out of a few thousand trading companies are designated as general trading companies. Many trading companies, especially larger ones, have their own manufacturing facilities. The government uses a license system for trading companies; that definition could be used. However, this license is issued to any company whose exports exceed a certain level. Therefore, even if a company's exports are entirely its own manufactured products, it can still qualify as a trading company. According to that definition, there are currently about 4,500 trading companies. However, that is not a very useful definition; it would be more meaningful for our purposes to define a trading company as one whose exports or imports include a minimum of 50 percent of other independent manufacturers' products. Although there are no data available that would enable us to classify companies by this definition, all KGTCs and many large trading companies will qualify as trading companies according to this definition.

There were forty-seven subsidiaries in the United States whose parents could be defined as trading companies. As was true in the case of the manufacturers' subsidiaries, most of the traders' subsidiaries were also established after 1975. However, the actual exports accounted for by these subsidiaries could not be estimated on the basis of available data. Consequently, exports by Korean trading companies are treated as residuals in this analysis. In other words, we will first estimate exports accounted for by all other trade channels, and then whatever is left we will assume to be exports by Korean trading companies. Because the activities of trading companies include manufacturing, exporting, and overseas sales, their trade channel functions may be highly diverse and differ considerably from one product market to another.

Japanese Trading Companies

The Association of Foreign Trading Agents of Korea lists fifteen Japanese trading companies, which include all nine of the JGTCs. Because foreign companies in Korea were not allowed until recently to take title in foreign trade, these companies were classified as *offer agents*, a common term used to denote importing commission agents. This association has over two thousand members, more than three-quarters of whom are Korean import commission agents.

Japanese trading companies, however, are bigger than other trading agents and have been long established in Korea. Many of them were operating in Korea even before the Japanese annexed it in 1910. The first ones to come back to Korea after its liberation from colonial rule in 1945 did so in the early 1960s, and all of them had established branch offices by 1967. They have been active in both exports and imports. For example, one large JGTC has three offices (Seoul, Pusan, and Pohang) in Korea, with a staff of twenty-six Japanese and more than one hundred Korean nationals. Their trade consists of exports to and imports from Japan, as well as third-country trade. As shown in table 6-7, their exports to third countries, including the United States, have been widely diversified. In footwear, for example, Japanese trading companies have acted as intermediaries for Korean manufacturers. Even now one JGTC acts as the exclusive agent for a large American importer of footwear.

Because trading companies were not allowed to take title of goods

Table 6–7
Involvement of Japanese Trading Companies in Korean Trade (1980)
($ million)

	Exports from Korea to		Imports to Korea from	
	Japan	Third Country	Japan	Third Country
Textiles	329 (40.0)	178 (21.7)	153 (7.8)	n.a.
Chemicals	173 (21.1)	57 (7.0)	421 (21.4)	n.a.
Metal	44 (5.4)	113 (13.8)	647 (32.9)	n.a.
Machinery	21 (2.5)	58 (7.1)	234 (12.0)	n.a.
Foodstuff	170 (20.7)	133 (16.2)	509 (25.9)	n.a.
Others	85 (10.3)	280 (34.2)		
Total	822 (100.0)	819 (100.0)	1,966 (100.0)	264

Source: Unpublished data from Sumitomo Corp.

in foreign trade until recently in Korea, JGTC branch offices could not perform some of the trading functions. However, if the functions of the head offices in Japan are also included, Japanese trading companies may be considered to be full-line trading service companies, performing all three categories of trade channel functions.

American Retailers and Importers

Many American retail chain stores, department stores, and specialized importers have buying offices in Korea. Korea Export Buying Offices Association (KEBOA) is an organization that represents foreign buying offices and buying agents. As of February 1983, KEBOA has a list of 366 members. The KEBOA members can be divided into four types:

Type 1: Buying offices for foreign retailers, 20

Type 2: Buying offices for foreign importers/importing agents, 157

Type 3: Korean trading companies acting as buying agents, 123

Type 4: Liaison offices operating on commissions, 66

Types 1 and 2 are staffed by the salaried employees of foreign retailers and importers. Types 3 and 4 are commission agents, whose relations with foreign buyers are not as stable as in type 1 and 2 offices.

Out of 366 members, KEBOA lists 135 as American offices. There were nineteen American buying offices among the top forty performers, based on 1982 export figures. These included six retailers, while the other thirteen were specialized importers. American retailers with buying offices in Korea include such well-known companies as J.C. Penney, Sears Roebuck, K-Mart, Tandy Electronics, and Associated Merchandising, which represents many established department stores. Retailer buying offices in Korea are much bigger and better organized than the buying offices of American specialized importers. All of the retailer offices were established around the 1972-1973 period. Exports arranged by the six retailers' buying offices added up to $668 million in 1982.

These buying offices operate mainly as trade facilitators; the purchasing authority rests with the buyers in the United States, who make regular visits to potential suppliers all over the world. Buying offices provide information and negotiation services for the buyers from the head office. Thus buying office functions are limited to negotiation, documentation, market research, quality control, and, to a certain extent, promotion. They are loath to take risks in terms of product quality or delivery dates in dealing with Korean manufacturers. In cases where they perceive an unacceptable level of risk, they will ask large trading companies to act as go-betweens.[6]

As joining KEBOA is not mandatory, there may be smaller commission agents who provide purchasing services to American importers but are not members of KEBOA. There is no way of knowing how much trade is facilitated by these unknown agents. Even for KEBOA members, the export amounts arranged cannot be estimated accurately; KEBOA states that the total purchases reported by its members amounted to $2,153 million in 1981, while it estimates that the actual total surpassed $4,500 million.

In breaking down the total exports from Korea to the United States by different channel types, we are forced to rely on very inexact methods. A major difficulty lies in the fact that the actual functions performed by channel members do not match the export amounts they report. Because all the exports should be performed, at least on paper, by registered trading companies only, we find much double counting when we add up all the figures reported by different channel members.

Data problems notwithstanding, we shall attempt to fit all the pieces together to approximate the total picture. First, we will estimate contributions by different channels for one year's exports from Korea to the United States. Next will come the more difficult task of tracing dynamic changes in the contributions of different channels over time.

Of the five channel types shown in table 6-8, the first two types represent intracorporate exports that do not involve any trade intermediary. One is the intracorporate trade of American multinational corporations that have export-oriented manufacturing subsidiaries in Korea. The other is that of Korean manufacturers that have their own marketing subsidiaries in the United States. These subsidiaries will sometimes have to go through local middlemen in the American market, including large retailers that are represented in type 3. However, since the manufacturers perform most of the international trade functions themselves without help from other trading companies, this channel should be distinguished from the others.

The third channel type is that of American retailers and importers who have extended their purchasing arms to Korea through branch offices or commission agents. To be more exact, we must separate retailers and specialized importers. Large American retailers who have buying offices in Korea are really integrating backward to bypass trade middlemen, while specialized importers are just performing their primary function when they have representation in Korea. It is true that buying offices and commission agents do not make purchasing decisions themselves, but act on the decisions of the buyers. However, the fact that the American retailers have buying offices in Korea is evidence that they purchase directly from Korean manufacturers.

It should be mentioned at this point that the retailers who have buying offices in Korea do not necessarily make all their purchases

Table 6–8
Contributions of Different Channels in Korean
Exports to the United States (1981)
($ million)

Channel Type	Estimated Exports	Share
Intracorporate trade of U.S. multinationals[a]	$1,099	19.7%
Korean manufacturers' exports to their marketing subsidiaries[b]	$ 744	13.3%
Japanese trading companies[c]	$ 485	8.7%
U.S. retailers and importers purchasing directly through their branches or agents in Korea[d]	$ 882 ($2,018)[e]	15.8% (36.2%)[e]
Residual, mainly Korean trading companies exports to their subsidiaries or to independent buyers in the U.S.	$2,370 ($1,234)[e]	42.5% (22.1%)[e]
Total	$5,580	100.0%

[a] Based on the OECD study of 1977 data. (See table 6–5.)

[b] Bank of Korea estimates. (See table 6–6.)

[c] Based on data from Association of Foreign Trading Agents of Korea data.

[d] Based on KEBOA reports.

[e] Figures in the parentheses are based on the estimate of the KEBOA. If the share of this channel increases, the residual should be reduced by the same amount.

directly from Korean manufacturers. These companies also purchase from American importers and domestic wholesalers in the United States, depending on the market situation. In that way they can lessen their risk of being left with unsold inventory. The same can be said about Korean manufacturers who have subsidiaries in the United States. It does not necessarily follow that they sell all their exports through their own subsidiaries. They also go through other types of intermediaries as the market situation dictates.

The estimate of exports through this third type, $882 million, should be considered conservative. This amount is based on figures substantiated by documents submitted to the government. The actual amount could be higher because some of the arranged exports are not reported. KEBOA thinks the amount unreported could reach as high as $2,018 million. KEBOA does not publish export amounts by destination. The estimates are based on a breakdown of the reports of the top forty buying offices, which account for about two-thirds of the total exports reported by KEBOA.

The fourth type is the Japanese trading companies. We have already mentioned that Japanese trading companies were the first to establish trading bases in Korea. The Association of Foreign Trading Agents publishes figures for the exports arranged by Japanese trading companies. Because Korea taxes the branches of foreign trading companies on the basis of their total imports only, the amounts of exports they report should be free from systematic bias or distortion. Based on 1980 and 1981 export figures, it can be assumed that about one-half of Japanese trading companies' exports are to countries other than Japan, out of which the share to the United States is not known. The author's survey of eight Japanese trading companies shows that the exports to the United States, out of their total exports from Korea, ranged from about 10 percent to 80 percent, the average being 26 percent for the seven companies that responded to the question. Thus we make the assumption that one-fourth of Japanese trading companies' exports from Korea are destined for the United States market.

The remaining exports to the United States that cannot be attributed to the preceding four channels may be of diverse types. There are non-Japanese foreign trading companies that may have exports to the United States; the prominent ones would be the trading companies based in Hong Kong. There are seven Hong Kong based trading companies listed out of the top forty buying offices and sixty-eight Hong Kong companies among the 366 members of KEBOA. Some of their exports may be destined for the United States. There are also some offer agents, the commission agents on the import side, who export for their foreign clients. However, total exports by offer agents amount to less than 1 percent of Korea's total exports.

Therefore, most of the residual, which is estimated to be between 22 percent to 43 percent of the total exports to the United States, should be exports by Korean trading companies. That includes exports by both KGTCs and other trading companies. It also includes the amount Korean trading companies sell to their subsidiaries in the United States. We noted earlier that Korean trading companies have fifty-two marketing subsidiaries in the United States, some of which are fairly large, employing as many as forty-eight Korean nationals.

Having estimated the contributions of different channels for one year, our next task is to trace the dynamic changes in different channels. There are two difficulties involved here: most data do not go back before 1976, and the available data for 1976 to 1982 are not broken down by destination. We will first look at the data for total exports and then make some educated guesses concerning the Korea-United States trade.

There is no information on the overall share of the intra-MNC trade channel. Because many of the Japanese direct investments in manufacturing in Korea are also for export markets, there are likely to be some additional flows by channel type 1. However, outside of Japan and the United States, there would be few exports of type 1. A similar statement can be made about type 2 channel exports. The United States is still the only country where Korean manufacturers make substantial efforts to penetrate the market.

That leaves us with three other channels whose exports, arranged by foreign retailers and importers, Japanese trading companies, and KGTCs, are shown in table 6-9. The table clearly shows that the share of exports arranged by Japanese trading companies has been declining since 1976. For non-Japanese retailers and trading companies, the trends are mixed. If we consider the fact that the figures for 1976 to 1978 include exports by two large Japanese trading companies, the share of foreign retailers and specialized importers should have increased slightly over this period.

Our survey data also support this conclusion. A sample of thirty-one foreign companies represented in Korea (eight Japanese trading companies, nine retailers, and fourteen specialized importers and non-Japanese trading companies) was surveyed during April and May of 1983. Asked about the trend of their exports after the introduction of the KGTC system, the companies answered as shown in table 6–10.

Table 6–9
Export Arrangements Made by Different Channel Members as Percentage of Korea's Total Exports
($ million)

	Korean General Trading Companies[a]		Foreign Retailers and Importers		Japanese Trading Companies		Korea's Total Exports
	Amount	Percentage	Amount	Percentage	Amount	Percentage	Amount
1976	1,472	19.1	870[b]	11.28	1,202	15.58	7,715
1977	2,719	27.1	1,044[b]	10.39	1,280	12.74	10,046
1978	3,427	30.0	1,244[b]	9.76	1,297	10.20	12,711
1979	5,046	33.5	1,047	6.95	1,562	10.38	15,055
1980	7,716	41.0	1,566	8.95	1,640	9.37	17,505
1981	9,105	42.8	1,823	8.58	1,938	9.12	21,254
1982	10,459	47.9	2,188	10.01	1.735	7.94	21,853

Sources: KGTCs: See Kukje Corp., *Chonghap sangsa ŭi kinŭng kwa silch'e* (Seoul: 1982), 152; Foreign Retailers and Importers: Korea Export Buying Offices Association; Japanese Trading Companies: Association of Foreign Trading Agents of Korea.

[a] KGTCs' contributions include arrangements made by other channel members.

[b] Includes exports by two Japanese Trading Companies.

This table indicates that the majority of Japanese trading companies reported that their exports were not increasing. Large retailers responded eight to one that their exports were increasing, while the responses of the importers and non-Japanese trading companies were mixed.

We also asked foreign companies how they perceived the role of KGTCs with respect to their own operations. The answers, as shown in table 6-11, are also consistent with the export performance above. Foreign retailers view KGTCs as complementary with their functions, while Japanese trading companies view them as competitive.

The KGTCs' share of Korea's total exports started from the low level of 19.1 percent in 1976 and increased annually to reach 42.8 percent in 1981 and 47.9 percent in 1982. As we mentioned earlier, export figures reported by the KGTCs include sales to foreign retailers and trading companies, exports by companies that belong to the same business groups, and exports by smaller companies that do not have trading company licenses. Thus the figures for the KGTCs do not accurately reflect the contributions made by the KGTCs themselves. Nevertheless, assuming that the ratios of this double counting remained relatively stable, the fact that the KGTCs' share increased at such a rapid rate can be taken as evidence that exports generated by their own marketing efforts have also increased significantly over this period.

Table 6–10
Export Trends: Post-KGTC Period

	Increase	Decrease or No Change	Total
Retailers	8	1	9
Importers	8	6	14
Japanese trading companies	1	7	8
Total	17	14	31

Table 6–11
Perception of KGTCs by Foreign Companies

	Complementary	Competitive	No Relationship
Retailers	6	0	3
Importers	5	3	6
Japanese trading companies	0	7	1

Many of the KGTCs' export increases have been made in the third world, however. That partly reflects the Korean government's intention of diversifying to export markets other than the United States and Japan. As a result, the KGTCs' share of Korea's exports to the United States is only 26.5 percent compared to their share of 42.8 percent of Korea's total exports. The KGTCs' low share of the exports to the United States reflects the fact that there were already established trade channels such as American retailers and importers and, to a lesser extent, other foreign trading companies. In addition, large Korean manufacturers and large non-GTC trading companies have also established their own marketing channels, further limiting the potential for KGTC penetration of the U.S. market. In fact, the KGTCs that sent a relatively high percentage of their exports to the United States are the ones that have large manufacturing bases of their own, such as textiles in the case of Daewoo and Samsung and footwear in the case of Kukje.

Despite the fact that KGTCs have a relatively small share of Korea's exports to the United States, they do have nineteen marketing subsidiaries in the United States. The dates of approval by the Bank of Korea for these subsidiaries are shown in table 6-6. It shows that KGTCs made major efforts after 1976, as did other Korean companies. The number of Korean nationals working in the United States also indicates the importance of the efforts of KGTCs. All in all, it is likely that the KGTCs' share of Korea's exports to the United States have increased over the period from 1976 to 1982.

In view of total export trends by different channel types, we can make the following statements about trade channel evolution in Korea-United States trade during the period from 1976 to 1981:

There is no reason to claim any systematic change in the share of intracorporate trade by American MNCs.

Korean manufacturers' direct exports (selling to their subsidiaries in the United States) definitely increased over this period, starting from an almost negligible amount to probably more than 10 percent of total exports in 1981.

The share of American retailers and specialized importers seems to have increased slightly over this period. The share of the large retailers increased faster than that of the specialized importers.

The share of Japanese trading companies has decreased over this period. It can be estimated that the share decreased from around 16 percent in 1976 to 8.7 percent in 1981.

The share of large Korean trading companies, especially KGTCs, has apparently increased over this period, although it is not possible to make an accurate calculation of their share.

Environmental Changes and Channel Evolution

The most significant shift in the Korea-United States trade channel in the last decade has been the increase in the role played by Korean manufacturers and KGTCs. Which factors have contributed to this evolution? Our task in this section is to relate several changes in the economic and regulatory environment to the trade channel evolution that we examined in the previous three sections. However, the conclusions we draw here rely almost entirely on circumstantial evidence. The information available at this point is not sufficient to establish definite cause-effect relationships.

As we hypothesized earlier, two factors contributed to the increase in the role played by Korean companies, both manufacturing concerns and trading companies. The almost fifteenfold increase in total dollar value of their exports allowed Korean companies to establish their own marketing arms in the United States. That move was concentrated during the two-year period from 1976 to 1978, when forty-six (out of seventy-nine existing in 1981) marketing subsidiaries were established. Here we must point out the possibility of the *bandwagon* effect, meaning that companies moved overseas, especially to the United States, in a competitive fashion.

The period from 1976 to 1978 can be described as the one in which the export drive of the Korean government reached its peak. The goal of surpassing the $10 billion export target was a political as well as an economic slogan for the government. This excessive export push by the government, together with the bandwagon effect, apparently drove many companies to move into the United States, in some cases prematurely. The interview study of eight subsidiaries in the United States revealed that about one-half of them incurred heavy losses because of bad inventories and bad accounts receivable. Nevertheless, the point is that Korean companies for the first time moved into foreign markets on a large scale and gained valuable experience through trial and error.

The second factor that forced Korean companies to move into the United States was the change in the product composition of Korean exports. As we have seen, the major product lines that increased most rapidly in volume were iron and steel products, consumer electronics, transportation equipment, and footwear. Marketing channels for industrial products tend to be short and direct, forcing manufacturers to reach out to end-users. Also the channel-dominating power of large retailers is not present in industrial product markets, making channel penetration by manufacturers easier. In consumer electronics and other durable goods, after-service requirements force many manufacturers to set up their own facilities in foreign markets. Thus the change in product composition seems to have significantly stimulated the direct involvement of Korean manufacturing companies in the United States market. This can be supported by the fact that the majority of the manufacturers' subsidiaries in the United States are in the steel, electronics, and automobile tire industries.

Another major evolution in the channel, the more active role played by American large retail chain stores and department stores, seems to have been caused by the rising quality of Korean export products. Large chain stores moved into Korea in the first half of the 1970s and have increased their direct purchasing steadily ever since. Retailers' increased direct purchasing should have reduced the role of American importers and foreign trading companies. Retailers expressed the view that as Korean manufacturers achieved higher product quality, they would want to increase their direct purchasing. One executive pointed out that the bargain-hunting importers who dominated the scene in the early 1970s have now moved to Southeast Asian countries and China and that current buyers are looking for stable suppliers of quality products.

The decline of Japanese trading companies, at least on the export side, may be just one symptom of a more general phenomenon: as Korean manufacturers move forward to the United States and American retailers move backward to Korea, there is simply less room left for trading companies. If this statement is true, what happened to Korean trading companies? It is our contention that the trading companies that export heavily to the United States tend to be the ones with their own manufacturing bases. Thus, even though it looks as if the Korean trading companies have become more active, it may just be the portion of their trade in the products they manufacture, rather than the portion of their pure intermediary-role trade, that increased more rapidly.

If this statement is true, then the KGTC designation system itself may not have contributed to any great extent to the more active channel involvement by KGTCs in the United States market. KGTCs have contributed to the diversification of export products to include industrial and capital-intensive products and also the diversification of markets to third world countries. However, in the United States market, the KGTC system itself has not contributed to the deeper penetration of the market. The penetrations that have been achieved by the KGTCs would have just as likely been achieved by the manufacturing companies in their respective groups.

Last, the question remains about the impact of increased import restrictions on channel evolution. The way export quotas imposed on Korea by other nations are allocated by trade associations in Korea favors established companies that have previous export records. To the extent that this is so, import restrictions tend to hinder channel evolution. During the interview study of retailer buying offices in Seoul, some of the officers expressed their desire to purchase directly from small, reliable specialty-line manufacturers but pointed out that they are forced to deal with large quota-holders who are, in many cases, KGTCs themselves or KTGC-related companies. This tendency is most notable in the case of textile quotas, which have been in place the longest and whose impact on total trade volume is the largest.

Large quota-holders can obtain substantial premiums on their quota-holdings during periods of excess demand. Under those circumstances, they do not feel the need to make risky efforts to penetrate the market. The fact that a substantial proportion of nondurable consumer products is still exported through foreign buying offices might be partly explained by the lack of market penetration efforts by large quota-holders, including some KGTCs. All in all, the import restrictions that were placed in effect during the 1970s have probably acted to slow the pace of channel evolution during this period.

We have looked at major environmental changes and their effect on trade channel evolution. Let us move a step further and ask how the channel evolution as described above has affected the performance of channel members. Because it is not possible to quantify the impact of channel evolution, we can only make some conjectural statements about it.

The attempt at deeper independent penetration of the American market by Korean companies is only about six years old. Since market penetration efforts take a long time to pay off, it still seems to be too early to assess whether or not these penetration efforts have had a definite impact on either the growth of sales or the profitability of the firms. However, these companies have incurred substantial costs in the course of market penetration. The benefits so far seem to be mostly intangible, but are probably not insignificant to the firms. One benefit is increased market information. Some foreign companies interviewed stated that Korean companies that established marketing subsidiaries in the United States have become much better informed about fashion trends and the market situation in the United States as a result. Having a marketing arm in the world's largest market is likely to broaden the outlook of many Korean managers who had been accustomed only to dealing in Korea with visiting foreign buyers or to selling in the smaller and more restricted Korean domestic market. In the medium to long term, the deeper involvement in the export channel may be expected to increase the stability of export earnings of Korean companies. Profitability improvement perhaps will come later.

Conclusion

The evolution that took place in the 1970s in Korea's export channel to the United States can be summarized as *channel shortening*. Even though there emerged a new channel member, Korean general trading companies, the most significant changes we found were the increasingly active roles taken by Korean manufacturers and American large retailers. Many of the KGTCs already existed as trading companies before the Korean government introduced the KGTC designation system in 1976. It is argued here that the more active role played by KGTCs could probably have been achieved even without the KGTC designation system. This point is supported by the fact that the KGTCs that are more active in the American market are mainly selling the products they manufacture themselves. It is not the intermediary trading function of the KGTC that has established a presence in the United States market, but the marketing function for manufacturing companies associated with or owned by the KGTC.

The major factors that contributed to the shortening of trade channels were increases in trade volume and changes in the product composition of Korean exports to the United States. The rapid increase in export volume made it economical for Korean manufacturers and American retailers to establish branches or subsidiaries in the trade partner country. The increased volume of industrial products and consumer durables make it both possible and necessary for Korean manufacturers to establish marketing subsidiaries in the United States. We have also speculated that the import restrictions put into effect in the 1970s may have hindered certain changes in the channel that might have otherwise taken place.

Large American retailers represented in Korea expect to play an even more active role in the future. As Korean manufacturers fulfill the American retailers' requirements for stable supplies of quality products, the American retailers will gradually increase their direct purchasing from Korea. This will, of course, depend on how well Korea maintains its competitive position compared to other Asian suppliers such as Hong Kong and Taiwan. Changes in the product composition of Korea's exports also affect large American retailers.

Some of them are already changing their import mix to include more hard goods, including electronics and consumer durables. Apparel, though still the most important product category for American retailers, is declining in relative importance.

The trends that forced the evolution in trade channels in the 1970s are expected to continue in the 1980s. As Korea's export product composition shifts from the labor-intensive to the more skill- and technology-intensive, and as the overall quality level of export products improves, one may expect the trend of channel shortening to continue in the future. Moreover, as Korean manufacturers gain more experience in operating in the United States market, they can be expected to become more deeply involved in the domestic American marketing channel and perform more distribution functions.

7 Growing Trade and Growing Conflict between the Republic of Korea and the United States

John S. Odell

Bilateral trade between the Republic of Korea and the United States has grown rapidly in the last two decades, bringing benefits to both countries. Yet simultaneously the tempo of conflicts between the two states over commercial issues also began to increase in the 1960s and especially in the 1970s. While bilateral protectionist frictions are quite familiar to newspaper readers, little systematic research has been devoted to them. What factors are most likely to lead the two governments to clash over commerce, and what determines the outcomes of their bargaining? This chapter reviews the most important United States-Korea disputes, and it describes how trade conflicts are handled in the two countries. It then suggests factors that increase the chances of an official dispute and may influence the outcome, and concludes with some implications for practice.

The explosion of Korean exports is now well known in many countries, not least in the United States. In 1960 Korean goods shipped to America totaled a mere $5.1 million. By 1970 the figure had reached $370 million. In 1974 Korean exports to the United States passed the $1 billion mark, and in 1980 they exceeded $4 billion. Thus, even in the 1970s when the world economy was relatively stagnant and protection policies were spreading, Korea expanded her exports to the United States by another 1000 percent. (These data are in current dollars.) The United States has remained South Korea's leading foreign market, taking 29 percent of her exports in 1979.

During the same time the United States also multiplied its own exports to Korea. From a 1960 level of $153 million, American exports expanded to $636 million in 1970 and to $4.7 billion in 1980. The United States has directed an increasing share of its total exports to Korea, which became its eleventh-largest trading partner in the world in 1980. The huge deficit in bilateral trade, typical of the 1950s, steadily narrowed over the subsequent years. The leading commodities moving in this bilateral commerce are shown in tables 7-1 and 7-2. In short, the two economies are complementary in significant respects, and each side has continued to profit from their mutual exchange.

Recent Conflict Experience

As their commerce expanded, however, the two governments began to find themselves engaged in official disputes over trade. An interstate trade conflict can be understood generally as an interaction in which one government responds with a complaint, a countermeasure, or with resistance to a request or trade action by another government which the first believes harmful to its trade or economy. Such a dispute ends either when the governments agree to an explicit settlement of their claims or when communications referring to the episode cease. The outcome refers to the terms of the settlement, or the behavioral equivalent in cases without explicit settlements.

Thirteen significant conflicts fitting this general definition occurred between Washington and Seoul from 1960 to 1981. The effort to identify them began with a search of the U.S. government publication listing all official agreements for this entire period and went on to other U.S. official sources.[1] *Far Eastern Economic Review* was read for 1961 through 1981, and various other nonofficial publications were checked for particular dates. Published research works, interviews in Seoul and Washington, and documents from the Korean government yielded additional information.[2]

A conflict has been included in this study when the value of trade at stake was more than US$50 million during the year prior to the outcome. Other disputes affecting small amounts of trade, including several recent U.S. investigations of alleged Korean export subsidies and dumping, are excluded. As an exception, cases of small trade value are included when the trade at stake nevertheless amounted to 10 percent or more of either country's exports.

All thirteen disputes appearing in these sources involve Korean access to the U.S. market, and all began with an American action. If there have been conflicts over access to the Korea or another market, these have left no traces in any of the sources consulted. The thirteen clashes arose in three sectors: textiles and apparel, footwear, and color television receivers. Three cases occurred during the 1960s, seven during the 1970s, and three in 1980-1981.

These disputes have varied in their distributional outcomes, that is, the degree to which each government achieved its initial objectives (requests, demands, faits accomplis) on the issues of disagreement. In

Table 7–1
Leading Exports from Republic of Korea to the United States

Year	Category							
	84	63	89	72	65	85	76	77
1968								
Value (million)	$62	$54	$34	$11	$11	$10	—	—
Share (%)	31	27	17	6	6	5	—	—
1978								
Value (million)	$958	$224	$317	—	$60	$400	$400	$301
Share (%)	26	6	8	—	2	11	11	8

Key:
63 Wood and cork manufactures (plywood and veneers)
65 Textiles, yarns, fabrics, and made-up articles
72 Electrical machinery (1968; category was redefined later)
76 Telecommunications and sound reproduction equipment
77 Electrical machinery, not elsewhere specified
84 Clothing and accessories
85 Footwear
89 Miscellaneous manufactured articles

Source: U.S. Department of Commerce, *U.S. General Imports*, FT-155, 1968 and 1978.

Table 7–2
Leading Exports from the United States to Republic of Korea

Year	Category					
	04	71	26	72	28	73
1968						
Value (million)	$128	$56	$44	$27	$15	$12
Share (%)	25	11	9	5	3	2
1977						
Value (million)	$372	$201	$318	$347	$132	$109
Share (%)	16	9	13	15	6	5

Key:
04   Cereals and preparations of cereal, flour, etc.
26   Raw textile fibers and their wastes (cotton)
28   Metalliferous ores and manufactures
71   Nonelectrical machinery
72   Electrical machinery
73   Transport equipment

Source: U.S. Department of Commerce, *U.S. Exports,* FT-455, 1968 and 1977.

order to make comparison possible, each outcome is here classified as either closer to the initial objectives of the United States government, closer to those of Seoul, or as an intermediate or mixed result. The procedure is to identify or estimate the initial position of each government on those issues where they disagree and then to locate the settlement roughly in the range established by those initial positions. Examples are given below. It should be borne in mind that initial positions and outcomes refer not to companies but to their governments. It is not assumed that the U.S. government's position regarding shoe imports, for instance, is the same as that of the U.S. shoe industry. The conflict experience is summarized in table 7-3.

Textiles and Apparel

Nine of the disputes arose in the textile/apparel sector. Each of the first three in the 1960s began with American requests for restraint on Korean exports of cotton textiles and garments, and the results in these early cases were all closer to the initial United States position than to that of the Korean government.

The United States first called for quantitative limits in December 1962. Earlier that year the United States had succeeded in negotiating a multilateral Long-Term Arrangement (LTA) regulating trade in cotton textiles and apparel. Under the terms of the LTA Washington then complained that Korean products were disrupting the American market. The Korean government took the position that its exports were a

Table 7–3

Trade Disputes between Governments of the United States and South Korea (1960–1981)

Outcome	Dispute
More favorable to Korean initial position	None
Mixed or intermediate	1972 textiles and apparel 1974 textiles and apparel 1977 footwear orderly marketing agreement
More favorable to U.S. initial position	1963 textiles and apparel 1965 textiles and apparel 1967 textiles and apparel 1976 footwear countervailing duty case 1977 textiles and apparel 1979 color television receivers 1979 textiles and apparel 1980 color television receivers 1980 textiles and apparel 1981 textiles and apparel

Sources: Texts of bilateral agreements; contemporary press reports; interviews with Korean and U.S. official negotiators and industry representatives. The procedure used in classifying outcomes is discussed in the text.

minuscule portion of the U.S. market and could not possibly be responsible for much harm. In 1962 Korea exported to the United States a total of only 11 million square yards of textile products, while all U.S. imports came to 1,165 million square yards.[3] All imports combined had captured much less than 10 percent of the American market. But Washington maintained, then and later, that other exporters had previously agreed to restraints on the condition that no third state would be allowed to enter the market to take up their shares. The Americans insisted that numerous small suppliers taken together did constitute a significant disruption.

The result was that over period of six months the United States named ten specific fabrics and garments, and negotiations established annual limits on each. The Korean government accepted limits on the growth of a key industry, which reportedly caused a large number of layoffs in apparel companies.[4] Actual 1963 exports were substantially larger than those of the previous year, but in the early 1960s Koreans were just getting these exports started.

In January 1965 Korea first signed a comprehensive bilateral agreement with the United States, providing for three more years of limits on cotton fabric and garment exports. This agreement appears to have been a major setback for Korea and a complete success for Washington. In spite of Korean preferences for eliminating or loosening the restraints, they accepted a sharp increase in the number of specific items controlled, from ten to eighteen. The aggregate limit was set 22 percent below the 1964 level of actual exports. In the second and third years the limits were to be raised by 5 percent. Washington achieved its objective of a comprehensive agreement and was not required to pay any compensation for these Korean concessions. From 1963 through 1966 Korea's cotton textile exports to America remained stagnant, in quantity terms.

The third round ended in December 1967, when the basic terms of the cotton agreement were extended for another four years. The aggregate limit was boosted by 34 percent compared with 1966 trade, and provisions were added allowing Korea to 'swing' small amounts of quota from one item to another. The number of products covered and the growth rate remained the same.

The first two textile/apparel disputes of the 1970s ended with outcomes in the intermediate range, making them more favorable to Korea than almost all others analyzed here. In 1969 the Nixon Administration began trying to have Japan, South Korea, Taiwan, and Hong Kong add new restrictions on their exports of wool and synthetic textile goods as well as cotton. These countries had been increasing their synthetic exports rapidly for several years, but U.S. imports had still captured less than 4 percent of the domestic market by 1968.

The first American ploy was to suggest a multilateral agreement covering all the fibers. Many months of confrontation dragged by as Tokyo refused to accept American demands. U.S. officials did not make any quantitative requests of the three small states until mid-1971. At that time Taiwan agreed tentatively to a new comprehensive bilateral five-year restraint accord that would limit synthetics' growth to 11 percent in the first year and 1 percent less in each subsequent year, and would calculate limits starting with the level of trade in a base period of April 1970 through March 1971.[5] It was reported that the United States had proposed the same declining growth rates to Korea.[6]

Korea and Hong Kong continued to resist agreement, however. They maintained that the United States had failed to show that exports in these additional areas were disrupting the American market, and Korean negotiators showed that their development plans depended heavily on rapid growth in synthetic exports. Later Seoul offered to accept a growth limit of 40 percent per year, the level of recent actual growth. They subsequently offered to cut this to 25 percent, the rate assumed in the national development plan.[7]

In September 1971 President Nixon threatened all four states with unilateral quotas unless they accepted U.S. terms by 15 October, and all four yielded to this intense pressure. The Korean agreement sharply widened restrictions against Korean exports. The number of controlled products jumped from eighteen to thirty-five, and these limits were to be in effect for five years. Growth for man-made fibers was limited on the sliding scale, starting at 10 rather than 11 percent. Provisions for flexibility between categories were the same as in the 1967 agreement.

But in this case Korea, and only Korea, also secured major offsetting gains from the United States, which agreed to provide Korea with a $100 million concessional loan plus $275 million worth of food aid over the next five years, in addition to aid commitments already made. The new commitments were not officially described as compensation for the textile agreement, but the amounts were calculated so as to match Korea's net losses in trade.[8] The United States also boosted Korea's quota for cotton products.[9]

In November 1974 the two governments initialed a new bilateral multifiber agreement. The United States had continued to seek a multilateral regime for textiles trade, and in late 1973 some fifty governments concluded the Multifiber Arrangement (MFA) in Geneva. The new rules permitted terms more favorable to exporter states than the 1972 bilateral settlements had been, and so those agreements were renegotiated.

The Korean team took a long list of requests to Washington, and they were able to achieve a substantial share of their objectives in this case. The number of restricted items was cut from thirty-four to twenty-one, growth was limited to 7 percent in the first year, 6.25 percent in the second, and 6.75 percent in the third year of the new agreement. These growth rates were slightly higher than those set for Hong Kong, which was a Korean aim. Korea's flexibility to swing unused quota from one apparel item to another was boosted from 5 percent under the previous agreement to 7 percent. The new agreement increased from 5 to 11 percent the scope for carrying over shortfalls from one quota year to be used in the next. And it added a new provision whereby Korea could overship in one year by 6 percent and charge those goods against the following year's quota (called carryforward). Because of the growing size of Korea's clothing exports, even a 1 percent change in permitted swing or carryover now meant a difference of millions of square yards of goods. Washington, for its part, also succeeded in 1974 in extending restrictions for another three years in basically the same structure, with the added gain of a new multilateral arrangement to legitimize and reinforce those on wool and man-made fibers.[10]

At the expiration of this agreement in 1977, another predictable textile/apparel dispute occurred. Its outcome was decidedly less favorable for the Korean side. The United States wanted Seoul to accept controls for another five years, and also wanted to make them more restrictive than ever. Washington asked Korea to forgo all growth in 1978, and to cut subsequent yearly growth to 1 percent in large-volume items that were "sensitive" to U.S. producers.[11] The MFA provided in general terms that extended restrictions should permit annual growth of at least 6 percent. The Korean government preferred no restrictions, as usual, and strenuously resisted demands to make them more severe.[12]

After difficult bargaining Seoul again accepted another five-year agreement including limits on twenty-nine specific items, as opposed to twenty-one in 1974. Growth was eliminated for 1978 and was limited to an average of 6.5 percent in the aggregate during subsequent years. But most apparel exports, the biggest volume products, were to be held to annual growth rates ranging between 1 and 3.9 percent. Seoul eked out only one slight improvement in flexibility provisions.[13]

Late in 1978 the American clothing and textile complex credibly threatened legislative action that might have jeopardized the entire Tokyo Round trade negotiation unless textile protection were tightened further. President Carter responded in November by pledging to tighten protection.[14]

In early 1979 Carter's negotiators flew to East Asia seeking fresh concessions, which would be departures from the five-year accords recently concluded. Of course Korea did not wish to accept any further tightening of restrictions; nonetheless Seoul did agree to forgo the use of its provisions for carryover and carryforward during that one year. This concession was not included in the 1979 official agreement but was made in a side letter.[15] In this case the United States, while basically achieving its objective, also compensated Korea to some extent within the textiles area by raising the limits on certain synthetic garments for the next four years.

Meanwhile, President Carter's Special Trade Representative Robert Strauss was negotiating at home with leaders of the American industry to get their agreement not to fight the general Tokyo Round agreements, which were now on the verge of completion. The industry was able to extract from the administration a 'White Paper' pledging to impose further restrictions on Hong Kong, Korea, and Taiwan. The objectives were to prevent import increases in 1979, to keep subsequent imports from these three in line with the growth of the United States domestic market, and to eliminate sudden increases or "surges."[16]

Thus, almost immediately, American negotiators appeared again in East Asia seeking further new concessions on 1980 trade. They sought to fulfill the President's commitment, especially by reducing flexibility. Seoul was asked to give up all carryover and carryforward on all apparel items, as in 1979, and also to reduce swing by 1 percent. They wanted to cut Korea's quota for synthetic sweaters, a major item.[17] The United States also sought a new administrative mechanism for controlling the trade that would give Washington the authority to halt imports of surging items not under specific limits, without consulting with Seoul first.[18]

The Korean and Hong Kong governments were outraged at a second effort to interfere with their exports after they had already concluded five-year restraint agreements. Each sat through four rounds of tough talks refusing to accept American terms. At the end of 1979 Washington went so far as to threaten Hong Kong with unilateral termination of its bilateral agreement, and Hong Kong then accepted cuts for 1980.[19]

After publicly denying that they would accept more cuts in flexibility, Korea's team also found it necessary to do so. The 1980 settlement eliminated carryover and carryforward for 1980, reduced swing by 1 percent on eleven clothing items, including four of the most important ones, and cut sharply the quota on sweaters. The new administrative mechanism was adopted, but it also included features that the Korean government considered improvements over the previous system. After a very long struggle the U.S. team granted Korea a small compensating increase in wool products for 1980 through 1982.[20] The actual signing of the 1980 agreement was delayed some seven months by the deep political turmoil in Korea that followed the assassination of President Park Chung-hee.

In 1981 the same scenario was replayed a third time. Washington sought and received reductions in Korean flexibility for 1981 trade. Korea gave up carryover, carryforward, and 1 percent of swing for eleven apparel items, including four major products, and gave up all flexibility for sweaters. The Korean government secured a small addition to their quota for yarn and fabric.

Footwear and Television Sets

Between 1960 and 1981 the two states also engaged in two major disputes over trade in footwear. In July 1975 the U.S. Treasury Department ruled that the Korean government was granting a 1 percent subsidy on shoe exports through a program of preferential export financing. The United States wanted Seoul to end the subsidy or to offset its effects on the U.S. economy.

Earlier in the decade Washington had also complained about other export promotion policies in this sector. Then and later, the Korean

government strongly objected to American threats to impose countervailing duties, disputing the U.S. charge that their promotion measures
were causing material injury to the American industry. They also maintained that the United States itself used similar policies and that such
complaints directed at Korea, and not at other, far larger, shoe exporters, were discriminatory. Nevertheless, in March 1973 the Korean
government had eliminated two of the programs, and they had imposed
"voluntary" quantitative limits on exports of rubber footwear from
1973 through 1975.[21]

In January 1976 Washington imposed a countervailing duty of 0.7
percent on nonrubber shoe imports from Korea. With respect to the
much larger category of rubber shoes, Korea agreed to extend its "voluntary" restraints through 1976, and the United States waived the imposition of this countervailing duty on rubber shoes.[22]

The second dispute occurred the next year. In the winter of 1977
the U.S. International Trade Commission sided with the American
industry and ruled that imports of nonrubber shoes were causing it
serious damage. The ITC proposed a tariff-rate quota to relieve the
pressure. The new Carter administration decided to reject this broad
plan and instead to negotiate bilateral protection agreements with Taiwan and Korea.[23]

The key United States objectives were a limit on 1977 trade substantially lower than 1976 levels, a five-year agreement, and sublimits
on shoes made of different types of materials. With Korea the U.S.
team reportedly began by asking for a massive cutback, from the 1976
level of 44 million pairs to the 16 million pairs Korea had shipped in
1975.[24] Reportedly the Koreans initially took the position that they
could not accept a limit lower than their 1977 export capacity (60 million pairs), and that for only one year.[25] Soon the Americans moved
up to proposing a limit of 30 million pairs the first year and the possibility of some growth thereafter or a flat limit of 34 million over the
life of the agreement, at Seoul's option.[26]

The outcome in this case was in the intermediate range, one of the
three of this period. Korean exports were to be cut back and limited
for four years. The aggregate limit was set at 33 million pairs for the
first year and at an average of 36.25 million over the life of the agreement—not far below the midpoint between the two opening positions.
This result, according to an American participant, was within the range
of the U.S. team's mandate but on the "generous" end.[27] In addition,
the Korean team secured a provision allowing 9 million more pairs to
be admitted during the first quota year without being counted against
the limit, on the grounds that they were already "in the pipeline" on
the starting date. The agreement also included provisions for the

administration to be in Korean hands and for swing, carryover, and carryforward.[28] Both governments achieved their objectives to some extent.

The only other conflicts involving substantial amounts of trade concerned Korean access to the American market for color television receivers. During the early 1970s, imports, almost entirely from Japan, filled 16 to 18 percent of this U.S. market (on a quantity basis). In 1972 sets from Taiwan began to snatch a small part of the Japanese share. A wave of new sets, mostly from Japan, hit American shores in 1976, pushing the import market share up to 33 percent.

Zenith Radio Corporation and a coalition of labor unions had been pressing for official action against imports. In March 1977 the ITC held that imports of color TV sets were causing serious injury to the American industry. As a remedy for this injury, the Carter administration two months later got the Japanese government to agree to a pact cutting shipments back sharply from the 1976 levels and capping them there for three years.[29]

At this time, Korean plans to build a color television export industry were just beginning to bear fruit. Korean exports to the United States rose from a negligible 1976 level to $72 million in 1978. In 1977 the Korean government decided that it was only a matter of time before it too would be hit with restrictions, and so it encouraged companies to expand exports as rapidly as possible to establish a market foothold.[30] The companies expanded their production capacity threefold in 1978 to 1.1 million units per year.[31] Taiwan's exports, mostly from American companies there, also proliferated after Japan limited her exports.[32] The Japanese government and other American companies complained that Taiwan and Korea were undermining the 1977 arrangement.[33] By this time most of the Japanese companies were moving their color television production to factories in the United States and shifting into the export of video recorders from Japan.

In November 1978 U.S. negotiators began pressing the Korean government to cut back television exports and control them. Korean representatives resisted, saying they were a new entrant and still a small factor in this market. They did not see how they, as opposed to Taiwan, could be causing injury. The Koreans also pointed out that their exports were mainly of sets with small screens and said that sets of that size were not even produced by most U.S. companies. They argued that any restrictions that reduced the level of recent trade would be inconsistent with GATT. At one point the Korean chief negotiator even threatened to boycott American nuclear energy and aircraft exports in retaliation if Korean interests were not protected.[34]

These arguments had little effect, apparently. Both Taiwan and

Korea complied with the United States demands—in Taiwan's case, two days before she was formally derecognized by Washington. The United States-Korea agreement of December 1978 slashed Korea's color television exports for the next twelve months back to 204,000 units, or half of the expanded 1978 level. It also permitted, however, an exception for 122,000 more sets to enter in the first year without being counted against the quota, on the grounds that these were already in the pipeline at the time of negotiations. The self-restraints were to remain in effect until June 1980.[35]

In 1979 capacity utilization in Korean factories fell to 34 percent.[36] Late that year a second TV dispute got underway as Seoul insisted that the restraints should be lifted in June 1980, while Washington sought an extension. Later Korean officials bargained for an annual limit of 750,000 units, and they sought to have small-screen sets freed from restrictions.[37]

The United States-Korean agreement of July 1980 extended but loosened restrictions on Korean television exports. The new limits did exempt small-screen sets, and the ceiling on others was set at 385,000 for the next twelve months and 565,000 for the year beginning July 1981.[38] Thus in the third year of restraints, trade would be allowed to rise back to the level attained in 1978. Seoul secured provisions for carryover of 11 percent and carryforward of 10 percent. In 1980 restrictions were also extended for Taiwan, but the Japanese agreement was allowed to lapse. Japan's exports had dwindled to a fraction of the 1976 level. In 1982 the Korean agreement also expired.

During the mid-1970s Washington also began several investigations of charges by American companies that Korean companies were dumping goods in the United States and that they were benefiting from Korean government subsidies. A number of these investigations ended when the United States government dismissed the allegations, so that no interstate conflict arose. Such was the result in cases involving leather apparel, cordage, saccharin, steel wire rope, and steel wire nails, for example. The United States did take administrative action against specialty steel, mushrooms, handbags, and bicycle tire exports from Korea, but the amounts of trade in these cases fell below the $50 million threshold used in this study to select significant conflicts.

How the Two States Handle Trade Conflicts

In sum, the 1970s saw a major increase in the frequency of trade disputes between the two governments, and there was some variation in the outcomes of these conflicts. There are also some interesting differences between the institutions and processes through which Korea and America handle international commercial frictions, and these should be kept in mind as we proceed to an analysis of this experience.

South Korea's political institutions are among the most centralized in the nonsocialist world, and those of the United States are among the most decentralized. In the case of Korea, interstate disputes over access to foreign markets are unlikely to provoke major differences of preference among Koreans, regardless of the nature of their institutions. Not many Koreans prefer barriers against Korean exports. Even so, when the Korean government decides the time has come to yield to U.S. power, the exporting industry is no doubt often disappointed. At that point the Korean system does become relevant. The traditionally strong position of the government vis-à-vis business and labor insures that the latter have little hope of blocking or circumventing an unwelcome decision.

The centralization and the government's strong structural position are rooted in the culture, which is unusually homogeneous and which traditionally lacked strong intermediary institutions.[39] More specifically, the entry of the Korean military into politics with the 1961 coup certainly strengthened the backbone of what has been called Korea's hard state, in Myrdal's sense.[40] The military were perhaps the most modernized segment of the society at that time, and they were determined to give top priority to modernizing South Korea's economy and giving order to her politics. Park Chung-hee and his associates made it clear that they were not afraid to use police powers to quell opposition, if necessary, in order to clear the way for their policies, after, as well as before, the transition to elected civilian government.

The major groups that pose challenges to government economic policies in other societies were already severely weakened by this time or were held in check by the Park Administration from thereafter. The North Korean attack and the Korean war had dealt a fatal blow to the chances a potential left might have had in South Korea. The new military government banned from politics most leaders of progressive political parties. Labor unions were prohibited from engaging in political activity. In the early 1960s only a tiny fraction of the labor force worked in manufacturing, and while that fraction swelled over the years, those new workers also shared heavily in the benefits of rapid growth.

The generals and colonels lost no time in showing the business sector its place. One of their first actions was to arrest most of the country's business leaders and to threaten to confiscate their assets because of alleged corruption under the Rhee administration. Only bank shares were confiscated and most businessmen were exempted from prosecution, but the message that the government intended to dominate was no doubt received.[41]

Throughout the next two decades, two elements of the Korean political-economic structure continued to keep business weak and government strong. Particularly after 1972, the government's tenure in office did not depend on pleasing the business sector to elicit election campaign contributions from it, as is the case in other countries including Japan; conversely, Korean business has depended heavily on government for credit. Korean companies typically have high debt-equity ratios, and they have little access to credit not controlled by the government. In practice government allocation of credit has been highly discretionary. Business behavior is governed by the realization that the Korean government can put a company out of business by shutting it off from credit.[42]

The color television dispute occasioned a recent manifestation of the relationship. From the beginning of the production of color sets, President Park forbade domestic television broadcasting in color, on the grounds that Korea was too poor for such a luxury and that permitting it would introduce an unhealthy social division. The companies and the Ministry of Commerce and Industry tried to appeal the decision on economic grounds. During the negotiations the United States also raised the issue informally, suggesting that the Korean government's pleas not to harm this industry were undermined by its own action. Even though the petitioners in this case included the largest and second largest business groups in Korea—Samsung and Lucky—President Park simply refused.[43]

Political parties and the legislative wing of the government also both failed to mobilize lasting alternative centers of power that could block economic policies of the executive. Korean opposition parties have long been frustrated by their own disunity, and the National Assembly has not been a serious constraint on the bureaucracy.[44]

President Park was known for his personal determination to promote economic development, especially exports. As a key part of its reform, the new government relied heavily on a rationally organized bureaucracy staffed by officials with advanced technical training. To plan and coordinate the entire development effort, the government created the powerful Economic Planning Board (EPB) and emphasized its importance by giving the director of the EPB the concurrent appointment of Deputy Prime Minister.

Differences of view between agencies are familiar in Seoul, as in other capitals, but the Korean system has special safeguards against centrifugal forces. The vice-ministers of all economic agencies and the Ministry of Foreign Affairs held formal meetings together twice every week, and the economic ministers also met once or twice a week. Most remarkable was Park's institution of the Chong Wa Dae Expanded Trade Promotion Meeting. The President brought together in one room all senior officials concerned with foreign economic relations and representatives of the major business and trade organizations, where he insisted on a report every month on how much they had accomplished for national exports. If private citizens had complaints about bureaucratic decisions, these too were aired, and Park sometimes issued decisions on the spot.

In responding to requests for restraints on exports, the Ministry of Commerce and Industry (MCI) is the most actively involved Korean institution. The Ministry of Foreign Affairs supplied negotiators in the 1960s because of a shortage of MCI leaders fluent in English; the Ministry of Foreign Affairs continues to lead delegations to multilateral economic organizations other than the financial ones. But MCI, with its many bureaus devoted to the promotion of particular industries, has greater expertise in the details of bilateral restraint talks. Since the 1960s the chief Korean negotiators have been the Director-General of the Trade Promotion Bureau and his superior, the Assistant Minister of Commerce, in the Ministry for Commerce and Industry. Park Pil-Soo, Kim Sun-kil, Lee Man-yong, Noh Chin-shik, Lee Eun-tak, and Kim Chul-su have each held the Director-General's post in recent years.

Business associations in the particular sector affected are also called on to play supporting roles. For example, the Korean Federation of Textile Industries was established in 1967 as the highest representative of that sector. In 1979 the government assigned it by law several functions related to the industry's health and its international relations (see chapter 8).[45] The Korean Footwear Exporters Association and the Electronic Industries Association of Korea operate in comparable fashion. The associations draft plans for their industry for submission to MCI, and they track and publish data on international trade in their products. When the government has adopted export restraints, it has given to these associations the tasks of allocating quotas and monitoring firms' compliance with regulations covering destination, quality, and sometimes price.

The process of deciding how to respond to a foreign request is not fully known. But according to a former negotiator who has also participated on the industry side, the industry association first drafts a proposal and sends it to the government.

The government adopts its initial position, and then holds more discussion. Finally the Minister of Commerce and Industry sets the final

mandate for negotiations. Some discretion is left to the chief negotiator. Negotiating strategy is established by the government, not by
the industry.[46]

According to a different industry association, once negotiations
begin, they are excluded from direct participation. The government
informs them of the result after a settlement is reached.[47] At least some
decisions rise all the way to the President. It was President Park's
personal decision to bow before the American textile ultimatum of
1971, over the protest of one of his negotiators.[48]

Over the long term, Korean bureaucracy and business modernized
and vastly improved their technical skills. President Park led the way
at the top, for example, by selecting Professor Nam Duck Woo, who
holds a Ph.D. in economics earned at a U.S. university, to serve as
Finance Minister from 1969 through 1974 and thereafter as Deputy
Prime Minister for four more years. Nam returned in 1981 as Prime
Minister. Four of the five chief trade negotiators during the 1970s and
early 1980s also came with American or British graduate degrees. One
of them had actually taught American politics as a faculty member at
an American university. By this time the Korean teams gave explicit
attention to the domestic political forces at work behind American
economic policies, as well as to market data. When the United States
began countervailing duty investigations, the Korean government,
lacking expertise in American law, began retaining experienced Washington law firms to fill that gap. This was a far cry from the days of
1962 when the United States first demanded textile export restraints.
When this word first arrived, the Spinners and Weavers Association
of Korea did not even know that the Long-Term Arrangement had
been created.[49]

American political institutions are much more decentralized than
those in Korea, permitting legislators and interest groups more points
of leverage for influencing trade policy. Such groups provide large
contributions to congressional and presidential election campaigns. And
while political leaders are more dependent on labor and business, the
latter are not vulnerable to the particularistic intervention that can
make or break a company in Korea. The structural fact that members
of Congress are elected independently from the chief executive gives
the legislative as well as the executive branch a political base for independent behavior in making policy.

It is important to emphasize that interest groups and legislators
favoring import protection are certainly not the only active, strong
forces in this system. The liberalization of United States trade policy
after 1934 depended crucially on the support of a political coalition in

which farmers, multinational corporations, other businesses, political leaders from the southern states, and organized labor (until the late 1960s) were prominent members. These efforts were necessarily led by the executive branch. Supporters of relatively open trade also succeeded in defeating the most ambitious proposals for protection, such as the Burke-Hartke bill in the early 1970s and the recent automobile domestic content proposal. Support for this coalition eroded significantly from the mid-1970s until the end of the 1981-83 recession.

These institutions are further decentralized by the creation of mechanisms for deciding some trade policy questions through a quasi-judicial process, partly removed from both the Congress and the President. As a price for agreeing to tariff reductions, members of Congress insisted on an escape clause. Under this mechanism, an industry that feels it is being seriously injured by imports may appeal to the ITC for protection. ITC recommendations for protection must be approved or disapproved by the President. American industries also have the legal right to seek government assistance if they can prove that foreign companies are benefiting from government subsidies or are otherwise dumping products in the United States. If U.S. agencies find the allegations to be true, they are required by law to impose countervailing or antidumping duties, whether or not there are economic or political reasons for avoiding these sanctions.

American institutions also include some safeguards against centrifugal forces. In addition to the President's personal authority and his influence as a leader of the Congress, a Trade Policy Committee has had overall responsibility for coordination since 1962. This committee is chaired by the U.S. Trade Representative and includes the cabinet secretaries from all economic departments as well as the Secretaries of State and Defense. The smaller Trade Negotiating Committee is composed of the USTR and the Secretaries of Agriculture, Commerce, Labor, Treasury, and State.[50] These agencies are normally represented on particular U.S. negotiating teams.

Conflicts of the sort considered in this study normally originate with pressures from the concerned private industry, and they are handled by the United States government on a product basis. That is, the chief responsibilities are given to officials who are chosen not so much for their expertise on particular foreign countries as for their knowledge of the industry and their expertise in trade negotiations in general. The textile and apparel sector has generated so many negotiations that a small bureaucracy is devoted exclusively to its protection. The Office of Textiles and Apparel in the Department of Commerce monitors imports in dozens of narrow categories and produces frequent, detailed reports. A permanent position of Chief Negotiator (with the rank of ambassador) has been created for this one sector in the office of the U.S. Trade Representative, and he is accompanied by a team of textile specialists from the other agencies. In the case of negotiations concerning footwear or electronics products, a similar model has been followed on an ad hoc basis. An interagency committee meets to study the situation and to determine the objectives and approaches to be taken by the American negotiating team. Some discretion is allowed to the negotiators.

Industries can and do inject their views before, after, and sometimes during negotiations. One important channel is through their congressional supporters. Also the 1974 Trade Act established a complex structure of more than twenty-five standing private sector committees, each representing a particular industrial or agricultural sector. These committees meet occasionally with American officials concerned with these sectors. Moreover, during bilateral talks an advisory team representing producers competing with imports has often traveled with U.S. official negotiators, in order to keep a close watch on concessions considered and to provide technical advice.

In some cases the President is personally involved. President Nixon discussed textiles and clothing with Japan's Premier Sato in 1969 and 1970. In 1976 and again in 1977 the Cabinet was deeply divided over the shoe issue. Retailers, importers, and consumer organizations lobbied heavily to oppose restrictions and were supported by some of the top advisers to President Ford and President Carter. Ford decided against trade policy changes for footwear, and no new interstate conflict resulted in 1976.

Theorists have argued that differences in domestic institutions affect interstate bargaining outcomes. The less centralized the policymaking process, the more opportunities there will be for foreign parties to penetrate the political system and form bargaining coalitions with like-minded groups inside, who then can lobby for an outcome more favorable to this transnational coalition. Presumably, if other things were equal, the more centralized of two states would have bargaining advantage over the less centralized.[51]

Analyzing Trade Conflicts

The rise in protection and protectionist pressures has been debated at length. Ultimately the broad explanation will resolve into the twin forces of expanding low-cost productive capacity in South Korea and elsewhere meeting the resistance to adjustment in the corresponding older industries in the United States and elsewhere. The circumstances of relatively sluggish aggregate growth and high general unemployment may have also made Washington more likely than before to bend to protectionist pressures.[52]

Broad conditions are not sufficient for explaining why conflicts arise in particular sectors and not in others, however. One might suppose, first, that the likelihood of a conflict over access to the American market varies with the degree to which imports have penetrated each sector. According to this view, the deeper the import penetration, the more responsive American authorities are to pleas for protection and the more willing they are to infringe on the precepts of free trade.

This hypothesis might be valid in general, but it does not seem to help much in interpreting this Korea-United States experience. These cases involve only three sectors, and the degree of import penetration that evidently triggered the first conflict varies widely, from 7 percent in textiles and clothing in 1963, to 26 percent in color television sets in 1978, to 47 percent in nonrubber footwear in 1976. Judging only from these cases, Washington must be sensitive to something other than, or in addition to, the degree of import penetration.[53]

Another sector-specific hypothesis holds that it is the industry's domestic political clout relative to its domestic rivals, and not so much its market conditions, that will determine whether American officials will provoke an interstate dispute on its behalf. The textile and apparel complex is famous for its domestic political resources in many countries. In the United States the segments of this industry, which do not share identical interests on all issues, aggregate to some 2.2 million workers and voters. More important, the segments long ago formed a political coalition for trade policy, which includes strategically placed members of Congress. This coalition used its leverage to extract campaign pledges to increase import protection from presidential candidates Kennedy and Nixon. These pledges account for the Kennedy program that produced the Long-Term Cotton Textile Arrangement and Nixon's long struggle with East Asian exporters over synthetic products. President Reagan made a similar pledge in order to gain textile support in 1980. As we have also seen, the Congressional textile caucus is strong enough to hold major national legislation hostage, if necessary, to overcome resistance to its demands. These political resources help explain why conflicts began over American textile trade even when the home industry still commanded 93 percent of the domestic market in the aggregate.

By the same token, the American nonrubber shoe industry, while sizable, has nothing like the political presence of the fabric and garment makers. Footwear employment declined from 237,000 in the early 1960s to 164,000 in 1976.[54] Also this sector's Washington lobby was

slower to form and less well financed. Several senators and representatives speak for the shoe industry, but they are relatively few in number. Even so, when import penetration approached 50 percent of the
U.S. market from all sources, Washington did respond with limited
additional protection.

In this respect the color television sector is an anomaly. It is a small
industry, employing some 48,000 people in 1978.[55] Judging from overall electoral strength alone, this industry should not have been able to
bend United States policy in its direction. The sector's political organization, COMPACT, was formed by the AFL-CIO, ten trade unions,
and four related companies. They were not joined by most of the color
TV manufacturing companies in the call for protection. The coalition
used the route of filing a petition with the International Trade Commission seeking relief from injury caused by imports. This administrative mechanism is so constituted that it takes into consideration only
the costs of free trade for the petitioners and not the costs of protection
for other more numerous American producers and consumers. It was
a ruling by the ITC that propelled the executive branch into negotiations with Japan and later Taiwan and Korea. Still, the President had
the authority to disapprove this protectionist response.

Given that there has been an increase in the frequency of conflicts,
how do we explain the pattern of their outcomes? One familiar hypothesis holds that the interstate distribution of power determines bargaining outcomes. The United States, being vastly stronger than Korea
in either military or economic terms, would be expected to have its
way in the end in every conflict. Seoul would have no choice but to
accept Washington's dictates.

South Korea's military vulnerability and dependence on the United
States add a dimension that is absent from other trade bargaining relations. From one angle, one might suppose that this security dependence adds to American strength vis-à-vis Korea on economic issues,
allowing the United States to extract greater trade concessions than
are granted by other developing countries in less exposed security positions. Korean trade negotiators themselves mention the military situation as a constraint on their bargaining. On the other hand, one
might suppose that the long U.S. military and economic commitment
in Korea has given Washington its own stake there, a special asset
meriting special treatment. Korean officials often try to persuade
Washington that the United States should demand *fewer* trade concessions in Korea than elsewhere, precisely because Korea has to bear
military burdens of mutual security. A third possibility is that, in general, trade issues are insulated from security conditions.

The results in these thirteen cases, summarized in table 7-3, certainly suggest the gross power difference between the two states. In none of these cases did Seoul achieve most of its initial goals, and in ten of these cases the United States accomplished its objectives more or less fully. The results here are skewed as a power analyst would have expected.

It is difficult to say whether the outcome would have been different except for Korea's military dependence on the United States. Latin American governments, not facing a comparable military threat, did better in twenty-five trade disputes with the United States.[56] But there were several other differences between the sets of disputes. Many of those were antisubsidy and antidumping conflicts, in which procedural rules tend to mute gross power differences. Some Korean cases of this type happen to be excluded here on the grounds that they involved less than $50 million of trade. Also the Latin American and Korean cases are not all drawn from the same sectors. Moreover, in some cases included in this paper, the Korean outcome was in fact somewhat more favorable than that of other exporters in the same sector: for example, in the 1977 shoe case and textiles in 1974 and 1972. In the latter instance, Seoul was able to link the settlement to security to her own advantage. In general, however, it appears that textile and apparel negotiations in the United States are largely insulated from international political concerns by virtue of their domestic political resources and separate bureaucracy.

While the stronger state generally prevails here, there is also more variation in these outcomes than would have been expected strictly on power grounds. In three of the cases that were generally American successes, Seoul also achieved significant compensation or improvements (textiles and apparel in 1967 and 1979, and color TV sets in 1980). And in three other cases: textiles and apparel in 1972 and 1974 and footwear in 1977, the result fell in the intermediate range. Under what conditions, then, does the outcome tend to shift away from the initial objectives of the superior power?

Import penetration might make a general difference in outcomes of trade disputes. The deeper the penetration, the more the United States government will dig in its heels and refuse to make concessions during bargaining; the less the penetration, the greater the Korean success. Unfortunately, we do not have enough sectors here to test this general proposition, and the idea is little help in understanding these cases. There seems to be no systematic correlation between penetration and outcomes. The first two textile cases went particularly badly for Seoul despite the low level of penetration, while the 1977 shoe case, despite relatively high U.S. penetration, was one of Korea's more successful negotiations.

It would also be reasonable to think that a government will do better in bargaining with the U.S. government over trade in a sector that is weak in American domestic politics and vice versa. In cases such as these involving access to the American market, the weaker the import-competing industry, the greater the flexibility that will be allowed to the American negotiator.

It happens that these three sectors also fail to confirm this general idea. As we have seen, the textile and clothing outcomes varied, even while this industry's domestic political position remained fairly stable. The 1972 and 1974 cases do not fit, nor does the severe cutback the United States dealt Korea on television sets in 1979 on behalf of a small sector of the American industry.

This Korea-United States experience does illustrate, however, how the choice of bargaining strategy and tactics can influence outcomes, shifting them away from American initial goals in some cases. Parenthetically, some of the more traditional strategies were not attempted in these cases. Seoul has almost entirely avoided retaliation and threats of retaliation. As far as is known, Korea did not form effective bargaining coalitions with other exporting states, and there were no coalitions formed between the United States and other importing countries in the context of these bilateral conflicts. Nor was there much sign of transnational coalitions: for example, between Koreans and American groups that shared a common interest, which have been used to affect outcomes in other encounters. South Korea does not seem to have been able to capitalize on the greater decentralization of the U.S. political system.

Korean officials have, however, used the old-fashioned tactic of delay to produce outcomes more favorable to them than would have prevailed otherwise. And they have also used a strategy that might be called technocratic. Broadly, this refers to long-term improvements in the bureaucracy's skills in economics, law, and negotiation, and in particular cases, the use of these skills to propose technical terms of settlement more favorable than those offered by the other side.[57]

When the United States came asking for restraints on synthetic as well as cotton textile exports in 1969, Korea and the other East Asian states resisted for nearly three years. Even after Taiwan succumbed to American pressure in the summer of 1971, Korea and Hong Kong continued their stubborn refusal to capitulate. Seoul argued that a blow to their key export industry would have indirect consequences for security. Even after President Nixon issued an ultimatum and threat of unilateral action, the American team still found it necessary to agree to a major package of financial compensation before the Korean government would accept the new restraints. Determined resistance and delay until the last possible moment ran the risk of provoking unilateral action by the much stronger power, but this tactic proved effective in shifting the outcome in Korea's favor, in this and in other cases.

The 1977 settlement regarding footwear illustrates clearly the effects of technocratic strategy and tactics. The American team sought to cut Korean exports sharply from their 1976 levels and to impose sublimits on shoes made from different types of materials. By this time the Korean economic bureaucracy included several officials holding Ph.D.s from American universities, as well as other highly trained members. The same trade officials were also responsible for negotiating textile agreements, and thus had accumulated considerable experience in the crafting of trade-restraining agreements. From this experience they had learned technical features that would ease the actual restraining effect, as well as features that might be accepted by the U.S. team because there was precedent for them. In the shoe case, the Korean team bargained hard to define the sublimits in such a way as to leave the greatest flexibility for Korean companies to fill the aggregate quota. They also got provisions for swing, carryover, and carryforward, as in textile agreements, and most important, they made sure that the administration would be in Korean, and not American, hands. The imaginative provision admitting nine million pairs through the pipeline may have actually originated with a technocrat on the American team.[58] The combination of these elements meant that in calendar year 1977, Korean shoe exports to the United States were actually higher than in 1976; the cutback was delayed until 1978.

Conclusions

This review of the growing trade and growing conflict between the two governments suggests a few modest implications for practice. Since this has not been a comprehensive analysis of economic or foreign policy, the conclusions must necessarily be selective as well.

From the standpoint of the United States government, it would be difficult to improve on the bilateral negotiating performance reviewed here, if performance is measured by comparing outcomes with initial objectives. If we take as given the occurrence of disputes and the actual U.S. objectives, American negotiators have a record of returning with many successes and no failures.

If, however, we examine the process of setting objectives, this experience suggests that U.S. officials may be able to increase their own leverage in that respect by encouraging more balanced interest group pressures. The active participation of shoe retailers and consumer organizations as well as shoe manufacturers during the 1976 debate increased the Ford administration's scope for policy control. It is well known that American exporters, importers, retailers, and consumers are difficult to mobilize into an effective force proportionate to their numbers. But such coalitions do form more often than is normally recognized. The most recent potent example is the active lobbying in 1983 by farm organizations, led by Senator Robert Dole, Chairman of the Senate Finance Committee, on behalf of more liberal treatment for imports of Chinese textiles. This unusual intervention was triggered after the United States unilaterally clamped restrictions on Chinese textile exports and Peking retaliated by banning Chinese imports of American cotton and soybeans and reducing imports of wheat.[59]

Clearly U.S. officials are not able to orchestrate the activities of interest groups, but they can at least reduce the barriers they place in the way of some. The private industry advisory teams accompanying U.S. textile negotiators, for example, are normally restricted to the protectionist interests. Those domestic interests favoring imports could also be offered a regular place at the table.

More generally, many governments, including the United States government, could reduce the frequency of interstate commercial conflicts by devoting greater attention to domestic industrial adjustment measures that might prevent their problems from spilling over into international relations. Policies for offsetting market failures, as well as more ambitious measures for 'positive adjustment' to trade, have been described and debated in specific terms in recent studies.[60]

From the Korean government's standpoint, the fundamental international power imbalance obviously limits the range of effective options. The long-term strategy of developing the bureaucracy's technical skills has nonetheless helped shift some bargaining outcomes in Korea's favor. Korean officials, while continuing this improvement and the search for imaginative technical proposals in particular disputes, might continue or intensify careful monitoring of domestic American politics. The relative political strengths of different sectors can be factored into long-range export planning and can be used tactically in evaluating the limits of U.S. negotiating flexibility. More effort might be put into the search for opportunities for transnational coalitions with congruent American groups or political leaders. Long-range planning for exports might also emphasize relative shifts into sectors where import penetration is low.

More broadly, the most meaningful fact was that the two societies were increasing their overall trade with each other at a rapid rate, despite the experience of sectoral conflict between their governments.

The conflicts had important consequences, but they were certainly not the only significant developments underway. All in all, the conclusion may be that there is not a great deal more that the Korean government can do beyond what it is already doing. This selected experience seems to recommend continuation of the practice of determined bargaining accompanied by a willingness to yield to superior power in the end, if necessary to produce agreement. The costs of nonagreement might well have been higher than the costs of accepting these agreements with the United States. If Washington as well as Seoul will observe in the future a continued willingness to find acceptable agreed settlements to trade disputes, their partnership will continue to be mutually beneficial.

8 Limited Partners: Transnational Alliances between Private Sector Organizations in the U.S.-Korea Trade Relationship

Karl Moskowitz

The welcome result of Korea's economic growth and the expansion of bilateral trade with the United States is that the former government-to-government relationship of aid dependency has become a complex market-to-market relationship that is private and competitive. Government authorities have hardly been eclipsed, however. Government regulations and trade agreements between the two governments affect the conduct of the U.S.-Korea trade relationship profoundly. At present almost half of Korea's exports to the United States fall under import restrictions of one sort or another. American firms in Korea contend with a pervasive government-business relationship, dominated by the Korean government, in which the role permitted the foreign firm is limited and not always clear.

Though we must acknowledge the powerful role of government, we recognize that most economic exchanges between the United States and Korea are undertaken as private transactions between for-profit business entities. Yet the growth in trade over the past two decades and the expansion of business relations has not been due only to the quest for profits by business or to paternalistic guidance from government. Between the two is a third category of actor that influences the behavior of government and business. This third category is that of private sector organizations. Private sector organizations are not-for-profit entities, such as industry associations and business councils, that serve the interests of their memberships as a group.[1]

Private sector organizations are involved in the day-to-day conduct of business relations between the United States and Korea. They have a role in the trade disputes and business problems that arise between the two partners—both in raising the issues and influencing attempts at resolution. They have acted to promote business ties between the two countries. In the United States political pressure from industry associations is behind the restrictions on Korean exports. In Korea

149

government-business coordination through industry associations often results in serious nontariff barriers to American access to the Korean market.

The concept of transnational relations and transnational organizations developed by Keohane and Nye apply to relations among private sector organizations in the U.S.-Korea trade relationship.[2] Keohane and Nye differentiated transnational phenomena from interstate phenomena, which by definition can only occur between governments. Transnational organizations are located in two or more states; they include nongovernmental actors; their actions influence societies and governments directly, not through formal interstate structures, to cause a result that would not occur without their actions. Transnational interactions are actions within one state that have effects in another state, although none of the actors need be a transnational group or a partner in a transnational relationship.

The definition of transnational organization does not exclude business entities; all MNCs are transnational organizations.[3] Our concern, however, is the role of not-for-profit private sector organizations. As the conduct of the economic relationship has grown in magnitude and moved from the hands of government to the hands of business, the potential scope of transnational ties among private sector organizations has increased accordingly. In considering the roles of private sector organizations in the U.S.-Korea business relationship, we will be looking at the following points:

> First, evidence of transnational relationships. Have alliances been formed between United States and Korean industry associations or business groups that help in the attainment of each group's objectives?

> Second, if we find evidence of alliances between American and Korean organizations, how strong are the ties, and how effective are they for both sides? Do the alliances actually produce results that would not otherwise be expected from the market?

> Third, if no transnational links are found, do the organizations nonetheless participate in transnational actions that influence the U.S.-Korea trade relationship, such as drives to restrict imports or reduce tariffs?

The third point leads directly to the principal limitation of this study. Industry associations may perform a variety of promotional and technical services for their members. However, the fundamental purpose of every industry association is to act as a political pressure group, representing the industry's position to the government and endeavoring to influence government policy. Thus the key point to understand is the relationship between an industry association and its home government. Actions that are transnational in effect, such as successful pressure from an industry association to restrict imports, may involve only an industry association and its home government, though the effects are felt by the industry and the government in a second country. To understand the dynamics of such actions, one must understand the patterns of the relations between the government and interest groups in a particular country. Nonetheless, there are still reasons to look at transnational ties between private sector organizations in the U.S.-Korea business relationship. Government-business relations in the United States and in Korea have already been studied at some length.[4] It is these transnational relationships between the two partners that have yet to be studied.

The first category of private sector organization is that of industry or producer associations. The members are producers of a specific product and, often, other firms whose interests are linked to the product. To explore the nature of industry association involvement in the U.S.-Korea trade relationship, we shall select examples according to two criteria. The first is that the products consistently represent the highest volume in the trade between the two countries. The second is that the industries be important in their respective national economies and foreign trade profiles. These are the industries in which we would expect strong industry association interest in the U.S.-Korea trade relationship. For the United States the broad industry sector is agriculture, while for Korea it is textiles.

Agricultural exports have always been important to the United States. During the past few decades, rising demand from abroad and increasing productivity on American farms turned agriculture into a major export industry, dependent upon exports for prosperity. In current dollars, the value of agricultural exports more than doubled over the past decade to reach $43.7 billion in fiscal 1981. More than half of America's wheat, soybean, cotton, and rice crops are exported, along with one-fourth of feed grain production.

Agricultural commodities have comprised the largest category of American exports to Korea since 1945. Although agricultural exports as a percentage of total American exports to Korea declined over the past decade, in 1982 they still accounted for some 29 percent of U.S. exports to Korea. As the statistics in tables 8-1 and 8-2 show, the decline has only been relative; Korea has steadily grown as a market for U.S. agricultural products, moving up to become fifth or sixth largest in the past few years. The potential market for a variety of

Table 8–1
Korea's Rank as a Market for Selected American Agricultural Exports

Fiscal Year	Fats, Oils	Hides, Skins	Wheat	Corn	Soya Beans	Cotton	Tobacco	Rice	Overall Rank
1978	6th	2nd	4th	7th	15th	1st	12th	63rd	7th
1979	2nd	2nd	4th	3rd	11th	2nd	10th	18th	6th
1980	4th	4th	5th	9th	13th	3rd	9th	1st	6th
1981	6th	2nd	5th	7th	10th	2nd	9th	1st	5th
1982	7th	2nd	6th	4th	10th	2nd	28th	3rd	7th

Source: USDA statistics.

Table 8–2
U.S. Exports of Agricultural Commodities to Korea by Purchase and Financing Terms ($1,000,000)

Fiscal Year	U.S. Government Financing Arrangements			Cash	Total
	Concessionary PL 480	Nonconcessionary GSM*[a]			
1971	183.54[b]	62.8		56.82	303.16
1972	196.83[b]	62.18		54.72	316.73
1973	263.33[b]	109.24		113.23	485.9
1974	15.28[b]	48.4		597.72	661.4
1975	78.17	60.19		746.64	885.0
1976	62.95	204.25		455.73	722.43
1977	72.1	128.42		718.5	919.02
1978	63.31	432.18		560.33	1,055.4
1979	42.9	395.1		948.89	1,386.0
1980	30.0	454.62		1,133.1	1,617.0
1981	27.5	560.5		1,713.0	2,300.0

Source: Commodity Credit Corporation (USDA).

[a]GSM-5 provides for U.S. government financing at government market rates (government cost of credit); GSM-102 provides for U.S. government guarantees for private financing arrangements.

[b]These figures include a separate barter category.

American agricultural products led the Foreign Agricultural Service (FAS) of the U.S. Department of Agriculture (USDA) to open an Agricultural Trade Office in Seoul in 1979.[5] The importance of exports to American agriculture, the large market in Korea, and the duration of the agricultural trade relationship make this sector an inviting case to study.

FAS takes the lead in foreign market development, and agricultural trade associations desiring to develop foreign markets work closely with it. Following the 1954 enactment of Public Law 480, the Trade Development and Assistance Act, trade association coordination with FAS became institutionalized in the FAS cooperator program.[6] In the program the trade associations, or cooperators, plan market development programs which, following approval by FAS, are implemented under FAS supervision. Budgets are funded by contributions from the cooperators and FAS according to matching formulas. Often, industry associations in the particular country for which a market development program is aimed join as cooperators in program planning and funding. There are several ongoing cooperator relationships in Korea, and at the time this study was done five American agricultural trade associations maintained offices in Seoul.

Wheat: Farmers and Flour Millers

In 1982 Korea imported 1.9 million metric tons of wheat, all from the United States. The origins of this market and the virtual American monopoly of it go back to the Korean War, when large-scale shipments of wheat flour for relief purposes made wheat products an important part of the Korean diet.[7] Subsequently, imports of wheat under PL 480 and other aid programs were a key element of American economic assistance. These imports stabilized the food supply and generated counterpart funds that provided a major portion of the Korean government's revenues. Korea's milling industry entered a boom period in 1955. To process the aid wheat, capacity expanded from 3,000 barrels per day in 1954 to almost 43,000 in 1958. Milling was highly profitable; flour was one of the so-called 'three whites' (*sambaek*) upon which the first Korean fortunes were built after the Korean War.[8] Expansion continued until the early 1970s, when a shakeout reduced the number of milling companies to thirteen and capacity to the current 55,000 barrels per day.

Rapid growth in the Korean market occurred in the 1960s. Wheat imports under PL 480 increased from 251,000 tons in 1961 to 935,000 in 1969, while total imports rose to 1,176,000 tons in 1969 after Korea began cash purchases in 1966. The growth was due to a complex of factors, but the overall strategy was to provide low-cost food to rapidly expanding cities and industrial areas. Imports rose to new peaks of 1,748,000 tons in 1972 (1,120,000 under PL 480) and 1,829,000 in 1973, and then fell back as wheat prices soared and the PL 480 program was discontinued. PL 480 financing of wheat exports to Korea resumed in 1976 and continued on a reduced basis through 1981, but Korean wheat imports have regained only the levels of 1972-1973; the Korean wheat market has matured at about two million tons per year.[9]

Working to develop this market for American wheat is a long-standing cooperator program, represented on the American side by U.S. Wheat Associates, an industry association supported by producer check-off contributions, and in Korea by the Korean Flour Mills Industrial Association (KOFMIA) and end-user associations such as the Korean Confectioners Association (KCA). KOFMIA was established under the Ministry of Agriculture and Fisheries (MAF) in 1955, when Korea was embarking upon its program to build milling capacity. KOFMIA has a monopoly on wheat imports: it makes the purchases, charters the transport, and allocates the wheat to its member mills. This monopoly gives KOFMIA tremendous influence. In addition, KOFMIA has been the custodian of the Flour Price Stabilization Fund, a role that increased its influence.

The market that the cooperators are working to develop is dominated by traditional end products, as is shown in table 8–3. Accordingly, market development programs emphasize new Western-style foods while still promoting traditional foods, such as noodles. However, per capita flour consumption is close to thirty-seven kilograms, and because Korean grain consumption already is high, the potential for expansion is limited.[10] The cooperator emphasis on new products and Western-style foods is defensive in nature. Its objective is to maintain current levels of wheat consumption by leading consumer tastes and diet habits as incomes rise and lifestyles change.

Table 8–3
Consumption of Flour in Korea (1982)
(percentage)

Noodles	40
Bread and confections	25
Makkŏlli (native alcoholic beverage)	15
Traditional Korean wheat foods	11
Food processing	6
Industrial use	3

Source: U.S. Wheat Associates.

The cooperator program supports several activities that are coordinated through the annual marketing plan. Technical services to KOFMIA and its members include consultation on milling technology by American experts, an annual mission to report on the new U.S. wheat crop, and at least one mission of KOFMIA and milling company executives to the United States to visit Washington, grain companies, and wheat-producing regions.

Technical support to the KCA focuses on baking techniques and bakery management. The centerpiece of the program is the Korea Baking School, founded by the cooperator program in 1973. Instructors were trained at the American Baking Institute under the auspices of the cooperator program. Alumni of the American and Korean schools either own or manage all major Korean bakery companies. The KCA contributes to the cooperator program by compiling recipe books and technical baking manuals for general distribution and by sponsoring technical seminars and homemaker education demonstrations.[11]

The cooperator program consists of American technical support, which is valuable to the Korean cooperators, who share the costs, and joint efforts to increase wheat consumption as the market changes, an objective beneficial to both parties. The visits back and forth foster direct personal ties between the American producers and the Korean millers, bakers, and the KOFMIA representatives who do the actual purchasing and transport of wheat. But do the ties between U.S. Wheat Associates, KOFMIA, and KCA constitute a transnational alliance that produces results that would not occur otherwise?

Even after Korea became a cash buyer, free to choose suppliers, and despite Korean government stress on diversification of economic relations, American producers have continued to enjoy a virtual monopoly on Korea's wheat market. There is evidence that KOFMIA has resisted import diversification and has exerted pressure to continue to purchase all wheat from the United States.[12] However, there are too many forces at play to conclude simply that this was a victory for the transnational alliance. The major complication is that MAF ultimately decides wheat purchase policy. Although MAF's chief concern is the level of purchasing, not from where, MAF may be responding to government desires to purchase from the United States to dress up the annual trade balance or to utilize CCC credit arrangements because of foreign debt considerations, rather than responding to KOFMIA pressure. On the other hand, MAF is also conscious of the benefits derived from the cooperator programs for wheat and other commodities, as well as the familiarity of the present relationship.

The alliance has worked to Korea's advantage: PL 480 was resumed from 1976 to 1981, and CCC credit arrangements were extended to portions of the annual purchases. Implied Korean threats to diversify sources, combined with the sharp drop in volume in the mid-1970s stimulated American wheat interests to press for resumption of the financing. We might wonder whether the wheat producers would not have applied the same pressures even without the alliance. Yet the ties clearly strengthened the American producers' commitment to keeping the Korean market and gave them the knowledge that the Korean side would likewise work to maintain the relationship. Both increased the propensity to mobilize forces in favor of benefits for the Korean customers.

We cannot conclude that the transnational alliance built around the complementary U.S.-Korean trade in wheat has deflected strong, committed forces working against the interests of one partner or the other; so far it has never confronted such a challenge. It seems safe to conclude that the alliance has worked to delay policy changes in Korea that threatened the relationship and to maintain U.S. benefits for the Korean side that might otherwise have stopped. However, the effects of the alliance cannot be separated completely from other factors that may also have contributed to the favorable outcomes.

Corn: Farmers and Feeders

In contrast to wheat, the feed grain market in Korea is solely a result of economic development and the tendency of populations to consume more meat, poultry, eggs, and dairy products as personal income rises. The government has encouraged the dietary changes and supported the development of these industries, as well as a feed processing industry to supply them. From its inception in the late 1960s, the feed grain market has grown rapidly; imports of corn from the United States, which has a virtual monopoly on the market, are shown in table 8-4. The market is expected to grow strongly through the 1990s, as consumption rises with income and changes in dietary habits. The feed corn market has essentially been a cash market from the beginning.

The cooperator on the American side is the U.S. Feed Grains Council (USFGC); a booklet published by the Seoul office of USFGC lists thirty-six "major cooperators" on the Korean side, beginning with the MAF and including the National Livestock Cooperatives Association (NLCF), research institutes, universities, and the Korea Feed Association (KFA) and eight other industry associations. The actual market relationship has been with the NLCF and, very recently, the KFA, which were designated by the Korean government to be the sole agents for the purchase and import of feed grains.[13]

Table 8–4
Korean Corn Imports from the United States
(By Volume [1,000 metric tons] and Financing Arrangements)

Fiscal Year	PL 480	GSM 5	GSM 102	Cash	Total
1968	3				(3)
1969	28				170
1970	132	24		78	234
1971	163			244	407
1972	290			215	458
1973	243			157	400
1974	7			409	416
1975				342	342
1976				825	825
1977				1,205	1,205
1978	265	563		933	1,761
1979	115	905		1,651	2,671
1980	86	571		1,473	2,130

Source: Commodity Credit Corporation

As one might surmise from the list of Korean cooperators and the short history of the industry, program activities are weighted toward technical services for end-consumers of feed. Indeed, of the forty-six technical experts the cooperator program brought from the United States between 1972 and 1981, only five were specialists in feed processing or corn milling; the rest were all livestock, dairy, and meat specialists.[14] The objective is to develop a technical infrastructure to support these industries. Although the United States is the largest and most reliable supplier of feed grains in the world market, there is credible competition. By concentrating on technical services, the cooperator program is forging the links that will help marketing efforts in a market that was never based on aid and in which concessionary financing has not been a lead marketing tool. Not incidentally, the technical assistance program has also created a large market for American breeding and livestock service industries.

The transnational links built up around the complementary market relationship between the American feed grain industry and the Korean end-user industries are not as strong as in wheat. The duration of the ties is shorter; the relationship was never based on aid. The NLCF and most of the Korean cooperators represent the government more or less directly. Importing feed grains or developing the user industries is only one of many functions each performs. KFA, which recently won the right to import, may be comparable to KOFMIA, but it does not have a monopoly on imports, and the industry does not have the structure that underpins KOFMIA's power.[15] The relationship has never faced a serious challenge from foreign competition or a maturing market, nor has it had to deal with the winding down of an exclusive aid relationship. Perhaps by the time it is challenged, the cooperator program will have established effective alliances to resist threats to the American domination of the Korean feed grain market.

The Korean Federation of Textile Industries

Textiles are as important to Korea as agriculture is to the United States. In 1981 close to two-thirds of Korea's textile production was exported, accounting for 29.5 percent of exports, while the industry accounted for 27.4 percent of Korea's manufacturing employment. The United States is one of the largest markets for Korea's textile products, consistently taking about one-fourth of Korea's textile exports in recent years.[16]

Like American agriculture, the Korean textile industry has developed a complex of associations based on product type and industry segment. All are members of the Korean Federation of Textile Industries (KOFOTI), which represents the entire textile industry. KOFOTI lists eighteen industry associations and institutes as active members in addition to some twenty of the largest textile manufacturers and traders.[17]

KOFOTI performs several functions for the industry. It maintains a textile and fashion research center and it publishes industry news and information. It sponsors seminars and promotional activities; it has a liaison office that refers foreign buyers and businessmen to member firms. KOFOTI maintains ties with international textile bodies and represents the Korean industry in international meetings of the industry.

However, KOFOTI's most important function is to coordinate industry communication with the government and compliance with government policy. According to a recent brochure, "To the Government, KOFOTI furnishes the integrated views of the industry on the various issues, while it makes policy recommendations in the interest of the industry."[18] KOFOTI works with MCI to prepare for textile trade negotiations with countries that restrict imports, and KOFOTI officials accompany MCI negotiating teams to the talks.[19] When other nations set quotas on textile imports from Korea, KOFOTI administers the allocation of the quotas among its member companies and polices performance through two of its member organizations, the Garments and Knitwear Export Association and the Korea Export Association of Textiles.[20]

The Textile Industry Modernization Act of 1979 delegated to KOFOTI authority to develop a modernization program for the textile

industry. The act gave KOFOTI control over financial resources for
the program, as well as some control over industry capacity.[21] The
program, which must be carried out under the supervision of MCI,
reaffirms KOFOTI's power as the central textile industry association.
Symbolizing the close relationship with MCI is the Secretary General
of KOFOTI, Noh Chin-shik, who had years of negotiating experience
as a commercial attaché in Korea's Washington embassy and then as
the director general of the Trade Promotion Bureau of MCI, the office
that conducts trade negotiations with other countries.

Despite its power in Korea, KOFOTI's transnational ties with industry associations in the United States appear to be almost entirely
technical in nature.[22] The Korean industry does not enjoy the type of
long-term complementary relationship with American interests that
American agriculture has in Korea. Although we can identify a complementary relationship between Korean producers and American importers, retailers, and consumers of textile products, this is common
to a number of countries. It is impossible for KOFOTI to provide
cooperator program type services that would differentiate the Korea-
U.S. textile relationship and, over time, build up an exclusive alliance
with the American side of the trade.[23] One obstacle is the antagonistic
relationship with the powerful American textile industry. The American Textile Manufacturers Institute (ATMI), KOFOTI's counterpart,
works to restrict exports. ATMI and KOFOTI do have a technical
relationship, but their only transnational relationship that affects U.S.-
Korean textile trade is of actions to restrict trade.

Cotton: Planters, Spinners, and Weavers

Some industry associations that are members of KOFOTI are prominent in their own right and, independently of KOFOTI, are partners
in important transnational relationships. The most powerful is the
Spinners and Weavers Association of Korea (SWAK), which was
founded in 1947, and which, in some ways, overshadows KOFOTI as
a spokesman for the Korean textile industry.[24] In recent years SWAK's
chairman has been a man of political importance.[25] SWAK certainly
wields more clout in Washington than KOFOTI because SWAK represents the Korean cotton textile industry, an important customer for
American cotton exports. SWAK is a unique case: at the same time
that it is involved in conflicts with American counterparts over textile
exports, it also maintains an effective transnational alliance with American cotton producers.

The development of SWAK's American connection resembles that of KOFMIA, but began earlier. When U.S. occupation forces arrived in 1945, Korea already had a large textile industry.[26] The link between SWAK and the United States was forged at this time because cotton and some textile machinery were imported under the GARIOA program, and SWAK was founded in 1947 to manage the distribution of this aid. After Korea became independent in 1948, SWAK received MCI recognition as the association representing the textile industry; the American connection continued, with SWAK participating in the planning of the ECA aid program. The Korean War destroyed Korea's textile industry. Reconstruction of the industry was a prime objective of post-war aid efforts and SWAK played an important role in these programs. Indeed, reading the thirty-year history of SWAK published in 1977 is like reading a history of American aid to Korea since 1945.[27]

Let us return to the KOFMIA comparison. Like flour, cotton was one of the 'three whites,' and SWAK became the institution through which the Korean government manipulated aid cotton and the benefits derived from it. As in the case of KOFMIA, SWAK did the importing—in 1954 it established an office in Washington to coordinate the supply of aid cotton; SWAK allocated cotton to its member mills and managed the cotton supply stocks and related funds. In 1956 Korea began to receive cotton under PL 480 in addition to the cotton it received under other aid programs, and it was SWAK that managed the PL 480 shipments.

Free cotton to Korea ended in 1961, but virtually free concessionary sales under the PL 480 program continued. However, during the 1960s SWAK's present transnational alliance with the United States cotton industry really developed. Park Chung Hee took power in 1961 and, as part of his economic strategy, Korea instituted new policies to encourage industrialization and the export of manufactured goods. The textile industry, which recorded its first exports in 1957, expanded rapidly, and the Korean cotton market expanded with it, as is shown in table 8-5. As in wheat, Korea began to turn into a cash market for American cotton at the end of the 1960s. As Korea was making the transition to cash buyer, the burgeoning growth of its textile industry transformed it into one of the largest overseas cotton markets for the United States. Meanwhile, in the United States the decline of cotton consumption by domestic mills made exports vital to cotton growers and shippers. Both developments combined to change the relationship between SWAK and American cotton producers, and the present relationship emerged at the beginning of the 1970s, at the juncture when Korea turned into a cash market.[28]

The relationship between SWAK and American cotton interests resembles the KOFMIA-wheat producer relationship in that the mar-

Table 8–5
U.S. Cotton Exports to the Republic of Korea
(By Volume [1,000 metric tons] and Financing Arrangements)

Fiscal Year	PL 480	GSM 5	GSM 102	Cash	Total
1960	72				(72)[a]
1961	72				(72)
1962	246				(246)
1963	276				(276)
1964	243	10			(253)
1965	233	1			(234)
1966	226	3			(229)
1967	249	28			(277)
1968	277	48			(325)
1969	357	89		19	465
1970	243	188		5	436
1971	162	230		104	496
1972	82	246		158	486
1973	175	293		68	536
1974	7	270		464	741
1975		200		341	541
1976	54	808		349	1,211
1977	28	217		620	865
1978		680		599	1,279
1979	27	570		593	1,190
1980	22	153		1,253	1,410

Source: Commodity Credit Corporation
[a]Figures in parentheses supplied by author. These figures may not capture cotton supplied as part of separate military assistance.

ket connection began as an aid relationship; PL 480 and CCC financing continued to be employed as marketing tools until recently; and as the market turned to a cash basis, a cooperator program began in 1971 with Cotton Council International (CCI), a subsidiary of the National Cotton Council. The cooperator program and the joint monitoring of CCC agreement performance require constant communication between the trade associations. The benefits each partner obtains from the relationship likewise parallel the KOFMIA-wheat producer connection. For SWAK the benefit has been CCC financing arrangements that are more attractive than could be obtained on the open market and a reliable supply of cotton. For the American cotton industry, the benefit is a market that is large, virtually assured, and still has growth possibilities.

Even more so than the wheat alliance, the cotton alliance has successfully obtained benefits and deflected threats. Financing arrangements are the best examples. In the autumn of 1982 the U.S. government announced a blended credit market development program, which offered free credit to certain countries to purchase additional commodities that would not otherwise have been purchased.[29] SWAK, which had already completed the negotiation of its purchasing program and financing for the year, demanded that it be given some of the free credit. There were two problems: there was no additionality, because SWAK merely wanted a better deal on the cotton it had already agreed to buy; Korea was not in the poor country category at which the blended credit program was aimed. SWAK underlined its demands by not proceeding with its purchase program. SWAK's actions stimulated American cotton interests to mobilize political pressure, and eventually SWAK obtained some blended credit.

One can argue that SWAK won the concession through a successful threat, not a transnational alliance. But the forces mobilized on behalf of SWAK and the American cotton producers were the same as those routinely mobilized by the alliance. SWAK regularly receives CCC financing (GSM 5) of a portion of its annual cotton purchases, with the loans to be repaid in three years (recently shortened to two and one-half years). Cotton turns around—is processed and sold within six months to a year after purchase. Up to the point the textiles are produced and sold, the financing represents a working capital loan to carry goods in process and inventory, but after the products are sold, the financing becomes a simple loan to the Korean textile company. Because the same terms are given year after year, in effect members of SWAK have received hundreds of millions of dollars of long-term financing at the best current rate in the U.S. capital market, the Treasury rate. No other foreign cash market enjoys such terms, and political forces mobilized by the American side of the alliance have repeatedly deflected pressures to shorten the financing period to approximate the actual working capital turnaround time.[30]

A third example is the great cotton crisis of 1974. Experiencing a phenomenal boom in demand, members of SWAK and their counterparts throughout Asia contracted for huge amounts of cotton in panic buying at the peak of a market that collapsed shortly thereafter, strangled by recession. Recession then strangled the textile industry, and both cotton and product piled up in mill warehouses. The crisis threatened the American cotton industry, because foreign buyers began to default on contracts. An FAS crisis management team eventually arranged a work out, but only after protracted negotiations. The Korean situation was the worst, because SWAK members had contracted for the most cotton in question, but even though the negotiations were difficult, the Korean situation was solved before others in Asia and, once settled, SWAK insured compliance.[31] This debacle is difficult to cite as a benefit. But because the alternative to a negotiated work out would have been bankruptcies in both Korea and the United States,

and the disintegration of the marketing connections that were beneficial to SWAK (and the American industry), we can assume that the
transnational alliance did work as a strong incentive for the Korean
side to cooperate in a negotiated work out.

One problem for the alliance caused by the 1974 crisis was a sharp
loss of prestige and influence for SWAK among Korea's economic
leadership.[32] SWAK apparently compensated for this by associating
itself more closely with the Blue House. In any event, like KOFMIA,
SWAK has successfully resisted Korean government diversification
policies that threaten the American monopoly. Again, this benefit is
impossible to quantify, and there may be alternative political-economic
explanations for SWAK's success in protecting the American market
position. But because SWAK's very ability to extract benefits from
alliance rests on the American market position, we must attribute some
of the result to SWAK's influence.

Ultimately, the basis of U.S.-Korea trade in cotton, wheat, feed
grain, and other agricultural commodities is the complementary market
relationship between efficient large-scale producer and large-scale consumer, not the transnational alliances created by the trade. Given Korea's economic development, even without U.S. Wheat Associates,
KOFMIA, SWAK, CCI, and the other industry associations, these
commodities would still be moving from the United States to Korea in
large quantities. However, agricultural markets are volatile, and for
certain commodities highly competitive. This is where the transnational
ties are important.

Close ties formed initially in the particularistic aid relationship were
converted through the use of credit as a marketing tool, and the cooperator programs into transnational alliances that protect the relationship in an open, universal cash market environment. The ties that
now date back almost four decades constitute an information channel
that is highly effective for both partners: it gives American producers
and marketers the advantage over the competition of vastly superior
knowledge of the Korean agricultural market, and it gives advance
warning of changing policies to both sides. Though impossible to quantify and thereby prove conclusively, there is a clear pattern of economic
benefits, especially for the Korean side, attributable to the transnational alliances that would not be expected on the basis of a univer-
salistic market relationship. These benefits are not present to the same
degree in similar trade relationships with other major customers for
American agricultural products. One long-term benefit has been a certain stability in the market relationship that has helped it weather shocks
such as the soybean and cotton crises of 1974 and the transition from
a particularistic aid market to the present cash market relationship.[33]

There are serious pressures on the transnational alliances in the agricultural trade at the present time. Due to several factors, mostly policy-related rather than economic, the powers of the Korean industry association partners in the alliance are under siege. The Korean government desires to diversify economic ties, to give more business to Korean GTCs and enable them to do barter trading for agricultural products from foreign-exchange-poor third world nations, and to show progress toward the long-promised liberalization of the Korean market and the diminution of industry association power. KOFMIA lost control of the flour price fund and, in September 1983, KOFMIA lost its monopoly on wheat imports; within days the experienced head of KOFMIA's trading department was hired away by a large milling company, presumably to establish a rival trading operation. SWAK's power over its members has declined. The feed grain alliance, which was never institutionalized in the same way, was the first to experience the breakup of importing monopolies and the new incentives for KGTCs to enter the trade.[34] In the United States, cost-conscious Treasury officials challenge CCC credit arrangements for SWAK that go beyond the original purposes of the credit programs.

We have viewed the repeated delays in the implementation of these changes as successes of the alliances. As these inevitable changes do take hold, however, it is unlikely that there will be rapid changes in the existing market relationships. Continued American domination of the Korean agricultural import market will be attributable in part to the well-entrenched transnational ties and the superior information channels they have nurtured over the years.

At the opposite end of the spindle and loom, SWAK's products compete in the U.S. market with the products of American spinners, weavers, and apparel manufacturers, another segment of the cotton industry also represented by the National Cotton Council and CCI. Although there are some technical links, and although the objective of the CCI-SWAK cooperator program is to promote the domestic market for cotton products in Korea, the relationship is competitive and antagonistic. The American textile industry exerts pressure against overly friendly credit arrangements for Korean cotton purchases and against the cooperator program. These pressures have not been notably successful, but the American textile industry has usually managed to restrict imports. Here the relationship between SWAK and its American counterparts is part of the antagonism between the U.S. textile industry and those segments of the Korean textile industry that export to the U.S. market.

As we stressed at the beginning of this chapter, the fundamental point to understand about industry associations is their relationship to

their home governments and political systems. Though we have focused on the development of transnational alliances between industry
associations in the United States and Korea, we can make a few observations about the formal relationships of these associations with
their respective governments.

In the United States provisions are made for industry to participate
in certain government deliberations. The FAS cooperator programs
are one example of industry participation. Another example is the
Industry Consultations Program, which is jointly administered by the
Department of Commerce and the United States Trade Representative.[35] There are seventeen Industrial Sector Advisory Committees for
Trade Policy Matters (ISACs) in the program, and these ISACs probably represent the closest institutional parallel in the United States to
the relationship between Korean government and industry through
industry associations. The parallel does not extend to power, however.
American industry associations wield great influence in Congress, the
White House, and at certain levels of the bureaucracy. In comparison,
ISACs can exert little influence on policies to favor specific industries;
their role is largely informational.[36] ISACs are not channels through
which the U.S. government can guide industry behavior.

Currently there is a national debate in the United States about
whether it should adopt a coordinated industrial policy that would
entail more government direction of industry for national economic
goals and, therefore, closer ties between government and industry
groups. Until such a system is implemented, and probably after, it is
safe to assume that interaction between government and industry associations in the United States will continue to be a complex political
process. The success of individual industry groups in advancing their
interests in this process depends upon political acumen, political align-
ments, and the realities of the particular moment.

Our examples are probably more revealing about the nature of
Korean industry associations and their interaction with the government. The success of Korea's economic development has been due to
effective government management of economic affairs. As Leroy P.
Jones and SaKong Il stress in their book on the relationship between
government and business in Korea's development, the dramatic results
have been due not just to good policies, but also to a policy implementation system that rests upon an intimate and pervasive government-business relationship. This relationship is dominated absolutely
by the government and is characterized by constant monitoring, government manipulation of incentives and sanctions to channel industry
behavior, and the ability of the government to make policy adjustments
rapidly.[37]

Although Jones and SaKong did not discuss them in detail, industry associations constitute the principal channel through which the government-business interaction occurs; it is through industry associations that the Korean government implements its policies, enforces routine compliance, gathers information, and monitors performance. Industry associations are also the principal conduit through which industries bring their concerns to the government. The three we have discussed, KOFMIA, KOFOTI, and SWAK, are typical in this regard. Moreover, as the cases of SWAK and KOFMIA demonstrate, the pattern of the Korean government controlling industry behavior through industry associations goes back to the very beginning of the Republic of Korea and was not a new institutional development of the Park government. What was new were Park's policies.

First, each association receives approval from the ministry responsible. This charter grants the industry association a monopoly as the representative of the industry to the government. The power of the industry association rests on its relationship with the government, not on the solidarity of member firms or ties it may have formed with politicians. (Informal political connections can be influential, and, as SWAK demonstrates, placing a politically connected personage in the chairman's seat may be a way to gain access. However, political or bureaucratic connections are more a technique for interfirm competition in Korea than industry influence.) Second, the ministry delegates to the association certain powers for it to administer, such as the import of designated commodities, the allocation of aid or credit, the allocation of export quotas imposed by other countries, the administration of prices and reserve funds, and the implementation of industry modernization programs. Like KOFOTI, industry associations in virtually all industries the government regards as vital are given statutory powers through special industry modernization laws.[38]

In order to stay in business, firms must cooperate with the industry associations; if a flour mill does not receive wheat, it cannot produce flour, or if a spinning company cannot get cotton at the same effective prices as other firms, it will be at a disadvantage. Participation in the planning of industry development and restructuring programs may be equally vital to a firm's survival. Perhaps in recognition of the critical importance of membership, the chronology section of SWAK's recent commemorative history solemnly records each instance when a firm's membership has been revoked.

The third characteristic is that Korean industry associations are dominated by the biggest firms in the particular industry. The twenty textile manufacturing and trading firms that are on KOFOTI's board are the largest in Korea and, where appropriate, are simultaneously

members of SWAK and the other seventeen industry associations in
KOFOTI. The chairman of KOFOTI is the chairman of the Dainong
Group, which operates more spindles and looms than any other textile
manufacturer in Korea. In this respect, Korean industry associations
are similar to those in other nations. However, in the Korean case the
reasons for big firm domination may be different. One might be that
the government encourages this because it uses the industry associations to coordinate policy, insure compliance, and communicate at the
industry level, and must have the cooperation of the largest firms.
Similarly, the associations are the best channel for the big firms to
communicate and cooperate at the industry level. In the case of certain
associations, such as SWAK or KOFMIA or KOFOTI, participation
is required in order to stay in business, and big firms must protect
themselves by participating directly in the administration of the privileges and powers the government grants to these associations. The
executive positions of Korean industry associations are often occupied
by former bureaucrats from the ministries that supervise them (KOF-
MIA, KOFOTI) or by politically prominent personages (SWAK), a
situation typical of industry associations in all countries and likely to
become more prevalent in Korea in the future.[39]

In SWAK we can identify three phenomena in U.S.-Korea industry
association relations: (1) a mutually beneficial transnational alliance
with American cotton producers and shippers similar to other U.S.-
Korean agricultural trade alliances; (2) the antagonism between the
Korean and American textile industries typical of relations between
American and Korean industries in which imports into the United States
are an issue; and (3) the lack of transnational ties with industry associations or other economic interest groups in the United States that
benefit from the import and distribution of SWAK's products, which
seems to be true of Korea's major exports to the United States, especially of consumer goods. How do we explain these phenomena?

The easiest to explain is the rivalry between United States and
Korean industry associations, because it simply reflects the antagonism
between competing national industries. The explanation of the well-
developed transnational alliances in agriculture is not difficult. The
market relationship is essentially complementary, not competitive. High
productivity, exportable surpluses at competitive prices, and a receiving market that is complementary, however, are not enough to establish an alliance; these factors only constitute the base upon which one
may be constructed. Apart from the long aid relationship that laid the
foundation, the crucial factor has been effective marketing by FAS:
cooperator programs that deliberately aim to create transnational ties
through technical assistance and joint market development efforts, and

the use of Pl 480 and CCC credit. In fact, FAS and CCC proudly cite Korea as proof of the strategy of developing foreign markets with credit and then weaning them over to cash.[40] The centralized purchasing authority Korean industry associations exercise under government supervision probably facilitated the growth of effective working relationships.

A similar complementary relationship exists in theory between efficient, low-cost Korean producers of export products and American importers and distributors. Yet Korean industry associations have failed to establish effective links with these groups. A number of factors explain this, chiefly the power of protectionist forces, but we could sum them up by observing that Korean industry associations have not been able to differentiate sufficiently the complementary relationship and the benefits that a particularistic alliance would yield, although it would seem impossible to differentiate the relationship to that extent.

KUSEC, US/KEC and AMCHAM

Given the absence of effective transnational industry association links outside of agriculture that protect bilateral trade relationships or that serve as channels for communication over trade problems, can we expect to find effective ties among broad-based business councils? In contrast to the focused actions of industry associations, the activities of business councils are aimed at improving the general business environment. At the national level this means paying attention to taxation, national economic policies, and government regulation of industry. Similarly, transnational business councils are concerned with the broad political environment that influences business relations. Besides the promotion of business ties, bilateral organizations usually pay attention to the particular issues that may trouble a relationship.[41]

A few business councils deal specifically with the U.S.-Korea business relationship. The Korea-United States Economic Council (KUSEC) was established in 1973 under the auspices of the powerful Korean Traders Association (KTA). The chairman of the KTA, always a man of national prominence with cabinet-level experience in economic affairs, serves concurrently as the chairman of KUSEC, while the vice-chairman of the KTA serves as president.[42] In its functions, and in its bilateral concept, KUSEC is the same as bilateral Korea-X Trading Partner committees established with every nation with which Korea has diplomatic and trade relations. Nevertheless, the stature of its chairman and its association with the KTA lend KUSEC an aura of

importance that overshadows the others. KUSEC states that its functions are:[43]

Making arrangements for consultations between American industrial and commercial leaders and their counterparts in Korea, including, where necessary, contacts with Korean officials.

Conducting necessary studies and providing for exchange of information on matters of trade, investment, and technical cooperation.

Sponsoring conferences and joint meetings with its American counterpart organization on a yearly basis to provide for further contacts and exploration of economic opportunities.

Dispatching and receiving economic and trade missions between
the two countries.

Serving as an information and contact center for American businessmen and investors seeking Korean counterparts.

Providing studies and policy guidance for American businessmen
seeking opportunities in Korea.

Helping various American groups and organizations with exploratory visits in the Republic of Korea.

The express purpose of KUSEC is to promote and facilitate business ties with the United States outside the formal interstate relationship. KUSEC's ability to provide high-level access to the Korean
government and to Korean business has been one of its key functions.
In the mid-1970s, KUSEC often hosted investment missions from the
United States; in recent years it has hosted missions from U.S. state
governments seeking investments from Korean companies. Aside from
promoting investment, one motive of KUSEC's founders was to improve broad business ties because they sensed a trend toward protectionism in the United States that they hoped these ties could help
avert.[44]

KUSEC's counterpart organization is the United States-Korea
Economic Council (US/KEC), which recently reorganized as the U.S.-
Korea Society for Business and Cultural Affairs. Despite the equality
implied in the title, US/KEC has never been in the same league as
KUSEC. With a membership drawn from American corporations,
banks, and some interested individuals, US/KEC maintains a small
office in New York with one not quite full-time employee. Aside from
luncheons and a newsletter, US/KEC sponsors meetings with visiting
Korean dignitaries—often key economic policy officials. US/KEC was

most active in the mid-1970s when there was a surge of American business interest in Korea and US/KEC's ties with KUSEC could be quite useful.[45] The driving force behind US/KEC has always been a prominent businessman who has taken a personal interest in the organization. Since the investment surge crested, it is the more general activities that may be coming to the fore, as is implied in the new name for the organization. In its hosting of meetings with visiting Korean economic bureaucrats, US/KEC is not dissimilar from a few informal organizations that have appeared on a regional basis, such as the Korean-American Chamber of Commerce of the North Pacific Coast, a group in San Francisco organized by an interested businessman. These groups also receive cooperation from KUSEC.

KUSEC and US/KEC are promotional in nature, promoting not only business relations, but also bilateral ties in general. They have never constituted a working transnational alliance as we have defined the term. They have not served as channels for serious discussion of bilateral business issues that might lay the groundwork for eventual resolutions of the problems. Given the extreme differences in stature and in relations with the respective home governments, such roles cannot reasonably be expected.

A third private sector organization that does focus its attention on difficulties that arise for American firms in Korea is the American Chamber of Commerce in Korea (AMCHAM), which is affiliated with American Chambers elsewhere in Asia and with the Chamber of Commerce of the United States. AMCHAM's membership is composed primarily of representatives of American businesses in Korea.[46] AMCHAM serves a number of functions, but almost all fall into the category of information and communication. Members are organized loosely into committees on such subjects as taxation, joint ventures, or patents and intellectual properties; it is through the committee meetings that information on individual experiences is shared. This enables AMCHAM to keep track of developments affecting foreign business in Korea. For individual members, the sharing of experience and discussion of apparent trends in Korean government policies that affect foreign business is useful. For visiting businessmen, AMCHAM likewise serves as a source of realistic and practical information based on the experiences of the membership.

AMCHAM is the channel through which the American business community in Korea communicates its views to the U.S. government. Its officers meet regularly with the American ambassador, while embassy commercial and economic officers participate in committee meetings. Making its views known does not mean that diplomatic pressure will be brought to bear on its behalf, however, so AMCHAM representatives occasionally go to Washington to visit Capitol Hill, government offices, and major business associations such as the United States Chamber of Commerce to discuss current problems.

AMCHAM has no power. It enjoys visibility because Korea values foreign participation in attaining its investment and technology acquisition goals, and because of the extraordinary degree of government and business centralization in Seoul, where AMCHAM is recognized as the only body representing the American business point of view. Consequently, the Korean government occasionally solicits AMCHAM's views on the business environment.[47]

Although AMCHAM is a problem-oriented organization, it suffers from two inherent limitations as a transnational channel for communication on bilateral business issues. First, it is a local organization and its focus is not on the bilateral relationship but on the problems of its members in Korea—to which it wants to draw bilateral attention and action. Second, members who represent large American firms are a few layers beneath top management and cannot represent to Washington or to Seoul the opinions or the political weight of top management.

The roles of KUSEC, US/KEC, and AMCHAM have changed because of Korea's economic achievements and fundamental changes in the world economy during the 1970s. From the early 1970s through 1978-79, everything was rosy; Korea survived the first oil shock handily and its economy grew to the degree of magnitude and sophistication that increasing numbers of American firms whose technology or services Korea wanted were attracted to participate in the 'miracle on the Han.' American protectionism posed a difficulty, but Korea was able to increase exports to the United States, even of restricted goods. KUSEC and US/KEC brought in American investors, and AMCHAM members had few complaints; many were enthusiastic about their firm's participation in such a dramatic growth scene. As the 1970s turned into the 1980s, however, much of the bloom faded from the rose.

Rising energy prices and a world recession undermined Korea's plans for industrial development. President Park was assassinated in 1979, and the resulting paralysis of the bureaucracy made business initiatives difficult. The new Chun government took drastic actions that alarmed foreign business.[48] The Chun government also made changes in the economic bureaucracy, diminishing the powers of the EPB and shifting the authority to deal with foreign investors from the EPB to the Ministry of Finance. This was termed a step down the road toward desirable economic decentralization, but the initial result was the decentralization of economic decision-making power within the government, which only added to the headaches of dealing with the government in the normal conduct of business.

By the end of the 1970s, Korea's successful growth and absorption of technology and management skills had changed the nature of the foreign participation Korea desired and had, to Korean eyes, rendered obsolete foreign investment agreements negotiated in the 1960s when Korea had required the foreign investor to provide the technology, capital, and management skills. Disputes with joint venture partners multiplied and so did difficulties with reinterpretations of statutes by the government, sometimes retroactively, that had profound repercussions for some foreign firms. Korea still desired foreign investment and technology, but it wanted advanced commercial technologies. However, the investment environment no longer seemed as attractive. Not only was it often more difficult to deal with the government bureaucracy and, sometimes, Korean partners, but there were also problems in such matters as laws and practices concerning patents that worried potential investors in high technology industries.[49]

The problems experienced by American businesses in Korea, by Korea in attracting the foreign investment it desires, and the ongoing problems of American protectionism and Korean barriers to market access all underscore the absence of a high-level bilateral business council that can address matters of concern and gain attention in Washington and Seoul. The KUSEC-US/KEC connection is not likely to grow into such a role. US/KEC, even in its new incarnation as the U.S.-Korea Society for Business and Cultural Affairs, does not represent the American business community. KUSEC's prestige and high-powered leadership give it potential, but it is still a creature of the KTA, and is impossible to separate from the Korean government's economic strategy. Given the nature of American protectionism and the nature of government-business relations in Korea, one might wonder whether a high-level transnational business council could have any influence on the resolution of bilateral issues.

Private Sector Organizations: The Current Transition

At the very time the research for this chapter was collected and written up, roughly from mid-1982 until the end of 1983, the roles of private sector organizations in the U.S.-Korea business relationship seemed to be undergoing changes, particularly in Korea. Having been pressed for years about industry association powers that amounted to nontariff barriers to trade, the Korean government promised to reduce such powers as part of Korea's comprehensive 'trade liberalization' package to be put into effect over the mid-1980s. If the government actually fulfills this commitment, the powers of some industry associations may be reduced considerably.[50]

We have seen that this has already begun to happen in the agricultural sector, where the Korean government has experimented with 'liberalizing' agricultural imports and stripping away the powers delegated to the industry associations. The objective of these changes has not been for the MAF to turn control of agricultural imports over to the private sector, because it will still be MAF that ultimately decides import levels. One objective is apparently to push more business to the large KGTCs that have grown up since the mid-1970s. Another objective might be to lessen the bonds with American suppliers, as Korea intentionally diversifies imports.[51] It is difficult to call this move a liberalization, because to the extent that the objective is to favor KGTCs or diversify suppliers, it reflects continuing government guidance of economic affairs. In any event, the trend is for the agricultural trade associations like KOFMIA to lose the privileges that once made them so powerful. The same might happen to other Korean industry associations.

Despite the likely loss of some powers, industry associations in Korea may actually be gaining influence. The decentralization of economic decision-making power within the bureaucracy has shifted more power to the individual ministries. It has always been at the ministry and the bureau level that the client industry has gotten a sympathetic reception, whatever the overall economic situation. Now that there is more power at the ministry level, the not unexpected result seems to be a tightening of the ministry-industry nexus, creating deeper ties and giving the industry associations more informal influence over government decisions. It is also at the ministry level that industries can make effective use of various informal inducements to influence bureaucrats. If the liberalization trend in Korea continues and extends to the political sphere as well, perhaps we can predict the further strengthening of ties between the regulators and the regulated in the style of Japanese and American industry-regulator ties. Should this speculation be borne out, then the barriers to access to the Korean market will not be lowered as easily as the pronouncements concerning liberalization state.

On the American side no changes are in progress, and one can only speculate about the future role of industry associations. If the industrial policy idea in the United States is ever implemented in the manner that some proponents desire, by aiding new high growth industries and pruning older, less competitive industries, then restrictions on Korean exports such as textiles and perhaps steel may fall and closer alliances between Korean exporters and American importers of these products may emerge (assuming, of course, that Korea is still an efficient producer of these goods). On the other hand, barriers to high technology exports from Korea may rise or bilateral trade might become contingent on reciprocal trade agreements. At present, however, the trend in the United States seems to be toward more industry group pressures for protection from imports, and the most likely development is that such protectionist measures would be embodied in any comprehensive industrial policy.

These concluding speculations only underline the point that both the potential influence and the limits of transnational interactions between private sector organizations in the U.S.-Korea trade relationship are determined by the way each partner organizes and manages relations between economic interests and government authority in its political and economic system.

9 The American Role in the Development of Management Education in Korea

Hak Chong Lee

As an economy develops and becomes more complex, the proportion of professional and managerial manpower to the total work force naturally increases. Thus, we recognize that economic development depends in part upon the supply of qualified technical, managerial, and administrative manpower.[1] Korea, as a developing nation, has been no exception. Since the Korean War, which brought vast destruction to the country, Korea has not only rebuilt its economy and industries but has also gone on to achieve spectacular economic growth over the past two decades, lifting herself into the ranks of the newly industrializing countries. Over the past two decades, the Korean economy expanded more than 500 percent in real terms, while the technical, managerial, and administrative work force more than tripled (table 9-1). Manufacturing employment also tripled and the employment in sales and services more than doubled, while agricultural employment stayed constant.

At the present time, despite some difficult constraints, Korean universities and colleges are endeavoring to meet the demand for graduates with degrees in business and management. In 1982 there were over forty-five thousand undergraduate students majoring in business and international trade in about one hundred colleges and universities, while there were over five thousand MBA students at more than seventy colleges and universities. Some two hundred graduate students were enrolled in doctoral courses (table 9-1). These are Korean students in Korean universities, most of whom will go to work in Korean companies—companies whose corporate environment, style, culture, and way of doing business is uniquely Korean. Yet, the curriculum these students learn can be instantly recognized and understood by the students and faculty of leading business schools around the world. This is the case because the American role, both direct and indirect, has been critically important in the development and transformation of management education in Korea.

Management education is an important prerequisite to economic growth. No country can expect to sustain economic development suc-

Table 9–1
Korea's Gross National Product, Employment, and College Enrollment

Korea's Gross National Product (1982 current U.S. dollars)

	1957	1962	1971	1981
GNP (million)	10,438	12,640	28,717	61,010
Per Capita GNP	460	477	873	1,575

Employment Statistics	1961	1970	1980
Total employed (1,000)	7,963 (92.0%)	10,153 (97.8%)	13,705 (94.8%)
Technical	224 (2.6)	323 (3.1)	548 (3.8)
Managerial	69 (0.8)	96 (0.9)	182 (1.3)
Administrative	340 (3.9)	593 (5.7)	1,266 (8.7)
Sales	849 (9.8)	1,028 (9.9)	1,983 (13.7)
Services	426 (4.9)	679 (6.5)	1,085 (7.5)
Agricultural	4,525 (52.4)	5,148 (49.6)	4,652 (32.2)
Manufacturing	1,350 (15.6)	2,198 (21.2)	3,990 (27.6)
Other	178 (2.0)	88 (0.9)	
Unemployed	693 (3.0)	225 (2.2)	749 (5.2)

Enrollment Statistics in Korean Colleges and Universities

	1955	1963	1971	1981
Undergraduate total	61,274	105,338	155,369	535,876
Business administration	3,078	10,685	10,878	32,503
International trade	255	546	2,565	12,775
Total business enrollment	3,333(5.4%)	11,231(10.7%)	13,443(8.6%)	45,278(8.4%)
Graduate enrollment:				
Masters total		2,476	6,682	39,153
Business total		99(4.0%)	1,407(21.1%)	5,444(13.9%)
Doctoral total		216	618	5,578
Business total		1	15(24.3%)	211 (3.8%)

Sources: Bank of Korea, *Korean National Income*, 1982; Economic Planning Board, *Korea Statistics Yearbook*, 1960–1982; R.O.K., *The Fifth 5-Year Economic and Social Development Plan*, 1981; International Labour Organization, *Yearbook of Labor Statistics*, 1982; Korean Ministry of Education, *Educational Statistics Yearbook*, 1963–1982.

cessfully without a management education establishment which provides the necessary managerial and technical personnel. From the 1950s, even before Korea's economy began to grow, management education and training was considered to be one of the high priority areas for development in Korea. The fact that Korea was able to develop a modern professional management curriculum with substantial American contributions and aid was an important factor in Korea's ability to achieve rapid economic development during the past two decades.

Formal business education has been in existence in Korea for almost eighty years, but the development of real management education has taken place only in the past twenty-five years. College-level business education can be traced back as early as 1905 when the forerunner of the present Korea University, Posung College, established a commerce department. Yonsei University, at that time Yonhi College, also set up a commerce curriculum in 1915. These were the beginnings of formal business education at the college level in Korea. Business education under Japanese colonial rule was directed mainly at training students for financial institutions and small business establishments. This style of curriculum is generally characterized as commercial education, not business education. Commercial education is distinguished from professional management education in that it is primarily concerned with the study of business transactions and covers sales, bookkeeping, and business law, with the major emphasis on learning methods and procedures.

The real beginning of formal business education at the university level came after the liberation of Korea from Japanese colonial rule in 1945. Sweeping changes were undertaken in the higher education system in Korea, including the upgrading of three-year colleges to university status as well as the establishment of new colleges and universities. While some colleges and universities established independent faculties for commerce and economics, others included commerce as part of the school of law and economics. However, the course contents of business education at the time continued to be primarily of the commercial education type. The curricula emphasized accounting, sales, and commercial law, and mainly stressed technical knowledge, methods, and procedures. Most of the instructors had been trained under the Japanese, and their overall orientation was predominantly toward Japanese-style instruction, with much emphasis on the study of commercial and financial transactions.

Professional management education began in the late 1950s with the introduction of the teaching of American management concepts. A number of Korean professors who had gone to study management in the United States after the Korean War began to return to Korea in the latter 1950s. In 1958 a six-year project funded by the U.S. International Cooperation Administration (ICA) to develop management education in Korea was launched. Under this project, Washington University (St. Louis, Missouri) Graduate School of Business Administration provided assistance to two leading private universities, Korea University and Yonsei University, to develop business administration programs. American concepts of professional management education introduced through this project became the framework for the development of management curricula in Korean colleges and universities during this period.

Beginning in 1957, many Korean universities restructured their or-

ganizations, establishing separate schools for business administration
with management departments, independent of the faculties of economics, law, or public administration. Existing commerce departments
were upgraded to management departments or business administration
departments, with basic changes in curriculum content to emphasize
professional management training. The professional orientation was
further extended to the graduate level in the 1960s with the establishment of graduate schools of business administration at major universities. Along with the two-year master of business administration (MBA)
programs, nondegree continuing education programs were also established by these graduate schools of business.[2]

The Role of the United States in the Development of Management Education in Korea

There were two important direct contributions from the United States
in the development of management education in Korea: a project sponsored by the ICA in the 1950s and another project sponsored by the
Ford Foundation in the 1960s. The importance of these projects cannot
be overestimated, for their impact, their catalytic effects at a critical
time, and their long-term influence were far greater than the number
of people and funds involved. Even now their influence is seen in
management curricula in Korean colleges and universities and, not
least, in managers who today play leading roles in the Korean business
community

The ICA Project

The ICA project was carried out from 1958 to 1964 with the Graduate
School of Business Administration of Washington University as the
prime contractor in assisting two leading private universities, Yonsei
University and Korea University, to modernize their business administration curricula, and to train their faculty. The project was the first
major direct assistance that Korea received from abroad for this purpose. The specific goals and tasks of the project were:[3]

To modernize the curriculum structure through the development
of appropriate general education and professional business management courses

To modernize and improve instructional materials by rebuilding the library resources and helping individual Korean professors to acquire current management literature

To improve teaching methods and introduce the case study method

To retrain and develop Korean faculty through graduate business administration programs at Washington University, enabling qualified professors to earn Master or Doctor of Business Administration degrees from the university

To develop capabilities for research and management consulting to fill the needs of the Korean business community

The major activities of the project focused on curriculum development at two Korean universities, training of Korean professors at Washington University, and joint research and management consulting for the Korean business community.

Curriculum Development. Under the ICA project, Washington University faculty members were assigned to Korea University and Yonsei University in Seoul to serve as resident professors. Their responsibilities included the coordination of the project with the two Korean universities, curriculum and course development, teaching and, in the later stages of the project, supervision of the doctoral dissertations of Korean professors who had returned from Washington University after completion of course work.

Prior to the ICA project, business courses in Korean colleges and universities dealt mainly with commerce. Although there were many courses, there was much duplication and very little overall integration in the course structure. At that time Korean schools were slowly integrating Western concepts of professional management into their curriculum. The ICA project accelerated the modernization process by introducing the curriculum standards recommended by the American Association for Collegiate Schools of Business (AACSB).

The AACSB standards emphasized a liberal and broad education in business administration to train generalists to work in a constantly changing business environment. The standards also emphasized a core concept and an overall integration of the course structure. The standard curriculum recommended by AACSB consisted of two years of undergraduate liberal education and two years of upper-level professional education including both core subjects and specialized courses. The first two years of liberal education was to provide a sound foundation for the professional training to follow. The core in the professional curriculum covered basic analytical courses and all basic business administration areas: economics, statistics, business law, production, marketing, personnel, accounting, and finance. Specialization followed the core courses, and all the upper-level professional courses were integrated into a final capstone course in business policy.

The AACSB curriculum design introduced at Yonsei University and Korea University became the model for all other Korean colleges and universities. During the six years of the project, nine management professors from Washington University served as resident project directors or resident advisors on two-year assignments to help carry out the program. These resident professors also participated in teaching and course development at the two universities, helping the Korean faculty with up-to-date course materials and new instructional approaches, including the case method.

We should remember that when the ICA project was launched in 1958, management education in the United States was undergoing an intense reevaluation. The Ford Foundation and the Carnegie Foundation had underwritten extensive studies on how to improve management education and had recommended curriculum modernization for American schools of business administration.[4] Because Washington University was at the vanguard of the changes taking place in the United States, Yonsei University and Korea University had the benefit of adopting the most up-to-date management curriculum even before many business schools in the United States.

Faculty Training. During the ICA project, twenty-three professors from Yonsei University and Korea University, practically the entire faculty in business administration at the two universities at that point, spent periods ranging from a semester to four full years in residence at Washington University. While senior professors audited graduate business courses and collected teaching materials, young faculty members were enrolled in graduate degree programs. Korean professors earned six Master of Business Administration and three Doctor of Business Administration degrees during the project period. They were among the first MBAs and DBAs in Korea, and returning from the United States, they played leading roles in the development of Korean management education. Because some of the Korean professors had to return immediately after completing course work in order to resume teaching, they finished their dissertations under the supervision of the faculty from Washington University in residence in Seoul.

Management Research and Consulting. Another aspect of the ICA project was to develop the capabilities of Korean professors to provide research and consulting services for Korean firms. These activities were very important to the business schools because they allowed faculty to offer guidance in professional management techniques to a business community that required their knowledge and expertise. Therefore this program was a natural extension of the development activities under the ICA project.

Prior to the ICA project, there were only a few professors capable of offering such guidance and expertise. As soon as the ICA project got underway, Korea and Yonsei Business Schools established research centers and began to engage in contract research and management consulting for business firms and the government, with the participation of the resident professors from Washington University.

Subsequently, the rapid growth of the Korean economy that began in the early 1960s generated tremendous demand from business and government for industrial research and management consulting—feasibility studies, market research, economic research for government planning, and so forth. Professors who had been trained under the ICA project played very important roles in meeting the needs of Korean industry. As economic development has progressed and the domestic and international environment has grown more complex, the demand for business research and consulting has steadily increased in Korea. Accordingly, management professors in Korean universities have been very active in meeting the expanding demands.

The ICA project also pioneered management development for Korean business, the most important source being continuing education programs for managers and executives offered by Korean business schools. The evening graduate programs in management which began in the mid-1960s provided professional training and education for managers and executives, many of whom had minimal professional management education. The evening programs continued to expand through the 1970s along with the rapid expansion in Korean business and industry (table 9-1). Yonsei Graduate School of Business alone has graduated over 1,300 MBAs and over 2,600 nondegree students since the evening graduate programs were instituted in 1965. The evening school has a current enrollment of four hundred students and awards about one hundred MBA degrees each year.

Another important source of management development was the top executive development program, also pioneered by the ICA project. With Washington University professors playing the leading role, the first Management Development Conference for top business executives in Korea was held at Onyang during July and August 1958.

This four-week conference became an annual summer program. Although Washington University professors took the lead in preparing and conducting the first conference, Korean professors gradually took on more of the work and had assumed complete charge of the summer program by 1962. This was the beginning of executive development programs in Korea.

Executive development programs are now offered each semester at Korea and Yonsei and at other leading graduate schools of business such as Seoul National University and Pusan University.[5] Over seven hundred top Korean executives have participated in the Yonsei programs to this date. Korea University and Seoul National University have each trained an equivalent number of top executives. In addition to technical and professional training, these programs help develop professional attitudes toward management values and ideologies.

This approach to management development spread rapidly to Korean business firms in the 1970s. Large firms such as Samsung and Sunkyong established their own management development centers, while leading banks such as the Bank of Korea and the Korea Exchange Bank also established educational centers for their employees. Soon other large industrial groups, such as Doosan, Hyundai, and Daewoo, instituted their own management training centers. Along with the in-house management development programs, on-the-job training programs were also initiated and fostered in large Korean business firms in the 1970s.

Management professors in Korean schools of business have been active participants in these corporate programs for management development and on-the-job training. Similar training activities in industry are now spreading to small and medium-size firms. Recently, the Korea Small and Medium Business Association established, with financial support from the Korean government, a management training center for the purpose of developing technical and managerial skills which are in short supply in small industries in Korea. In 1983, the first year of operation, the center provided training for more than 5,000 small business managers and executives.[6]

In addition to the joint business research and consulting for Korean industries and management development programs for Korean executives, the ICA project also initiated collaborative research in case writing between Washington University professors and Korean professors. A number of case studies were conducted on Korean firms, and the cases thus developed were actually used in the classroom and in the Management Development Conference held at Onyang. These first cases gave the Korean faculty experience in researching and developing case materials with specific relevance to the Korean situation and business environment.

The Ford Foundation Project. As the ICA project was drawing to a close, having successfully accomplished its goals, another American sponsored project got underway in 1963. This was the Ford Foundation project to retrain Korean professors in the United States. Stanford University offered its International Center for Advanced Management Education (ICAME) for the retraining of Korean professors for one year periods. In addition to Yonsei Universities and Korea University, three other universities, Sogang, Seoul National, and Choong-Ang, participated in the Ford Foundation project. In all, sixteen Korean professors from these five institutions were retrained at ICAME during the five years of the project. At the conclusion of this project, the Ford Foundation provided individual grants to two ICAME participants to finance their doctoral studies at the University of Washington in Seattle. Although not as broad in conception as the ICA program, the Ford program continued the process of faculty development, an ongoing process that takes many years.

Together, the ICA and Ford projects covered a period of ten years from 1958 to 1968, a decade when Korea was undergoing major changes socially and economically. The fact that these projects came at a time of fundamental change enabled them to have a critical impact on the development and direction of management education in Korea. If the ICA project had been undertaken earlier, say in the early 1950s, Korea might not have been able to take advantage of the assistance; if the project had taken place in the late 1960s, its impact would likely have been less. By coming when they did, the ICA and Ford projects engendered a close and, in a sense, synergistic relationship between the development of management education and increased professionalization and competence in the Korean business community. Moreover, professional management programs in Korean colleges and universities, developed with American assistance, began to provide technical and managerial manpower for Korea's economic development just as it began to accelerate in the mid-1960s.

The faculty members trained under the American assistance projects encouraged the active participation of all Korean management faculty in business executive training and consulting, thus promoting the positive interaction between the academic and business world that was stressed by the ICA program. The business managers who participated in the management development programs undoubtedly contributed to the economic success of Korea in the 1960s and 1970s.

The Continuing Influence of American Management
Education in Korea

American contributions to Korean management education did not end
with the conclusion of the Ford Foundation project in 1968. In fact,
the United States has continued to exert great influence on the development of management education in Korea up to the present. As the
demand for managerial and technical personnel increased in Korean
industry, there was an increased need for more management instructors in Korean schools of business to educate greater numbers of students. American graduate schools of business continued to be the most
important source for training Korean management faculty.

As the Korean economy began to grow rapidly in the late 1960s,
the schools of business were not able to expand rapidly enough to meet
the demands of Korean industry for management graduates. The Korean Ministry of Education (MOE) policy of regulating the size of
student enrollments in existing departments in Korean colleges and
universities hindered the expansion of enrollments in management degree programs. To overcome this constraint, Korean schools of business established new departments in accounting and international trade
with curriculum contents essentially identical to the management degree program curriculum.

In 1981 the MOE enrollment quotas that had limited the number
of students in Korean colleges and universities were drastically revised.
Management was one of the areas where the number of students allowed to enroll was greatly increased. One reason for the revision was
the sharply rising demand for managerial manpower from industry,
while another was high student demand for entry into the business
management programs. Korean schools of business, which had already
been burdened throughout the 1970s with too many students for the
limited faculty resources, were suddenly hit by drastic increases in enrollment. Consequently, the problems of classroom overcrowding and
faculty shortages have worsened to the crisis point over the past few
years.

The huge increases in student enrollment have also brought to a
head several major and much-debated issues concerning management
education in Korean colleges and universities. One issue concerns the
basic objectives and orientation of the management curriculum and
calls for reexamination of general education versus specialized education. From the early 1960s when the concept of core curriculum was
introduced from the United States, the concept of general and broad
management education with limited specialization came to be widely
accepted. However, economic development and increased profession-

alization in Korean business have brought about an increased demand in recent years for more specialized and technical training in functional areas such as accounting, finance, marketing, production, and international business.

Specialization within the management curriculum has its merits, but this specialization requires a wider range of courses than Korean schools of business can offer because of the severe shortage of faculty and the constantly increasing student enrollments. Consequently, the core concept together with the general management curriculum continue to dominate Korean schools of business, less from choice than from practical necessity. However, changes are taking place; greater attention is being paid to the changing environment of Korean business and more efforts are being made to identify and develop a style of management applicable to Korean conditions.

Another issue concerns the relative status of undergraduate and graduate management education. Up to the present, the major emphasis has been on undergraduate instruction. Recently, however, increasing demands for high-quality management faculty from Korean colleges together with demands from industry for high-quality professional managers have called attention to the need to expand and upgrade the quality of business administration education. However, the demand for undergraduate business education is so great and the number of faculty capable of graduate-level instruction so small that a major shift in resource allocation toward graduate management programs has not yet taken place. There is no doubt that the graduate programs will continue to gain more attention and resources, especially in the leading Korean universities.

Compounding these problems is a severe shortage of management faculty. Currently, there are more than 45,000 undergraduate and 5,600 graduate students majoring in business administration. However, there are only 822 full-time instructors teaching business administration in Korean colleges and universities, and the overall student-faculty ratio is more than 60 to 1.[7] Just to bring down the student-faculty ratio in business administration to around 30 to 1, which is the average for all disciplines in Korean colleges and universities, requires doubling the current number of management faculty.[8] Not only are classes overcrowded, but management faculty are also carrying extremely heavy teaching loads.

The quality of management faculty is a serious problem. Well-trained management professors are few in number and, to make the problem worse, they are all concentrated in a few schools in Seoul. Of 707 instructors who returned a management faculty survey questionnaire for this study, about three-quarters received their final degrees

from Korean universities. Only one-fifth, or 135 instructors, were educated in the United States, with 78 of them, or slightly over 10 percent
of those who responded, having doctoral degrees from American universities (table 9-2).[9] This indicates a real problem in the quality of
Korean management faculty, because doctoral programs in management in Korea have yet to achieve a high level of quality. The problem
is even more serious in business schools outside of Seoul (table 9-3).

     In order to alleviate the problem of faculty shortage, the Korean
government arranged a loan from the International Bank for Reconstruction and Development (IBRD) to finance the training of future
instructors for Korean colleges and universities. Under this $4 million
loan program, top quality graduate students are selected and sent to
graduate schools of business in advanced countries with full financial
support for their doctoral studies. Of the 82 students selected under
the program thus far, 79 chose schools in the United States. The remaining three chose schools in England, France, and West Germany
for their doctoral work. The IBRD loan program also supports retraining of Korean management instructors at graduate schools of business
in advanced countries. Up to the date of writing, 124 faculty members
have been admitted to the program. Of those selected, 104 have chosen
American graduate schools for their studies. Of the rest, thirteen have
chosen schools in Japan, six have gone to West Germany, and one to
England.

     The overwhelming preference for American schools by the Korean
doctoral students and management faculty indicates the continuing at-
tractiveness of American management education to Koreans and at-
tests to the continued strong American influence on Korean schools of
business. American advanced management education is highly regarded, and an American degree is considered to be a distinct advantage for Koreans in their professional development. There is also the
fact that for young Korean students English is the primary foreign
language, and many have read American textbooks and journals
throughout their university education. There is no doubt that many
Korean students and future professors of management will pursue advanced training in the United States in the future.

     According to our statistics, about one-fifth of all management in-
structors and about one-third of all doctoral degree-holders in Korean
schools of business received their final degrees from American universities. Many more have studied in the United States without receiving degrees. Considering the number of students and professors
currently studying management in American graduate schools of busi-

Table 9–2
Training Background of Korean Management Professors by Field and Country (June 1983)[a]

Field \ Degree	Korea BS	Korea MS	Korea PhD DBA	USA BS	USA MS	USA PhD DBA	Japan BS	Japan MS	Japan PhD	Other[b] BS	Other[b] MS	Other[b] PhD	Total BS	Total MS	Total PhD DBA	Total (%)
Accounting	2	109	30	—	8	8	—	3	1	—	—	1	2	120	40	162 (22.9)
Finance	—	41	13	1	12	12	—	1	2	—	—	2	1	54	29	84 (11.9)
Management sci.[d]	—	52	16	—	7	21	—	1	1	—	2	6	—	62	44	106 (15.0)
Marketing	—	33	18	—	11	9	2	4	—	—	—	3	2	48	30	80 (11.3)
Personnel and organization[e]	1	41	27	—	7	5	1	2	3	—	—	2	2	50	37	89 (11.3)
General management[f]	2	8	12	—	1	3	1	—	1	—	1	—	3	10	16	29 (12.6)
International business[g]	—	30	6	—	4	4	1	—	1	—	—	3	1	34	14	49 (4.1)
Economics[h]	1	41	26	—	5	14	—	2	2	—	1	5	1	49	47	97 (6.9)
Other	—	5	2	—	1	2	—	—	—	—	1	—	—	7	4	11 (13.7)
Total (%)	6 (0.8)	360 (50.9)	150 (21.2)	1 (0.1)	56 (7.9)	78 (11.0)	5 (0.7)	13 (1.8)	11 (1.6)	0	5 (0.7)	22 (3.0)	12 (1.7)	434 (61.4)	261 (36.9)	707 (100.0)
Total (%)	516 (73.0)			135 (19.1)			29 (4.1)			27 (3.8)			707 (100.0)			

[a]Based on management faculty survey data collected from 35 universities and 26 colleges. Three universities and 13 colleges did not respond, but there were no U.S. doctorates in these schools.

[b]Includes England, France, West Germany, Philippines, and Thailand.

[c]Includes insurance, securities, and real estate.

[d]Management science includes production, operations management, statistics, and management information system.

[e]Includes organization behavior, industrial relations, and organization theory.

[f]Includes business policy and strategy.

[g]International business includes international marketing, international finance, international management, and international trades.

[h]Includes only those professors with economics degree teaching in management or business administration department.

[i]Includes public administration, management of research and development, business law, hotel management, and business teacher education.

Table 9-3
Distribution of Korean Management Professors in Colleges and Universities[a] (June 1983)

Degree	Country / School	Korea (%)	USA (%)	Japan (%)	Other[b] (%)	Total (%)
B.S.	Total	6	1	5	0	12
M.S./ M.B.A.	5 leading schools[c]	5 (1.4)	6 (10.7)	0	0	11 (2.5)
	Other universities	169 (46.9)	36 (64.3)	8 (61.5)	3 (60.0)	216 (49.8)
	4-year colleges	186 (51.7)	14 (25.0)	5 (38.5)	2 (40.0)	207 (47.7)
	Total	360 (100.0)	56 (100.0)	13 (100.0)	5 (100.0)	434 (100.0)
Ph.D. D.B.A.	5 leading schools	22 (14.7)	44 (56.4)	1 (9.1)	5 (22.7)	72 (27.6)
	Other universities	105 (70.0)	25 (32.1)	9 (81.8)	17 (77.3)	156 (59.8)
	4-year colleges	23 (15.3)	9 (11.5)	1 (9.1)	0	33 (12.6)
	Total	150 (100.0)	78 (100.0)	11 (100.0)	22 (100.0)	261 (100.0)
Total	5 leading schools	27 (5.2)	50 (37.0)	2 (6.9)	5 (18.5)	84 (11.9)
	Other universities	277 (53.7)	62 (45.9)	21 (72.4)	20 (74.1)	380 (53.7)
	4-year colleges	212 (41.1)	23 (17.0)	6 (20.7)	2 (7.8)	243 (34.4)
	Total	516 (100.0)	135 (100.0)	29 (100.0)	27 (100.0)	707 (100.0)

[a]Based on management faculty survey data collected from 35 universities (including 5 leading schools) and 26 colleges. Three universities and 13 colleges did not respond, but there were no U.S. doctorates in these schools.

[b]Includes England, France, West Germany, Philippines, and Thailand.

[c]Five leading schools are Korea Advanced Institute of Science and Technology, Korea University, Seoul National University, Sogang University, and Yonsei University.

ness under various arrangements, the influence of American management education on Korean schools of business is likely to become even
stronger in the future.[10]

The Need for Korean-Style Management Education

Rapid economic development has brought about many changes in the
Korean business environment. Since the early 1960s the economy has
grown nearly five times in real terms, while an increasing number of
Korean firms have joined the ranks of the multinationals. As of 1982,
ten Korean industrial groups such as Hyundai, Samsung, Lucky, and
Daewoo were represented in Fortune's 500 largest international firms.

To a degree, the professional management curriculum developed
through the ICA project has filled the needs of Korean industry. However, the curriculum content in Korean schools of business is largely
based on American models and management practices developed in
the United States to be effective in the American business environment. There is no question that Korean firms operate in an environment which is different economically, culturally, and technologically.
Consequently, there has been greater attention paid in recent years to
making the management curriculum in Korean business schools more
applicable to the real conditions and problems of Korean business.
Research activities and publications on Korean business and management, which have grown tremendously, also contribute to the development of instruction materials relevant to Korean practices.[11]

Attempts at increased relevance in the management curriculum in
Korean schools can be approached in several ways. One way is to
develop applicable concepts and techniques through empirical research
and case studies based on the experience of Korean business organizations. The instructional material currently used in Korean schools of
business is based predominantly on American business and practices;
the differences in organizational and managerial behavior shown by
actual research on Korean business could be incorporated into the
existing material. Management education can also reflect the increasing
internationalization of Korean business; additional courses and materials related to international business management can be made part
of the curriculum.

A recent study on management education practices by the Korea
Association of Business Administration reveals that only 8 percent of
management instructors employ case study methods and only 5 percent
have undertaken case research. Even the instructors who use cases

devote less than six class hours per semester to case method instruction. Because Korean students are so accustomed to the didactic method of instruction, they experience difficulties initially with the case study approach in which there is no one correct answer; however, experience shows that once they become used to it, students participate readily and profit from the exercises.[12] Though the pace may be slow, the general trend is toward increased emphasis on both case research and case instruction.[13]

The development of management education specifically suited to the Korean business and cultural environment will take a long time, require much research, and necessitate shifts in instructional orientation. However, the current shortage in faculty and, consequently, the extremely heavy teaching loads seriously inhibit the processes of institutional and instructional movement toward this goal.

Conclusion

The United States has made very important contributions to the introduction and development of modern management education in Korea. Direct assistance from the United States provided crucial training and financial support for faculty and curriculum development at the critical point when Korea was turning from postwar reconstruction to rapid economic growth.

The six-year ICA project provided assistance to the schools of business administration at two leading universities for the purpose of modernizing their curricula and training their faculties. The project introduced the modern curriculum standards that had just been established in the United States by the AASCB. In addition, nearly the entire business administration faculties of the two Korean universities studied at Washington University during the course of the project. The curriculum approach and the faculty training supported by the ICA project later served as the model for management education policy development at all other Korean universities. Collaboration between Washington University faculty and the Korean faculty members in research and case writing gave the Korean professors invaluable experience in developing relevant teaching materials based on studies of actual business situations in Korea. The ICA project also stressed direct interaction between business school faculty and the business world; this led to the development at Korean universities of advanced seminars for senior managers and evening graduate programs, the involvement of business faculty members in corporate training programs, and management consulting and research by faculty members. Although not as broad in scope or effect, the Ford Foundation project continued the process of faculty development begun by the ICA project.

The ICA project was carried out from 1958 to 1964, and the Ford Foundation project lasted from 1963 to 1968. By the time the Ford Foundation project drew to a close, the Korean economy was growing rapidly and Korea no longer needed to rely on outside assistance for all its development needs. Nevertheless, the strong American influence on Korean management education has not diminished. Whether supported by government fellowships or by their own resources, the overwhelming majority of Koreans going abroad for advanced management degree work attend American institutions; the training of the future management faculty of Korean universities is now taking place at graduate schools of business in the United States. Concepts of business analysis originally developed in the United States are an important part of the management education curriculum, while most of the textbooks and instructional materials used in Korean schools of business are American.

The changing relationship between Korea and the United States in the development of management education in Korea reflects the larger changes in the economic and business relationship between the two countries. Korea was dependent on American aid in the 1950s and early 1960s when the ICA project was carried out. The need for modern management curriculum and faculty development could only be met by direct assistance from the United States. Since the late 1960s the Korean economy has grown rapidly with little outside assistance, and Korea has supported the independent development of her own management education programs. American influence on Korean management education has remained strong out of Korean choice. In management education, as in the overall economic relationship, the connection may be best characterized now as a partnership. As in the economic relationship, the United States remains the dominant partner and for the forseeable future will continue to be the most important source of influence affecting the further development of management education in Korea, but the relationship now benefits both partners.

The prospect for the future is that the partnership will grow stronger and closer through cooperative research and instructional activities. American schools of business are placing more emphasis on international business and business experience in other countries. In recent years there have been several joint research projects on international business questions by Korean and American scholars, and Korean management professors with particular expertise in international business studies have been invited to leading American institutions as visiting faculty members. Interest in such cooperative activities is growing, and the results will be beneficial for both of the partners. Joint research on Korean business problems, both domestic and international, will undoubtedly help in the development of instructional materials specifically relevant to Korea; these joint efforts and the exchange of faculty and increased scholarly communication cannot but be of benefit to American management education as well.

Notes

Chapter 1

1. Harold F. Cook, *Pioneer American Businessman in Korea* (Seoul: Royal Asiatic Society, Korea Branch, 1981), 35, 38-41, 48-50, 53-55, 57-61.

2. See Imsi Oeja Ch'ongguk (OSROK), *Oeja Ch'ongguk saŏp kaehwang*, 1949.

3. If American Forces payments for goods and services in Korea are included, the United States supplied virtually all of Korea's foreign exchange.

4. From USDA/FAS summaries of PL 480 agreements with the Republic of Korea.

5. *Pioneer American Businessman in Korea*, 89.

6. See W. D. Reeves, *The Republic of Korea* (London: Oxford University Press, 1963), and Leroy P. Jones and SaKong Il, *Government, Business, and Entrepreneurship in Economic Development: The Korean Case* (Cambridge: Harvard University Press, 1980), for discussions of the political and business corruption surrounding the manipulation of economic assistance.

7. An excellent summary by David Cole of American aid to Korea from 1945 to 1975 is found in Edward S. Mason et al., *The Economic and Social Modernization of the Republic of Korea* (Cambridge: Harvard University Press, 1980), 165-205.

8. For American perceptions about Korea, see William Watts, *The United States and Asia: Changing Attitudes and Policies*, (Lexington, Massachusetts: Lexington Books, 1982), and other works by the same author. According to a survey done by Michael Hong for this project, the frequency of articles in *The Wall Street Journal* concerning Korean firms and Korean economic affairs increased approximately eight times during this period.

9. Chalmers Johnson, "East Asia: Living Dangerously," *Foreign Affairs* 62, no. 3 (1984): 721-745; Ronald A. Morse and Edward A. Olsen, "Japan's Bureaucratic Edge," *Foreign Policy*, no. 52 (Fall 1983): 167-180.

10. The figure of 46 percent is taken from a report of a speech by Dr. Nam Duck Woo, the Chairman of the Korea Traders Association, *The Korea Herald*, 17 January 1984, American edition.

11. In February 1984, several articles in *The Wall Street Journal* reported of talks between American automobile companies and Hyundai and Daewoo's Saehan unit about the export of automobiles man-

ufactured in Korea to the United States. For one example, see the issue of February 29, 1984.

12. *Government, Business, and Entrepreneurship in Economic Development* is the best.

13. Gulf Oil, which experienced difficulties over tax liability when it left Korea, is one example. Union Oil is another.

14. There are actually many policies, which are more or less coordinated.

15. T. Jefferson Coolidge, Jr., "The Realities of Korean Foreign Investment Policy," *Asian Affairs* (July, August 1981): 370-385.

16. Korea Petrochemical Industry Association, *Petrochemical Industry in Korea 1983* (Seoul: 1983) includes a schematic illustration of the different production streams and the many firms involved.

17. An excellent source for information about possible connections between the security relationship and the political relationship and commercial transactions is the *Investigation of Korean-American Relations*, Report of the Subcommittee on International Organizations of the Committee on International Relations, U.S. House of Representatives, October 31, 1978. Rice is the one staple grain that is not involved in a private sector alliance, because the Korean government purchases rice directly through OSROK.

Chapter 2

1. See Richard D. Robinson, *Foreign Investment in the Third World*, U.S. Chamber of Commerce (Washington, D.C.: 1980), 1-12ff.

2. See Richard E. Caves, *Multinational Enterprise and Economic Analysis* (Cambridge: Cambridge University Press, 1983), 36-56, 195-226.

3. Singapore's experiences in the 1970s may be a good example.

4. See John M. Stopford and John H. Dunning, *Multinationals: Company Performance and Global Trends* (London: Macmillan Publishers, 1983), 30-31.

5. For U.S. affiliates, see U.S. Department of Commerce, *US Direct Investments Abroad, 1977 (Benchmark Survey)* (1981) and the same survey for previous years.

6. For further discussion, see Birgitta Swedenborg, *The Multinational Operations of Swedish Firms* (Stockholm: Industrial Institute for Economic and Social Research, 1979), 13-44; and John H. Dunning, ed., *Economic Analysis and the Multinational Enterprise* (London: George Allen Unwin, 1974), *passim*.

7. Warner Max Corden, "The Theory of International Trade," in

Economic Analysis and the Multinational Enterprise, edited by John H. Dunning.

8. Raymond Vernon, "International Investment and International Trade in the Product Cycle," *Quarterly Journal of Economics* 80 (May 1966): 190-207.

9. Steven Hymer, *The International Operation of National Firms: A Study in Direct Foreign Investment* (Cambridge, MIT Press, 1976); C.P. Kindleburger, *American Business Abroad* (New Haven: Yale University Press, 1969); Richard E. Caves, "International Corporations: The Industrial Economics of Foreign Investment," *Economica* 33 (February 1971): 1-27; John H. Dunning, *International Production and Multinational Enterprise* (London: George Allen Unwin, 1981).

10. Dunning, *International Production and Multinational Enterprise*, especially 21-45, 72-141.

11. Ibid.

12. The data on which this description and analysis is based is from the special survey of foreign direct investment conducted by the Economic Planning Board in 1979 and from the registry of foreign firms at the EPB. The survey included data from 548 out of 785 foreign firms in the manufacturing sector. Because of the incompleteness of the responses, the analysis in this chapter used only data from 397 sample firms. See the author's chapter, "Patterns of Foreign Direct Investment, Foreign Ownership, and Industrial Performance: The Case of Korean Manufacturing Industry," in Roger Benjamin and Robert T. Kudrie, eds., *The Industrial Future of the Pacific Basin* (Boulder, Colorado: Westview Press, 1984).

13. Larry E. Westphal, "The Republic of Korea's Experience with Export-Led Industrial Development," *World Development* 6 (1978): 347-380; Larry E. Westphal, Yung W. Rhee, and Garry Pursell, "Korean Industrial Competence: Where It Came From" (World Bank Staff Working Paper, no. 469, July 1981).

14. U.S. Tariff Commission, *Economic Factors Affecting the Use of Item 807.00 and 806.3 of the Tariff Schedule of the USA* (Washington, D.C.: Government Printing Office, 1971), A-90.

15. The 1975 data are not reproduced here, but are available from the author.

16. Kiyoshi Kojima, "Transfer of Technology to Developing Countries: Japanese Type versus American Type," in *Hitotsubashi Journal of Economics* 17 (February 1977); Id., "A Macroeconomic Approach to FDI," *Hitotsubashi Journal* 14 (June 1973). For comments on Kojima's hypothesis, see R. H. Mason, "A Comment on Professor Kojima's Japanese Type versus American Type of Technology Transfer," *Hitotsubashi Journal* 17 (February 1980).

17. This is based on total FDI on an approval basis, including sectors other than manufacturing. The actual arrival basis data is different. See the Economic Planning Board publication, *Major Statistics of the Korean Economy*.

18. The objective of the new policies adopted in 1973 was to prevent distortions from large FDI inflows and to increase host country (Korea's) gains.

19. According to arrival basis data, total annual FDI figures have not increased since 1976. Except for the $127 million in 1979, they have remained around the $100 million level. For the FDI policies of other host countries, see Robinson, *Foreign Investment in the Third World*.

20. We separated total sample data into subgroups according to size of investment, share of foreign equity, total assets, and so forth.

21. According to the EPB survey, in 1978 the FDI share of exports was about 17 percent. Although this is not large compared to some other developing countries, it is quite high considering the small level of FDI in Korea.

22. Korea's labor cost index (wage index divided by productivity index) rose from 100 in 1975 to 224 in 1980, whereas in Japan it only rose to 142 and in Taiwan it actually dropped to 96. See the author's paper, "Recent Development of the Korean Electronics Industry," mimeo, 1984.

23. During the 1972-76 period the textile sector induced $58 million in FDI, but in the period 1977-81 it induced only $3 million.

Chapter 3

1. Chalmers Johnson, *MITI and the Japanese Miracle: The Growth of Industrial Policy, 1925-1975* (Stanford, California: Stanford University Press, 1982), 305.

2. Dong Sung Cho, "Han'guk kiŏpkwan ŭi chŏngnip ŭl uihan kiŏpchŏngbu ŭi bunsŏk" (Analysis of Business-Government Relations in Order to Establish Korean Corporate Philosophy), in *Kyŏngyŏng chŏngch'aek kwa chang'gi chŏllyak kyehoek* (Business Policy and Strategic Planning), 2d. ed. (Seoul: Youngji-moonwha-sa, 1983), 45–73.

3. George Cabot Lodge, "Business and the Changing Society," in *The Dynamics of Business Government Relations*, Harvard Business Review Reprint Series, no. 21212 (1975), 57.

4. A. Elkins and D. W. Callaghan, *A Managerial Odyssey* (Massachusetts: Addison-Wesley Publishing Company, 1975), 400-405.

5. Murray L. Weidenbaum, *Business, Government, and the Public* (Englewood Cliffs, New Jersey: Prentice-Hall, 1979), 3, 14, and 167-240.

6. F. Luthans, R. M. Hodgetts, and K. R. Thompson, *Social Issues in Business*, 3d ed., (New York: Macmillan, 1980), 380-404.

7. "A Changing Balance of Power: New Partnership of Government and Business," *Business Week*, 17 July 1965.

8. George A. Steiner, *Business and Society*, 2d ed., (New York: Random House, 1975), 355-392.

9. Thomas C. Schelling, "Command and Control," in *Ethical Theory and Business*, edited by Tom L. Beauchamp and Norman E. Bowie (Englewood Cliffs, New Jersey: Prentice-Hall, 1979), 217-225.

10. Milton Friedman, *Capitalism and Freedom* (Chicago: University of Chicago Press, 1962), 22-36.

11. Leroy P. Jones and Il Sakong, *Kyŏngje kaebal kwa chŏngbu mit' kiŏpka ŭi yŏkhal* (Economic Development and Roles of Government and Businessmen) (Seoul: Korea Development Institute, 1981), 108-177.

12. See Stefan H. Robock, Kenneth Simmonds, and Jack Zwick, *International Business and Multinational Enterprises* (Homewood: Richard D. Irwin, 1977), 222–242; Franklin R. Root, *International Trade and Investment* (Cincinnati: South-Western Publishing Co., 1978), 534–603.

13. This section includes information from interviews with officials of the Ministry of Finance and the Bank of Korea. The references used are *Uri nara ŭi haeoe t'uja* (Korean Investment Overseas), The Bank of Korea, 1982; *Korea Annual 1982*, Yonhap News Agency, 1982; *Korean Economic Yearbook '82*, The Federation of Korean Industries, 1982.

14. Byung Soon Kim, *Han'guk kiŏp ŭi haeoe chikchŏp t'uja* (Foreign Direct Investment by Korean Companies), (Master Dissertation, School of Management, Seoul National University, 1980), 78.

15. The Foreign Exchange Control Decree, Section 15, July 1981.

16. *Uri nara ŭi haeoe t'uja*, 66-70.

17. See Ministry of Finance, *Oegugin t'uja annae* (Investment Guide for Foreigners), 1982; *Questions and Answers for Your Investment in Korea* (Economic Planning Board, 1975); Chan Jin Kim, *Oeja toip ron* (Theory of Foreign Capital Inducement) (Seoul: Iljogak, 1976); Korea, Chamber of Commerce, *Chikchŏp t'uja ŭi hyŏnhwang kwa munjejŏm* (Current Status and Problems of Direct Investment) (1972).

18. Chan Jin Kim, 125.

19. Chan Jin Kim, 127.

20. Dong Sung Cho, *Han'guk kiŏp ŭi kukche kyŏngyŏng sarye* (Casebook of International Business by Korean Companies)(Seoul: Kyŏngmunsa, 1984), 190-237.

21. Chan Jin Kim, 135, 137, 265-267.

22. *Korea Annual 1982* (Yonhap News Agency, 1982), 166.

23. Chan Jin Kim, 136, 138-139. These are arrival basis figures.

24. *Korea Annual 1982*, 165.

25. *Oegugin t'uja annae*, 8-11.

26. Root, 535.

27. Robert L. Kerstiens, "U.S. Government Restrictions on Foreign Investment," in *Readings in Multinational Enterprise* edited by Sang Kee Min (Seoul National University, 1981), 646.

28. Root, 559-561.

29. U.S. Department of Commerce, *Foreign Direct Investment in the United States: Report of the Secretary of Commerce to the Congress in Compliance with the Foreign Investment Study Act of 1972*, (April 1976), 141, 143-152.

30. Cho, *Han'guk kiŏp ŭi kyŏngyŏng sarye*, 229.

31. Selig S. Harrison, *China, Oil, and Asia: Conflict Ahead?* (New York: Columbia University Press, 1977), 134-135.

32. The review of the joint venture between Samsung Electric and Corning Glass Works is based on field interviews with the management of Samsung Corning and data collected from the company.

33. The review of POSCO's investment in Tanoma Coal Mine is based on field interviews with the management of POSCO, company data, and public information.

34. Cho, *Han'guk kiŏp ŭi kyŏngyŏng sarye*, 98–134.

35. The questionnaire asked for the respondents' perceptions of the investment climate of the host country, as well as their evaluations of each component of the incentives provided by the home and host governments respectively. Some of the responses are summarized in tables N-1, N-2, and N-3.

Chapter 4

1. For a discussion of this point, see P. J. Buckley and Marc Casson, *The Future of the Multinational Enterprise* (New York: Holmes and Meier, 1976); also Richard E. Caves, *Multinational Enterprise and Economic Analysis*.

2. See chapters 2, 3, and 5 for discussions of Korea's policies on foreign investment and technology acquisition.

Table N–1
Perceptions of Managers of the Investment Climate of Host Country
(percentages)

Item	U.S. Managers' Perception of Investment Climate of Korea			Korean Managers' Perception of Investment Climate of the U.S.		
Respondent	unfavorable	so-so	favorable	unfavorable	so-so	favorable
General attitude toward foreign investment	36	55	9	7	35	58
Political stability	5	45	50	0	7	93
Economic growth potential	0	23	77	0	21	79
Limitation on ownership	68	32	0	3	14	83
Stability of foreign exchange	14	77	9	0	14	86
Currency exchange regulation	55	45	0	3	18	79
Tax structure	36	46	18	24	59	17
Familiarity with country	9	36	55	3	31	66

Table N–2
Perceptions of Managers of Incentives of the Home Government
(percentages)

Incentive	Korean Managers on Korea			U.S. Managers on the U.S.		
Respondent	not helpful[a]	so-so	helpful	not helpful[a]	so-so	helpful
Tax incentives[b]	41	41	18	50	36	14
Capital assistance	24	14	62	59	23	18
Foreign risk insurance	52	45	3	46	18	36
Investment promotion	45	45	10	59	36	5
Political representation	17	52	21	50	36	14

[a]Includes answers of "nonexistent."
[b]Tax deferral and tax credit provisions are included.

Table N–3
Perceptions of Managers of Incentives of the Host Government

(percentages)

	U.S. Managers on Korea			Korean Managers on the U.S.		
Incentive	*not helpful[a]*	*so-so*	*helpful*	*not helpful[a]*	*so-so*	*helpful*
Tax concessions	27	23	50	41	38	21
Financial assistance	73	18	9	48	35	17
Foreign exchange guarantees	36	14	50	17	31	52
Investment information service	55	45	0	59	34	7
Arbitrations of labor disputes	41	23	36	62	31	7

[a]Includes answers of "nonexistent."

3. See Korea Development Institute, *Long-Term Prospect for Economic and Social Development, 1977-91* (Seoul: KDI, 1979); also Korea Petrochemical Industry Association, *Petrochemical Industry in Korea 1983* (Seoul: 1983).

4. Based on data collected by Republic of Korea, Economic Planning Board.

5. "The Dow Expansion," *Fortune,* May 1952, 105.

6. Alfred E. Kahn, "The Chemical Industry," in *The Structure of American Industry*, 3d ed., Walter Adams, ed. (New York: Macmillan, 1961).

7. Dow Chemical Company, *1958 Annual Report.*

8. Dow Chemical Company, *1966 Annual Report*, 1.

9. "There's Also Some Good News About South Korea," *Fortune*, September 1977, 171.

10. "Dow Chemical Fights Loss in Korea," *The Asian Wall Street Journal*, 27 May 1982.

11. Quoted in *The Asian Wall Street Journal*, 7 July 1982. Reprinted with permission.

12. Caustic soda is not emphasized in this study because it played a lesser role in defining the direction of Dow's expansion. For reasons that will become apparent later in the narrative, it was not a source of conflict in Korea between Dow and its local partners downstream.

13. "The Dow Expansion," *Fortune,* May 1952, 180.

14. The 20 percent includes revenues from vinyl chloride monomer; estimated from Dow Chemical Company, *1975, 1980,* and *1981 Annual Reports.*

15. Executive Office of the President, United States Committee on Wage and Price Stability (COWPS), Staff Report August 1976, *A Study of Chlorine, Caustic Soda Prices*, (Washington, D.C.: COWPS, 1976); William H. Martin, "Potential Competition and the United States Chlorine-Alkali Industry," *Journal of Industrial Economics*, July 1961, 234.

16. "Chemical Profile: Chlorine," *Chemical Marketing Reporter*, 5 August 1974, 9; 27 June 1977, 9; 14 April 1980, 9.

17. COWPS, 14.

18. F. M. Scherer, *Industrial Market Structure and Economic Performance*, 2d ed. (Boston: Houghton Mifflin, 1980), 68.

19. Alfred E. Kahn, "The Chemical Industry." The discussion of market structure draws heavily on Kahn.

20. George W. Stocking and Myron W. Watkins, *Cartels in Action* (New York: The Twentieth Century Fund, 1946), 489.

21. Scherer, 342.

22. COWPS, 7.

23. COWPS, 20-25; unit capital costs are 13 percent higher for the smaller plant and variable costs "as much as 29 percent higher."

24. COWPS, 28.

25. COWPS, 56; note that chlorine rates of return are calculated in terms of replacement cost, while the others are estimated on the basis of the book value of assets. Because the replacement costs factor in inflation, the figures in the text appear to underestimate the actual profit advantages of investments in chlorine.

26. COWPS, 27.

27. "Dow versus Dupont: Rival Formulas for Leadership," *Fortune*, 10 September 1979, 74. Reprinted by permission.

28. "Dow versus Dupont," 81.

29. Dow Chemical Company, *1962 Annual Report*, 6.

30. Ibid.

31. Dow Chemical Company, *1963 Annual Report*, 18.

32. Dow Chemical Company, *1967* and *1975 Annual Reports*.

33. Dow Chemical Company 1980 10-K Disclosure Form, 6-7.

34. For a detailed discussion of the events leading to MITI's decision, see Harvard Business School Case Services, *Caustic Soda in Japan (A) (B)*: (Boston: Harvard Business School, 1978); also "Japan's Investment Rules may be Liberal in Name Only," *Chemical Week*, 20 March 1974, 28.

35. Details from "Dow Chemical Fights Loss in Korea," *The Asian Wall Street Journal*, 27 May 1982; "Dow's Korea Partner Seeks Ouster of Venture Chief," *The Asian Wall Street Journal*, 10 August 1982.

36. COWPS, 21. Electricity costs amount to almost half of the total costs of chlorine production.

37. *The Asian Wall Street Journal*, 27 May 1982.

38. "Chlorine," *Chemical Engineering*, 5 October 1981, 125.

39. "Chlorine, Major Alkalies still in Doldrums," *Chemical and Engineering News*, 6 February 1978, 8.

40. "United States Will be Squeezed out of Basic Petrochemicals Trade," *Chemical and Engineering News*, 22 February 1982, 16, quoting data compiled by Exxon Chemical; Susan Curry and Susan Rich, eds., *The Kline Guide to the Chemical Industry* (Fairfield New Jersey: Charles H. Kline, 1980), 103, 110.

41. "Chemical Profile: Ethylene Dichloride," *Chemical Marketing Reporter*, 10 June 1974, 9; 16 May 1977, 9; 5 May 1980, 9.

42. *The Kline Guide to the Chemical Industry*, 103.

43. Only a price that included all these components would compensate the supplier for diverting production from its own affiliates to independent buyers.

44. For an analysis of the destabilizing consequences of this dual

market structure in the oil industry, see Brian Levy, "World Oil Marketing in Transition," *International Organization* 36, no. 1 (Winter 1982): 113-133.

45. See "Chlorinated Solvents: No More Discounts," *Purchasing*, 11 April 1979, 60-65; "Chemical Markets," *Journal of Commerce*, 27 September 1979; "PVC puts the squeeze on VCM," *Chemical Week*, 1 August 1973, 15; "PVC growth has led to big VCM expansion," *Chemical Week*, 13 February 1980, 26.

46. Indeed, a Dow official noted that in the mid-1970s (when Dow's chlorine plant had not yet come into operation and the KPCC was dependent on EDC imports) there were several occasions when the KPCC would not have been able to import EDC had Dow not been supplying the product to its joint venture on a preferential basis; *The Asian Wall Street Journal*, 10 August 1982.

47. The assumption here is that the Korean plant continually maintains a price proportional to its long-run production costs.

48. This of course is the familiar function of credible threats, examined in Thomas Schelling, *The Strategy of Conflict* (Cambridge: Harvard University Press, 1960).

49. For evidence that this consideration weighed heavily with the Korean government, see "Investors in Korea Gain Insight from Dow," *The Asian Wall Street Journal*, 26 October 1982.

50. It is interesting to note that Dow's bargaining position was stronger before it built the chlorine-caustic soda plant, because it was then providing the KPCC with preferential access to a crucial raw material, EDC; it is also worth noting, though, that given the presence of potential licensors of chlor-alkali technology and a ready availability of investment capital in Korea, a national Korean firm could independently have set up its own chlor-alkali plant.

51. "United States will be Squeezed out of Basic Petrochemical Trade," *Chemical and Engineering News*, 22 February 1982, 16; "Overcapacity: It Could Last for A Decade", *Chemical Week*, 7 April 1982, 44; "New Petrochemical Competition," *Chemical Week*, 23 September 1981, 13; but for evidence that by early 1983 the Canadian and Mexican plants had slowed down, see "Facing up to another Rough Year," *Chemical Week*, 19 January 1983, 26; the Saudi Arabian ventures were, however, going ahead, "Saudi Arabia set to Emerge as Factor in World Marketplace for Chemicals," *Chemical and Engineering News*, 20 December 1982, 65.

52. For a discussion of the advantages of this production chain for Middle Eastern nations in particular, see James F. Ross, "Which Raw Materials for Petrochemicals," *Hydrocarbon Processing*, 76-D-76-VV.

53. R. W. McPherson, C. M. Starks and G. J. Fryor, "VCM: What

You Should Know," *Hydrocarbon Processing* (March 1979), 75-87. Chlorine purchases accounted for only 16 percent of production costs. In 1972 the chlorine and ethylene requirements each came to about one-third of total production costs; see D. P. Keane, R. B. Stobaugh and P.H . Townsend, "Vinyl Chloride: How, Where, Who—the Future," *Hydrocarbon Processing*, (February 1973), 99-110. The price of EDC (and thus presumably value added) is approximately two-thirds that of VCM.

54. "Japan Looks Abroad for Growth," *Chemical Week*, 7 October 1981, 50; "EDC and VCM Imports Head Upward in Japan," *Chemical Week*, 18 November 1981, 33.

55. "Chloralkali Growth Slows," *Chemical Marketing Reporter*, 9 August 1982, 5.

56. "Dow: Headed for Overcapacity, It Veers from Basic Chemicals," *Business Week*, 31 January 1983.

57. Dow Chemical Company, *1981 Annual Report,* 3.

58. *Business Week*, 31 January 1983; "The Woes of Dow," *Financial World*, 1 June 1982.

59. "A Foreign Exodus for Dow," *Chemical Week*, 8 December 1982, 11.

60. See, for example, L. G. Franko, *Joint Venture Survival in Multinational Corporations* (New York: Praeger, 1971).

Chapter 5

1. Carl J. Dahlman and Larry E. Westphal, "The Meaning of Technological Mastery in Relation to Transfer of Technology" in *The Annals of Political and Social Science,* special issue *Technology Transfer: New Issues, New Analysis,* edited by Alan W. Heston and Howard Pack, Vol. 458, November 1981.

2. This point is stressed by Dahlman and Westphal, "The Meaning of Technological Mastery" and also by Ku-Hyun Jung and Kee Young Kim, "Transfer of Technology and Management Know-How Through Multinational Corporations: A Case Approach," (Presented at the International Conference on Management Implications of the Transfer of Technology from Developed to Developing Countries, Seoul, Korea, 13-14 June 1978).

3. According to the Korea Development Institute, *The Long-Term Prospects for Economic and Social Development 1977-1991* (Seoul: 1978), the contribution of labor to GNP growth during 1967-76 was 40 percent and the contribution of capital was 22 percent, while the contribution of technological improvement was only 7 percent.

4. According to information compiled by the author from the Min-

istry of Science and Technology and from KAIST, some of the strategic base technologies are fine chemicals, fine materials, sophisticated industrial machinery, semiconductors, computers, and robotics.

5. Joan Woodward, *Industrial Organization: Theory and Practice* (London: Oxford University Press, 1965).

6. Louis T. Wells, Jr., "Foreign Investors from the Third World," in *Multinationals from Developing Countries* edited by Krishna Kumar and Maxwell G. McLeod (Lexington, Massachusetts: Lexington Books, 1981), 23-36.

7. James Utterback and W. J. Abernathy, "A Dynamic Model of Process and Product Innovation," *Omega* 3, no. 6 (1975): 639-656.

8. Kiyoshi Kojima, *Japanese Direct Foreign Investment* (Rutland, Vermont and Tokyo: Charles E. Tuttel, 1981).

9. Population and GNP from *1978 World Bank Atlas,* Consolidated Balance of Payments, 19 May 1978, cited by Westphal, Rhee, and Pursell, "Korean Industrial Competence: Where It Came From" (Washington, D.C.: World Bank, staff working paper no. 469, July 1981).

10. Goldstar Semiconductor, the joint venture established in September 1979 between American Telephone and Telegraph and the Lucky Goldstar Group is a recent example of a joint venture initiated by the government because of the strategic importance of the industry and the technology to national security and national welfare. The joint venture makes telecommunications equipment, electronic switching systems, and integrated circuits. At about the same time the government also arranged a similar joint venture between ITT and Samsung.

11. See note 10.

12. According to our survey, U.S. technology was imported by seventeen companies that are domestic-market-oriented and sixteen that are export-oriented. However, twenty-six domestic market-oriented companies imported Japanese technology, while only eleven export-oriented companies imported technology from Japan.

13. Jung and Kim, "Transfer of Technology and Management Know-How."

14. The incentives included tax reductions and special financing arrangements for exports and export production.

15. Upon obtaining the U.S. safety and emissions standards approvals, Pony exports increased, and Pony model automobiles have been exported to more than seventy countries.

16. In February 1984, *The Wall Street Journal* carried several articles reporting talks involving HMC and Chrysler. There were also

reports of talks between General Motors and Saehan Motor Company, a Daewoo Group affiliate, concerning the production of automobiles in Korea for export to the United States.

Chapter 6

1. In answering these questions, trade statistics and other secondary data have been investigated to find some evidences of structural changes in the trade channel. Extensive interviews were conducted with the different channel members during 1981 to 1983. The companies interviewed included six Japanese trading companies in Tokyo, five buying offices in Seoul, and eight Korean trading companies and manufacturers in the United States. In addition, thirty-one buying offices and agents were surveyed in Seoul. Because the question, as formulated, requires looking at the dynamic change of the channel, the problem of obtaining historical data became a major difficulty.

2. The countries that are known to have attempted to establish their version of GTCs include Brazil, Taiwan, Thailand, Malaysia, and Israel, among others.

3. See Han'guk Muyŏk Hyŏphoe (Korea Traders Association), *Han'guk chonghap muyŏk sangsa ŭi chillo* (Seoul: 1981), 33. For an analysis of KGTC performance, see the author's chapter, "The Sogo Shosha: Can It be Exported?" in *Export Promotion: The Public and Private Sector Interaction* Michael C. Czinkota, ed. (New York: Praeger, 1983).

4. See Bank of Korea, *Haeoe t'uja hyŏnhwang* (Seoul: 1982), 7.

5. Because this figure is based on the reports by the companies themselves, it may somewhat overestimate the actual figure.

6. This observation is based on the author's interviews with buying offices in Seoul.

Chapter 7

1. *U.S. Treaties and Other International Agreements.*

2. Other sources were consulted for the periods indicated: U.S., *Public Papers of the Presidents*, 1940 to the present; U.S., *Annual Report of the President on the Trade Agreements Program*, 1960 through 1981; *The Federal Index*, 1977 through 1981; *Korea News Review, Korea Business, F S International*, and several periodicals devoted to particular industries, for particular periods.

3. U.S. Tariff Commission, *Textiles and Apparel*, TC Publication 226, Vol. 1, Table 10 (January 1968). The history of Korea's economic policies and performance is discussed in Charles R. Frank, Jr., Kwang Suk Kim, and Larry E. Westphal, *Foreign Trade Regimes and Economic Development: South Korea* (New York: Columbia University Press, 1975), and in Anne O. Krueger, *The Developmental Role of the Foreign Sector and Aid*, Studies in the Modernization of the Republic of Korea: 1945-1975 (Cambridge, Mass.: Harvard University Press, 1979).

4. *Far Eastern Economic Review,* 25 July 1963.

5. I. M. Destler et al., *The Textile Wrangle* (Ithaca: Cornell University Press, 1979), 284.

6. *Daily News Record*, 28 September 1971.

7. *Journal of Commerce*, 11 March 1971; *New York Times*, 21 June 1971.

8. See U.S. General Accounting Office, "Economic and Foreign Policy Effects of Voluntary Restraint Agreements on Textiles and Steel," Report by the Comptroller General, to Representative Sam Gibbons, 21 March 1974, 29; and "Republic of Korea: Economic Assistance," *U.S. Treaties and Other International Agreements*, 28 UST 7591-92, 16 October 1971.

9. Interview with a participating Korean official.

10. *Far Eastern Economic Review*, 1 July 1974; *Daily News Record*, 16 September 1974.

11. Interview with a participating Korean official.

12. Interview with a Korean negotiator.

13. *Daily News Record*, 26 August, 31 August, 29 September, and 27 December 1977.

14. *National Journal*, 16 December 1978.

15. Interview with a participating Korean official. See U.S. Department of State, Press Release No. 228, 19 September 1979.

16. *Washington Post*, 13 February 1979; *New York Times*, 13 and 16 February 1979; *Journal of Commerce*, 20 February 1979; *Boston Globe*, 28 February 1979; *Far Eastern Economic Review*, 16 March 1979; U.S. Special Trade Representative, Press Release 302, 22 March 1979.

17. Interview with a Korean participant.

18. *Daily News Record*, 29 January 1980.

19. Interview with a Hong Kong negotiator.

20. Interview with a Korean official; U.S. Department of State, Press Release No. 263, 19 September 1980; *Textile Asia*, January 1980, 116; *Daily News Record*, 30 January, 5 February, and 29 September 1980.

21. Note, Korean Embassy Washington to U.S. Department of State, KAM 72/172, 17 August 1972; cable, U.S. Embassy Seoul to Secretary of State, 30 June 1972; Letter, Ambassador Dong-Jo Kim to William Eberle, U.S. Special Trade Representative, 19 June 1973; U.S. Special Trade Representative, Press Release No.183, 19 June 1973; Memorandum, Peter Suchman to David Macdonald, U.S. Department of the Treasury, 27 June 1975; U.S. Department of Commerce, Countervailing Duty File 580-028; Republic of Korea, Ministry of Foreign Affairs, *Quota Arrangements in Force*, 15 February 1975, 183-194. This 1971-1973 dispute is not included as a separate case in the present study because the amounts of trade at stake at that time were minimal.

22. U.S., *Federal Register*, 9 January 1976, 1587-89; Cable, U.S. Embassy Seoul to Secretary of State, 13 January 1976; U. S. Department of Commerce, Countervailing Duty File 580-028.

23. U.S. International Trade Commission, *Footwear*, ITC Publication 799 (February 1977); *New York Times*, 2 April 1977; *Journal of Commerce*, 4 April 1977.

24. *Footwear News*, 11 April 1977; *Korea News Review*, 28 May 1977; interview with a Korean trade negotiator. This report was described as exaggerated by some participants.

25. David Yoffie, *Power and Protectionism* (New York: Columbia University Press, 1983), 183; interviews with Korean negotiators.

26. Interview at the Korean Footwear Exporters Association.

27. Interview with an American negotiator. The word *generous* was the negotiator's term.

28. U.S., *Federal Register*, 22 June 1977, 32430-444. When this agreement expired in 1981, President Reagan decided to allow this form of protection to lapse.

29. See U.S. International Trade Commission, *Color Television Receivers and Subassemblies Thereof*, ITC Publication 1068, Appendix C (1980).

30. Interview with a Korean former cabinet minister.

31. Electronic Industries Association of Korea (EIAK), "U.S. Restraints on Korean Televisions, 24 March 1980.

32. *Home Furnishings Daily*, 7 November 1977.

33. *Wall Street Journal*, 14 October 1978.

34. Interviews with Korean officials and a U.S. negotiator; *Wall Street Journal*, 14 October and 24 November 1978.

35. *U.S. Treaties and Other International Agreements*, 30 UST 3880-91; *Wall Street Journal*, 9 January 1979. One Korean official maintains that Korea was cut back more severely than Taiwan because Taiwan had joint ventures with American companies. U.S. negotiators reject this interpretation, saying that the two rollbacks were calculated in

reference to the same base period, during which Korean exports were increasing much more rapidly.

36. EIAK, "U.S. Restraints on Korean Televisions."

37. *The Asian Wall Street Journal,* 2 July 1980.

38. Memorandum, Chulsu Kim to Stephen Lande, 15 September 1980, provided by Korean Ministry of Foreign Affairs.

39. David C. Cole and Princeton N. Lyman, *Korean Development: The Interplay of Politics and Economics* (Cambridge: Harvard University Press, 1971), 13-33.

40. Leroy P. Jones and Il Sakong, *Government, Business, and Entrepreneurship in Economic Development: The Korean Case* (Cambridge: Harvard University Press, 1980), 132-140.

41. Jones and Sakong, 69-70. Big business opposed the key interest-rate reform of 1965, but this opposition failed (Cole and Lyman, 89).

42. Jones and Sakong, 78-140 *passim.*

43. Interviews with Korean negotiators and business leaders and a U.S. negotiator. After Park's death and after the U.S. restrictions were in place, the Economic Ministers' meeting authorized local color broadcast.

44. See Cole and Lyman.

45. Korea Federation of Textile Industries, *Textile Industry in Korea 1980–1981* (Seoul: 1981).

46. Interview in Seoul.

47. Interview in Seoul.

48. Interview with a Korean participant.

49. Interviews in Seoul. In the early 1980s it was not clear that other Korean industries had yet matched the growing sophistication of the textile sector.

50. See U.S. Trade Representative, *A Preface to Trade* (1982).

51. The most explicit discussion of such tactics is found in Robert Keohane and Joseph Nye, Jr., "Transgovernmental Relations and International Organizations," *World Politics* 27 (October 1974): 39-42. See also Keohane, "The Big Influence of Small Allies," *Foreign Policy* 2 (Spring 1971): 161-182.

52. See IMF, *Developments in International Trade Policy*, Occasional Paper 16 (November 1982) for a treatment of these factors.

53. Ratios are U.S. imports from all sources divided by U.S. apparent consumption, measured on a quantity basis. Imports from all sources rather than from Korea alone are used on the assumption that Korea's penetration alone will always be too slight to trigger group political action in the United States, but that aggregate penetration may well trigger group political action that will sweep up small sup-

pliers as well as large ones. Sources: U.S., I.T.C., *U.S. Imports of Textile and Apparel Products under the Multifiber Arrangement, 1976-1982*, Publication 1392, Table 3 (June 1983); I.T.C., *Color Television Receivers and Subassemblies Thereof*, Publication 1068, Table 5 (1980); I.T.C., *Nonrubber Footwear*, Publication 865, Table 1 (1978).

54. U.S., I.T.C., *Nonrubber Footwear,* Publication 1139, Table 15 (1981).

55. U.S., I.T.C., *Color Television Receivers and Subassemblies Thereof*, Table 10.

56. John Odell, "Latin American Trade Negotiations with the United States," *International Organization* 34 (Spring 1980): 207-228.

57. Odell, "Latin American Trade Negotiations."

58. Yoffie, 187.

59. *Washington Post*, 20 January and 19 August 1983; *New York Times*, 1 August 1983; *Far Eastern Economic Review*, 11 August 1983.

60. See Development Centre of the Organization for Economic Cooperation and Development, *Adjustment for Trade: Studies in Industrial Adjustment Problems and Policies* (Paris: OECD, 1975); OECD, *The Case for Positive Adjustment Policies* (Paris: OECD, 1979); Richard Blackhurst, Nicolas Marian, and Jan Tumlir, *Adjustment, Trade and Growth in Developed and Developing Countries*, GATT Studies in International Trade, No. 6 (Geneva: General Agreement on Tariffs and Trade, 1978); Martin Wolf, "Adjustment Policies and Problems in Developed Countries" (World Bank Staff Working Paper, no. 349, 1979).

Chapter 8

1. For a thorough discussion of private sector organizations interested in international trade, see *Export Promotion by Private Sector Organizations*, International Trade Center (Geneva: UNCTAD/GATT, 1971).

2. This bare-bones definition has been taken from Robert O. Keohane and Joseph S. Nye, Jr., *Transnational Relations and World Politics* (Cambridge: Harvard University Press, 1972), xi-xvi, 72.

3. Most studies of transnational organizations in international business relations have focused on the multinational corporation.

4. See chapter 7 by John Odell. Leroy P. Jones and SaKong Il, *Government, Business, and Entrepreneurship in Economic Development: The Korean Case* is the most comprehensive treatment of government-business relations in Korea to date, while there is extensive literature on relations between the government and interest groups in

the United States. One excellent book on the complex factors that influence and hamper the formation of international economic policy in the U.S. government is I. M. Destler, *Making Foreign Economic Policy* (Washington, D.C.: The Brookings Institution, 1980).

5. See the FAS pamphlet, "Agricultural Trade Offices: One-Stop Service Overseas," (December 1980). Conversations with Evans Browne, the first director of the Seoul ATO.

6. See the FAS pamphlet, "Partners in Trade Promotion," (June 1980), which describes the cooperator program and lists the American industry groups that actively participate.

7. Actually, shipments of agricultural commodities to Korea began with the GARIOA program during the American Military Government period. CRIK and the reliance on American aid to feed large portions of the population was a result of the Korean War.

8. The 'three whites' were flour, cotton, and sugar, and symbolize the corruption of the Syngman Rhee regime. The Korean government manipulated the allocation of aid commodities, foreign exchange, and import licenses to obtain funds and political backing. As in the case of flour, unnecessary capacity was built to process all of the three whites, because allocation of raw materials and other privileges was done on the basis of installed capacity. The current capacity of 55,000 barrels per day is equivalent to 2,122,000 metric tons per year, according to Han'guk Chebun Kongŏp Hyŏphoe (KOFMIA), *Flour Milling in Korea 1983*, 2-3.

9. "North Asia Marketing Plan," U.S. Wheat Associates (?), Mimeo, which contains a market report on Korea and Japan and the proposed schedule and budget for cooperator activities for the Korean market for fiscal 1984.

10. "North Asia Marketing Plan," and conversations with Eul B. Yoon, Korea Director for U.S. Wheat Associates, in May and June of 1983. Visits by technical consultants to the baking industry are also included in the program.

11. "North Asia Marketing Plan," and conversations with Eul B. Yoon.

12. Interviews with KOFMIA officials and others concerned with the wheat trade, wheat supplies, and wheat processing in Korea.

13. U.S. Feed Grains Council, *10 Years of the U.S. Feed Grains Council in Korea* (Seoul: 1982). USFGC is the cooperator for the corn wetmilling (corn oil) industry in Korea. USFGC also represents sorghum and soybeans for feed use, although the American Soybean Association has a separate cooperator program in Korea.

14. *10 Years of the U.S. Feed Grains Council in Korea.*

15. There are many feed processors in Korea; the industry does

not have the same high concentration as the flour milling industry, and feed grains were never involved in the aid relationship of the 1950s. However, when CCC credit arrangements are made available, KFA does have the privilege of allocating them to feed processors.

16. Han'guk Sŏmyu Sanŏp Yŏnhaphoe (KOFOTI), *The Textile Industry in Korea 1982* (Seoul: 1982), 10-11, 22-23.

17. For a listing of the industry association and corporate board members, see *The Textile Industry in Korea 1982*, 25-28.

18. Ibid., 4.

19. See chapter 7 for a detailed analysis of trade negotiations. Large textile companies also send representatives to the talk sites.

20. Quotas are allocated on the basis of past export performance, but KOFOTI has discretionary control over about 5 percent of all quotas to use as incentives.

21. *The Textile Industry in Korea 1982*, 3; KOFOTI, *Sŏmyu kongŏp hyŏnhwang* (Seoul: 1980); *Sŏmyu yŏngam'80* (Seoul: 1980).

22. Agreements include technical standards and the use of trade symbols such as the symbol for cotton. Many of these technical ties are actually maintained by KOFOTI's member organizations.

23. The use of credit terms below market rates would only attract charges of political subsidies. Moreover, it is doubtful that the U.S.-Korea textile trade link has the same long-term characteristics that underlay the agricultural marketing program.

24. In fact, SWAK claims to have founded KOFOTI, according to Taehan Pangjik Hyŏphoe (SWAK), *SWAK Directory* (Seoul: 1982), 5. Statistics about the textile industry that appear in Korean newspapers usually come from SWAK.

25. Two recent chairman of SWAK were Choo Young Bock (Chu Yŏng-bok), a retired Air Force general who served as the Minister of National Defense from 1979 to 1982 before becoming SWAK chairman; in 1983 Choo was appointed the Minister of Home Affairs. His predecessor was Lee Hui Sung (Yi Hŭi-sŏng), Acting Director of the KCIA in 1979, Army Chief of Staff (1979), Martial Law Commander (1979), who took up the SWAK chairmanship in 1981 and then left it to become Minister of Transportation in 1982. Both men were in key positions during the 1979-80 transition from the Park government to the new Chun government.

26. Japanese textile companies had invested in large manufacturing plants during the colonial period, and textiles were one of the few industrial sectors of the colonial economy in which the Japanese permitted Korean participation; Kyongsong Bangjik, SWAK's oldest member firm, was founded by Korean entrepreneurs in 1919, while several other member firms were built up from Japanese textile fac-

tories that were seized as enemy property in 1945. SWAK, *Panghyŏp samsim-nyŏn sa* (Seoul: 1977),. 75-78, 635-650.

27. *Panghyŏp samsim-nyŏn sa* is the thirty-year anniversary commemorative history.

28. In fiscal 1978 Korea was the largest foreign market for American cotton. The information in this passage came largely from FAS publications on the American cotton industry and cotton exports, especially Robert B. Evans, *The Market for U.S. Cotton in the Republic of Korea*, (FAS-M-291, 1979?), *U.S. Upland Cotton's Competition in Foreign Markets*, (FAS-M-229, 1971), and CCC statistics on financing arrangements for U.S. cotton exports to Korea from the 1950s up to the present.

29. Based on interviews and conversations with FAS officials in June and November of 1982 and interviews at the Seoul ATO in April and June 1983.

30. Based on interviews with FAS, CCC, and U.S. Treasury Department officials.

31. Ray A. Goldberg and Laura L. Hall, "The Far Eastern Cotton Spinners Case," Harvard Business School Case 4-576-122 (Cambridge: 1976).

32. Interview with a former top official in the EPB, May 1983.

33. In the 1974 soybean export embargo, Korea was able to obtain soybeans by citing mutual defense needs because a large portion of the soybeans were for use by the Korean military.

34. One incentive was a reduction in the import duty on feed grains imported by KGTCs. Interviews with KOFMIA officials and the Seoul ATO.

35. This program, which is part of the private sector advisory committee system authorized by the Trade Act of 1974, provides for the appointment of policy advisory committees and technical advisory committees from different economic interests. Certain questions related to trade issues are referred to these committees.

36. The one ISAC that probably does have some strength is ISAC 15, Textiles and Apparel, one member of whom is the international trade director of ATMI, but any influence wielded by ISAC 15 is due to the political strength of the industry and the specialized bureaucracy that has been created to negotiate textile trade issues. See chapter 7.

37. See Jones and SaKong.

38. One is the Electronics Industries Association of Korea, another is the Korea Petrochemical Industry Association, while a third example is the Korean Society for the Advancement of Machine Industry (KOSAMI). One privilege KOSAMI has enjoyed for years has been the effective power to approve or reject applications for licenses to import foreign machinery into Korea.

39. The president of KOFMIA is Yi Hee Il (Yi Hŭi-il), a former

EPB official and Minister of Agriculture and Fisheries (MAF), who assumed the KOFMIA presidency in 1980.

40. It is clear that market development was not the objective of agricultural commodity aid to Korea in the 1950s. During the course of the 1960s the issue becomes fuzzier, but it has only been in the 1970s that PL 480 and CCC credit arrangements have been used solely as marketing tools.

41. *Export Promotion by Private Organizations*. The objective is to remove unnecessary obstacles to expanding business ties. For example, in recent years the Chamber of Commerce of the United States and counterpart organizations in some Asian countries have established bilateral consultative committees to advise on problems in the business environment in the Asian countries that prevent the host countries from attracting the foreign participation they desire.

42. The KTA is one of the four major business associations in Korea. The others are the Korea Chamber of Commerce and Industry, the Federation of Korean Industries, and the Federation of Small and Medium Industries. The past four chairman of the KTA have come to the post from the position of Prime Minister or Deputy Prime Minister, the latter being the most important economic post in the Korean government because the Deputy Prime Minister is concurrently the head of the EPB.

43. Korea-United States Economic Council, *Membership Directory 1981–82,* (Seoul: 1982), 1.

44. Interview with Kie-Hong (Daniel) Lee, who served as the Vice President of KUSEC during the 1970s, July 1981.

45. In the 1970s US/KEC arranged delegations of American businessmen interested in business deals in Korea. The U.S. Department of Commerce, ITA publication, "Marketing in Korea," OBR 80-82, July 1980, cites US/KEC and KUSEC as sources of information on investment in Korea. However, according to the former head of US/KEC, few actually came to it for such information (interview, April 1982). The delegations and the contacts and access to well-placed government and business representatives in Korea was US/KEC's most important service to American firms interested in investment in Korea.

46. AMCHAM membership is not limited to American firms. Many Korean law and accounting firms that serve the American business commmunity are members.

47. In 1981 and again in 1983 AMCHAM was asked to present the views of its membership on the business environment informally to representatives of the offices of the Korean government that manage economic affairs and foreign investment in Korea.

48. Among other measures, the government ordered a drastic restructuring of some heavy industries and the automobile industry that affected several joint ventures directly.

49. See chapter 4 and chapter 5.

50. For example, KOSAMI would lose its privilege of passing on import license applications for machinery.

51. A small tariff discount has been offered for certain commodities traded through KGTCs. Diversification of suppliers might give Korea opportunities to gain politically from purchases from third world countries, while allowing KGTCs the leeway to do barter deals with producer countries that are low on foreign exchange.

Chapter 9

1. Frederick Harbison and Charles A. Myers, *Management in the Industrial World* (New York: McGraw-Hill, 1959), 21-39; Eli Ginsberg, *The Manpower Connection: Education and Work* (Cambridge: Harvard University Press, 1975), 69-87.

2. MBA programs are generally of two types. One is a two-year day program consisting of 36 credit hours plus thesis, and the other is a two and a half year evening program, primarily for those working full-time, consisting of 30 credit hours of course work plus thesis. While degree program require full-time studies, nondegree programs are offered on a part-time basis.

3. Powell Niland and Joseph W. Towle, eds., *Business Research in South Korea* (New York: United Christian Board for Higher Education in Asia, 1976), 8-9.

4. Robert A. Gordon and James E. Howell, *Higher Education for Business* (New York: Columbia University Press, 1959).

5. A typical executive development program consists of about one hundred hours of study over 14-15 weeks, twice a week in the evening. The programs generally cover contemporary management concepts and current issues facing Korean business.

6. A typical management training program consists of 48-50 hours of concentrated study for one week, covering modern management concepts and techniques in functional areas of production, marketing, accounting, finance, and personnel. The program also covers the issues and problems facing Korean small and medium-sized businesses.

7. Korea Management Education Board, *An Evaluative Study of Korean Management Education* (December 1980), 225.

8. *An Evaluative Study of Korean Management Education*, 224-226.

9. Of the 78 professors who hold doctoral degrees from American schools, 14 are in economics and at least 10 are in industrial engineering, leaving only 54 professors who have completed doctoral programs

in management, or less than 7 percent of the total management faculty now teaching in Korean colleges and universities. Though the survey results do not include some colleges and universities because of their failure to respond, all Korean professors who have American doctorates are included in the survey results.

10. Although there are no official statistics available, it is reliably estimated that several hundred Korean students currently are studying management in graduate schools of business in the United States on private arrangements.

11. According to a study by the Korea Association of Business Administration, the number of articles in the area of management published in Korean academic journals during a recent five-year period (1976-81) was close to two and one-half the number of articles published during the preceding five-year period (1971-76). Furthermore, more than three times as many new textbooks on management were published during the last ten years (1973-82) as were published during the previous ten years (1963-72). Korea Association of Business Administration, *The Current Status and Tasks of Korean Management Education* (February 1983), 5-11, 224-227.

12. *The Current Status and Tasks*, 233-248.

13. Interviews with Korean management faculty who employ the case study method of instruction. *The Current Status and Tasks*, 241-255.

Index

About the Contributors

Dong Sung Cho is associate professor of business administration at Seoul National University. He received his D.B.A. from the Harvard Business School in 1976, and recently returned there as a visiting associate professor for 1983–1984. Professor Cho was a visiting fellow at the Institute for Developing Economies in Tokyo in 1983. Before joining the faculty of Seoul National University, he worked as a senior corporate planner for the Gulf Oil Corporation. Professor Cho has published numerous books and articles in Korean and English, and recently completed a two-volume work on Korean General Trading Companies.

Ku-Hyun Jung is associate professor of international business and marketing at Yonsei University in Seoul, Korea. He received his M.B.A. from State University of New York–Albany, and his Ph.D. from the University of Michigan in 1976. He has been a visiting professor at the universities of Michigan and Hawaii, and he will be a visiting professor supported by a Fulbright Fellowship at the Graduate School of Business at the University of Washington (Seattle) during 1984–1985. Professor Jung has written extensively on the subjects of export marketing and general trading companies. He is the author of two books, *International Business Management* and *Marketing Strategy,* both in Korean.

Kee Young Kim is the dean of financial affairs at Yonsei University, where he is a professor of management at the School of Business and Economics. He received his M.B.A. (1973) and his D.B.A. (1975) from Washington University in St. Louis, and has been on the Yonsei faculty since 1968. Professor Kim was a visiting research associate at the Center for Policy Alternatives at the Massachusetts Institute of Technology, and a lecturer at the School of Management of Boston University in 1981–1982. His most recent books in Korean are *Production and Operations Management* and *Quantitative Methods for Business Decisions* (coauthor), and he has written numerous articles in Korean and English on technology development, technology transfer, Korean export industries, and Korean multinational enterprises.

Hak Chong Lee is professor of management and director of the Computer Center at Yonsei University in Seoul, Korea. Before joining the Yonsei faculty in 1981, Professor Lee was on the faculty of State University of New York–Albany from 1963 to 1979. During these years he served also as a visiting professor and adviser at the University of Hawaii, Nanyang University in Singapore, and the Korea Institute of

Science and Technology. He was senior management consultant at the Advanced Management Institute of the Federation of Korean Industries. He jointly authored *Human Resources Administration: The Problems of Growth and Change* (Hougton Mifflin, 1971), and also published *Organization Adjustment under Computerization* (Nanyang University, 1971) and *The Impact of EDP upon the Patterns of Business Organization and Administration* (State University of New York, Albany). One of his recent articles in Korean is "The Computerization of a Korean Business Group," published in 1982.

Brian Levy is an assistant professor of economics at Williams College. He received his Ph.D. from Harvard University, and his publications include "World Oil Marketing in Transition," *International Organization* (winter 1982) and "State-Owned Enterprises in the World Economy: The Case of Iron Ore" (with Raymond Vernon), in *Public Enterprises in Less Developed Countries,* edited by Leroy P. Jones (New York: Cambridge University Press, 1982).

John S. Odell is associate professor of international relations at the School of International Relations of the University of Southern California. Professor Odell received his M.A. (1968) and his Ph.D. (1976) from the University of Wisconsin–Madison. An assistant professor of government at Harvard University from 1976 to 1982, he has published *U.S. International Monetary Policy: Markets, Power, and Ideas as Sources of Change* (Princeton University Press: 1982), and numerous scholarly articles on international politics, international trade bargaining, and international debt negotiations. He has received grants and fellowships from The Ford Foundation, the Carnegie Endowment for International Peace, and The Brookings Institution. A recipient of the Council on Foreign Relations International Affairs Fellowship, he will be working in the Office of the U.S. Trade Representative in 1984–1985.

About the Editor

Karl Moskowitz is an assistant professor at Harvard University, where he teaches modern Korean history and economic and social development. A graduate of Indiana University, he took his A.M. in Regional Studies, East Asia, and his Ph.D. in History and East Asian Languages from Harvard. He is the executive director of the Korea Institute, a research institute that he helped establish within the John King Fairbank Center for East Asian Research at Harvard University. Professor Moskowitz was assistant editor for Korea for the *Journal of Asian Studies* from 1980 to 1982, and has contributed articles on Korea to the *Journal* and other scholarly publications. His book *Current Assets: The Employees of Japanese Banks in Colonial Korea* is published by the Council on East Asian Studies at Harvard. Most recently, Professor Moskowitz directed a three-year research project on U.S.–Korean trade relations funded by a grant from The Henry Luce Foundation, some of the results of which are reported in this book; a Fulbright-Hays Faculty Research Abroad Fellowship from the U.S. Department of Education supported a year of work in Seoul for the project. Fluent in Korean and Japanese, Professor Moskowitz is a consultant to firms with interests in Korea and East Asia.